RESCUING
HISTORY
FROM THE
NATION

RESCUING HISTORY FROM THE NATION

QUESTIONING NARRATIVES
OF MODERN CHINA

PRASENJIT DUARA

THE UNIVERSITY OF CHICAGO PRESS

CHICAGO AND LONDON

PRASENJIT DUARA is professor of history at the University of Chicago. He is the author of *Culture, Power, and the State: Rural Society in Northern China, 1900–1942*, which won the 1989 John K. Fairbank prize of the American Historical Association for best book in East Asian Studies and the 1990 Joseph R. Levenson prize of the Association of Asian Studies for best book on twentieth-century China.

THE University of Chicago Press, Chicago 60637
The University of Chicago Press, Ltd., London
© 1995 by The University of Chicago
All rights reserved. Published 1995
Printed in the United States of America

04 03 02 01 00 99 98 97 96 95   1 2 3 4 5

ISBN 0–226–16721–6 (cloth)

Library of Congress Cataloging-in-Publication Data

Duara, Prasenjit.
    Rescuing history from the nation: Questioning narratives of
modern China / Prasenjit Duara.
        p.   cm.
    Includes bibliographical references and index.
    1. China—Historiography. 2. China—History—20th century.
    3. Civilization, Oriental.   I. Title.
DS734.7.D83   1995
951'.072—dc20   95-3205
                                                                             CIP

♾ The paper used in this publication meets the minimum requirements of the American National Standard for Information Sciences—Permanence of Paper for Printed Library Materials, ANSI Z39.48-1984.

To my parents,
Ira Duara and Punya Prasad Duara

CONTENTS

ACKNOWLEDGMENTS

THE OFFERING of gratitude for this book has forced me to reflect upon the impossible but necessary task of identifying the moment of its conception. I feel deeply uneasy having to exclude mention of all of those who helped me early on and indirectly and who are now shrouded in the "prehistory" of this project—a phase I regard, befitting the theme of this book, as equally important as its history.

But it is with pleasure and gratitude that I recall the year 1989–1990 spent at the Woodrow Wilson Center in Washington, DC, perhaps the first host of this project in recognizable form. Gratitude for the wonderful research support and access, for the kindness and friendship of Mary Bullock, the Asian Program Director, and the pleasure of a reading circle made marvelous by historians from all over the world, especially Jnaina Amado, Mercedes Villanova, David Ransel, and Philip Scranton. The move to the Chicago faculty the next year brought new meaning to the phrase "intellectual stimulation." It became, for good or for worse, a kind of permanent state of affairs, and the book took shape in exchanges with my colleagues (many of whom are cited throughout), in the lively workshops of the Center for Transcultural Studies (then known as the Center for Psychosocial Studies) run by Benjamin Lee, and, perhaps most of all, in unending discussions with the graduate students. The extraordinary intellectual energy of these students of China from the various disciplines, whether in class, in the office, or at Jimmy's, has, for me, been both intellectually formative and practically helpful—as they often brought relevant sources and information to my notice. I would particularly like to thank my assistants, Lee Chiu-chin and Juliette Chung.

Several of these chapters have been presented in some preliminary form at many places, and I am grateful to the hosts for the opportunity for discussion. These include the Institute of Modern History at the Academica Sinica in Taiwan, the Chinese University of Hong Kong, Fudan University in Shanghai, Harvard University, Stanford University, the University of California at Davis and Irvine, and the Woodrow Wilson Center. The book represents a coming together, a cross-hatching, of several ideas and themes I have written about over the last five years. I am thankful to the publishers of my previously published articles for granting me permission to re-use segments of that work. They include "Bifurcating Linear History: Nations and Histories in China and India" *Positions: East Asia Cultures Critique* 1, no. 3 (Winter 1993); "Deconstructing the Chinese Nation" *The Australian Journal of Chinese Affairs* 30 (July 1993); "Rescuing History from the Nation," Working Paper of the Center for Psychosocial Studies (1992); "Knowledge and Power in the Discourse of Modernity: The Campaigns against Popular Religion in Early Twentieth Century China" *Journal of Asian Studies* 50, no. 1 (February 1991); "State, Civil Society and the History of Chinese Modernity," forthcoming in Frederic Wakeman, ed., *China's Quest for Modernization: A Historical Approach* (Berkeley: Institute for East Asian Studies Publications); "Provincial Narratives of the Nation: Centralism and Federalism in Republican China" in Harumi Befu, ed., *Cultural Nationalism in East Asia* (Berkeley: Institute for East Asian Studies Publications, 1993); and "Modernity and Its Critics in India and China," *Proceedings of the Conference on Modernization in China* (Taipei: Academica Sinica, 1990).

Guy Alitto, Paul Cohen, David Laitin, Elizabeth Perry, Mary Rankin, William Rowe, David Strand, and an anonymous reader at the University of Chicago Press wrote extensive comments on the first version of the full manuscript. I took them with gratitude and utmost seriousness and I hope that they will find their labors to have not been in waste, if perhaps not fully rewarded, in the final product. Between law school and motherhood, Juliette somehow found the time to share in the project and to give me detailed, intelligent comments, while Nisha gave me reason to finish quickly so as not to miss a bit of these joyous years.

PART ONE

INTRODUCTION

HISTORICAL consciousness in modern society has been overwhelmingly framed by the nation-state. Yet, despite the certainty that a history belongs to a nation, the nation itself remains a highly contested phenomenon. Regimes, politicians, and ordinary people within a nation do not often agree on what the nation does or what it should mean. Little wonder then that scholars of nationalism have found it difficult to define such words as "nation," "nation-state," and "nationalism." Since Ernest Renan's lecture "What Is a nation?" delivered in 1882, a cottage industry has flourished seeking to define these terms, and Louis Snyder's attempt to clarify nationalism yielded a definition of no less than 208 pages (see Snyder 1983, 253).[1] If it is true that that which lives in history cannot be defined, then it is ironic that the nation seeks its ultimate moorings in history. And it is surely extraordinary that we still find it difficult to count histories that do not belong to a contemporary nation.

In this book, I explore the intimate relationship between the nation-state and nationalism on the one hand and linear, evolutionary history on the other, in a study principally of early twentieth-century China. My understanding of the nation and nationalism is informed not only by Chinese nationalism, but even more importantly by re-

1. In general, the discussions about the definitions of nationalism revolve around such factors as the relative proportions and role of objective and subjective criteria and how to distinguish ethnicity from nationalism. Less obvious questions, such as the meaning of heterogeneity in a nation, how some collectivities come to be included and others excluded, and how collectivities gain and lose national identification have barely entered the discussion.

cent developments around the world. In our time, the instability of
the concept of the nation is such that we are unable to even say
whether it is in ascendancy or in decline. What does emerge clearly
in the rapidity with which nations are being formed, destroyed, and
re-formed is the contingency and contestedness of nations. The contrast between these developments and the view of the nation as an
evolving unity is so striking that it behooves us to examine the formal
aspects of this history. Contemporary work on historical narrative,
in particular, the critique of a causal, evolutionary history has been
especially useful for my task. In evolutionary history, historical movement is seen to be produced only by antecedent causes rather than by
complex transactions between the past and the present. By bringing
together the critique of evolutionary history with the study of nationalism, there is an opportunity to decouple the deep, tenacious and,
as I will try to show, repressive connection between history and the
nation.

My principal argument is that national history secures for the contested and contingent nation the false unity of a self-same, national
subject evolving through time.[2] This reified history derives from the
linear, teleological model of Enlightenment History—which I desig-
nate with a capital *H* to distinguish it from other modes of figuring
the past. It allows the nation-state to see itself as a unique form of
community which finds its place in the oppositions between tradition
and modernity, hierarchy and equality, empire and nation. Within
this schema, the nation appears as the newly realized, sovereign
subject of History embodying a moral and political force that has
overcome dynasties, aristocracies, and ruling priests and mandarins,
who are seen to represent merely themselves historically. In contrast
to them, the nation is a collective historical subject poised to realize
its destiny in a modern future. This narrative, which I have sketched
here in its crudest form, depicts not only nationalist histories, but
underpins much modern historiography, both popular and professional. Although the narrative is as old as the modern nation-state
itself, the modernization paradigm of the postwar era has reinforced
many of its salient oppositions. More recent theories of nationalism
have broken with some of these oppositions but have remained tied
to others.

2. The *Oxford English Dictionary* defines the modern philosophical meaning of the
"subject" as: "More fully *conscious* or *thinking subject* . . . the thinking or cognizing
agent; the self or ego" (*The Compact Edition of the Oxford English Dictionary*, vol. II,
p. 3120. Oxford: Oxford University Press, 1971).

In this context, the early twentieth century in China is of particular interest not only because modern nationalism took hold during this period, but because it is when the narrative of History and a new vocabulary associated with it—such as feudalism, self-consciousness, superstition, and revolution—entered the Chinese language, largely by way of Japanese. It was these new linguistic resources, both words and narratives, that secured the nation as the subject of History and transformed the perception not only of the past but also of the present meaning of the nation and the world: which people and cultures belonged to the time of History and who and what had to be eliminated. Because our own historical conceptions have shared so much with the linear History of the nation, we have tended to regard History more as a transparent medium of understanding than as a discourse enabling historical players (including historians) to deploy its resources to occlude, repress, appropriate and, sometimes, negotiate with other modes of depicting the past and, thus, the present and future.

The book is divided into two parts. The next two chapters of Part One deal with the theoretical problem of the nation as the subject of History. Chapter 1 tracks the dialectic through which emergent nations embraced the narrative of Enlightenment History and how this History itself produced the nation as the self-same community progressing from ancient times to a modern future. I examine the prevalence of this narrative, its particular rhetoric, and its strategies of periodization in China through some influential general histories from the turn of the century into the Republican period (1911–49). In chapter 2, I develop a wider, "bifurcated" conception of history as an alternative to linear History. The past is not only *transmitted* forward in a linear fashion, its meanings are also *dispersed* in space and time. Bifurcation points to the process whereby, in transmitting the past, Historical narratives and language appropriate dispersed histories according to present needs, thus revealing how the present shapes the past. At the same time, by attending to the very process of appropriation, bifurcation allows us to recover a historicity beyond the appropriating discourse. Thus, through this conception, I try to salvage historicity even while overcoming or, at least, becoming self-conscious of the repressive teleologies of linear and simple, causal histories.

Part Two contains five empirically and textually weighted essays that attempt to write bifurcated histories. My aim is to flash a little light on areas darkened by the categories and schemas of the evolutionary History of the nation. The first two essays focus on how narratives and representations seek to appropriate or conceal complex historical realities incompatible with its view of the world. Chapter 3 examines the encounter between nationalist reformers and popular religion or "superstition" in the late 1920s, in which the representation of modernity (versus feudal superstition) not only concealed a complex social world but also had to conceal the changes of its own meanings. Chapter 4, probes the efforts of the 1911 republican revolutionaries to appropriate the romantic narrative of secret societies into a global social Darwinist discourse of the racial nation.

The next set of essays considers alternative narratives of the nation that contest, in muffled or incipient voices, the centralizing, statist narrative of History which has become hegemonic in China since the Republican revolution. Chapter 5 stubbornly risks joining what is, by now, a spent debate on the prospects of "civil society" in late imperial China. However, I join it from the angle of a more performative conception of history in which historical actors at the end of the nineteenth century, tried (momentarily) to re-narrativize their past in order to enable a present civil society. Chapter 6, "Provincial Narratives of the Nation" focuses on the search of the federalist movement of the early decades of the twentieth century for an alternative historical narrative to critique centralized authority and articulate its vision of the nation built from the locality upwards. The last essay evaluates critiques of modernity in China and India in the first half of the century by figures who utilized the alternative foundation of "culture" to challenge the claims of History.

Although my goal is to critique the nation as the subject of History, I am acutely aware that it is—as yet—impossible to radically displace the nation as the locus of history, if for no other reason than that our values, whether as historians or individuals, have been intimately shaped by the nation-state. It is doubtless because of the tie to the nation that I have found myself periodically returning to the study of India, where I was born and grew up. The field of Indian studies has witnessed a vigorous critique of national History, most famously by the school of Subaltern history. Although I am not a specialist in Indian studies, I have been influenced by the general framework of a still vaguely defined "postcolonialism" which informs much of this new scholarship in India and elsewhere. I think of postcolonialism as the critique of the ways in which modern, independent nation-states continue to operate within the old (colonial/Enlightenment) problematic of History and its hierarchy of different modes of living and time. I have tried to interrupt the narrative certainties of Chinese history by thinking about China from this relatively unfamiliar historiographical vantage point.

At the same time, I also use my interest and knowledge of India to conduct a comparative study with China in chapters 2 and 7 and in this way take comparative history itself out of its familiar problematic of History. In most comparative analyses conducted in Chinese historiography, China has been compared mainly with Japan and invariably to answer the question: Why was China slower to attain modernity than Japan? The comparative dimensions of this book (which are not restricted exclusively to India) will seek to dislodge the centrality or givenness of this narrative of History. My efforts at comparison search for the ways in which History is adopted in these different societies by linking up with indigenous narratives, for the different areas History seeks to obscure or appropriate, and for the different sites of impenetrability and resistances to its hegemony. In this way we may gain some insights into the wider history of History itself.

IMAGINED NATIONS: WHO IMAGINES WHAT?

In this work, I presuppose a specific conception of the nation that is critical of the claim that nationalism represents a unitary consciousness or identity. The remainder of this Introduction develops my conception of nationalism, which I see as a phenomenon that registers difference even as it claims a unitary or unifying identity. The expression "identity" has become controversial with developments in psycho-analysis, philosophy, and other fields. To the extent that it suggests a prior, *primordial* self that identifies with a social or cultural representation, the thrust of my work, here and elsewhere, is to put it radically under question. Without burdening ourselves with that enormous literature, let me say that I use "identity" to refer to a subject position produced by representations in relation to other representations. In other words, the "prior" self which identifies, or is sutured with a representation of, say, the nation, is itself another set of subject positions—say, woman, Korean-American, Baptist—produced by other representations. Thus the self is constituted neither primordially nor monolithically but within a network of changing and often conflicting representations.

I propose that we view the dynamics of national identity within this fluid network of representations. We will thus need to break with two assumptions underlying most studies of nationalism. The first is the privileging of the nation as a cohesive collective subject. Nationalism is rarely the nationalism of *the nation*, but rather marks the site where different representations of the nation contest and negotiate with each other.[3] Second, nationalist consciousness is not, by itself, a unique and unprecedented mode or form of consciousness. Although nationalism and its theory seek a privileged position within the representational network as the master identity that subsumes or organizes other identifications, it exists only as one among others and is changeable, interchangeable, conflicted, or harmonious with them. This is true not only with regard to other contemporary identities, but, as we shall see in chapter 2, also with regard to historical identities.

What is novel about modern nationalism is the world system of nation-states. This system, which has become globalized in the last hundred years or so, sanctions the nation-state as the only legitimate expression of sovereignty. The nation-state is a political form with distinct territorial boundaries within which the sovereign state, "representing" the nation-people, has steadily expanded its role and power. This system will be discussed in greater detail in the remainder of Part One.

The system of nation-states is, of course, related to the global economy of the modern, capitalist world-system which Immanuel Wallerstein and others have written about. In Wallerstein's earlier work, modern states were tied very closely to the imperatives of the global, capitalist division of labor which, in order to enable the asymmetrical flow of resources, necessitated strong states in the core regions of capitalism and weak states in the peripheries (1974). Wallerstein's model had been criticized by many for not sufficiently recognizing the relative autonomy of state-building in the new nations of the periphery (Meyer 1980; Duara 1988a, 3). In a recent piece, Wallerstein appears to have addressed the problem. He suggests that the formation of nation-states provides a means of mobility for some social formations in the periphery to attain "core" status (Wallerstein 1991, 81–82). The idea that the nation-state seeks to enable the transition

3. In this respect, the exploding, or rather, imploding of large categories such as nationalism may appear to make my conception resemble positivist, rational choice theory, which rests on the notion of the maximization of individual or group utility. Yet, in my view, utility is itself defined by a discourse, and even more important, it is often confounded by the play of multiple discourses or representations that constitute the individual or group. Throughout this book, instances of multiplicity, changeability, and ambiguity will be encountered in the representation of the self, which is often mediated or disguised by the polysemic quality of language.

to a modern capitalist society is compatible with my study, although I could be said to focus on how capitalist penetration is enabled by the emergence of the nation-state as the most important discursive conduit for the spread and conquests of Historical awareness over other, "nonprogressive" modes of time. At the same time, both the system of nation-states and the problem of national identity are sufficiently complex that they may also be discussed independently of the world economy. The variety of relationships that different representations of the nation may develop with capitalism, as well as the changing relationship between the global capitalist economy and global system of nation-states, while touched upon in this book, is the subject of another study.

Historically, what is unique and new about nationalism is not an epistemological category, such as a type of identity or a mode of consciousness. What was new was the global *institutional* revolution which, to be sure, produced its own extremely powerful representations of the nation-state. Totalizing, self-conscious political communities have, as we shall see, been around long before nation-states made their appearance. Moreover, in present times, the nation-state has not been able to exhaust the identifications of the individual, nor, for that matter, has it been able to confine the meaning of the nation to its representations. Modern nation-states have to confront or engage with other, including historical, representations of community. When we consider national identity in its ambiguities, changeability, fungibility, and interplay with other identifications, we see that it can be as subversive of the nation-state as it has been supportive.

Ever since Karl Deutsch (1961), analysts of nationalism have emphasized how the nation-state, in the print era and after, has been able to avail of the proliferating mass-media to facilitate the nation-building project. Few have emphasized how this same technology also enables rivals of the nascent nation-state to construct alternative representations of the nation, whether in Breton, the Baltic states, Tibet, or the Punjab. The state is never able to eliminate alternative constructions of the nation among both old and new communities. The most successful states are able to contain these conceptions within relatively depoliticized spaces; but even where such states are older, as in Western Europe, there are overt challenges to the established national form in almost every nation. Walker Connor (1972) has shown that there is scarcely a nation in the world— developed or underdeveloped—where ethnic mobilization has not challenged the nation-state. Defying the presumption of the nation-state to restrict the term "nationalism" to loyalty to itself, Connor insists on identifying these self-differentiating ethnic groups as, in fact, nations.

Connor's identification of nationalisms within the nation-state reveals the conflicted but isomorphic nature of political identities: ethnic mobilization develops into national identification identical to the one it opposes. But the relationship among different identities is more complex than this. Nationalism is often considered to override other identities within a society—such as religious, racial, linguistic, class, gender, or even historical ones—to encompass these differences in a larger identity. However, even when or where such an encompassment has been temporarily achieved, the way in which the nation is represented and voiced by different self-conscious groups is often very different. Indeed, we may speak of different "nation-views," as we do "world-views," which are not overridden by the nation, but actually define or constitute it. In place of the harmonized, monologic voice of the Nation, we find a polyphony of voices, contradictory and ambiguous, opposing, affirming, and negotiating their views of the nation.

Thus the legitimate object of the study of nationalism ought to include more than overtly national movements; the scope must be broadened so as to include nation-views and other narratives of the nation. In today's America, for example, the voices of various collectivities tell us how differently or contradictorily they imagine their Americanness. These are the voices not only of different ethnicities— the various groups of blacks, Jews, Asians, Hispanics—but of subgroups or minorities—women, gays, religious pacifists—who in seeking to reconcile their own identity with Americanness often pose a powerful challenge to hegemonic nationalism. Consider how two Americans—an American Indian and a lesbian activist—think of the 4th of July:

> "Oftentimes, I have been at pow-wows at the Fourth of July having an awful lot of fun, but it has absolutely nothing to do with being a citizen of the United States of America . . . I cannot personally remember a time when I was emotionally overtaken by total and indiscriminate pride in just being an American. My ethnic identity and tribal membership have always been for me and my family the overriding element of our lives." (Joallyn Archambault, director of American Indian programs, National Museum of Natural History, quoted in the *Washington Post*, 4 July 1990)
>
> "I would consider myself a very patriotic citizen. I get

teary-eyed on the Fourth of July. I love to sing 'The Star-Spangled Banner' at football. To me being patriotic means participating as an openly gay person and being able to do so comfortably with my family in what is considered an all-American institution—football." (Perry Radecic, legislative director of the National Gay and Lesbian Task Force, also quoted in the *Washington Post*)

Studies of nationalism have emphasized how nations have incorporated gender and gender roles into the body-politic through a variety of representational strategies (Yuval-Davis and Anthias 1989). Less attention has been given to the ways in which women have sometimes sought to defy or reject these representations. New work among Chinese women writers is beginning to reveal a certain defiance among these writers. Historically in China, the purity of the woman's body has served both as metaphor and metonymy of the purity of the nation (Schoppa 1989). The bodies of Chinese women raped by foreign invaders—Mongol, Manchu, or Japanese—were both symbol and part of the national body violated by these foreigners. The writer Xiao Hong, who came from the city of Harbin, rejects this representation in her novel, *Field of Life and Death*, which is set in the period of the Japanese occupation. According to Lydia Liu, nationalism in the novel "comes across as a profoundly patriarchal ideology that grants subject-positions to men who fight over territory, possession and the right to dominate. The women in this novel, being themselves possessed by men, do not automatically share the male-centred sense of territory" (Liu 1994, 58). In a deliberate subversion of the trope of the raped woman in nationalist discourse, Xiao Hong's protagonist turns out to have been raped by a Chinese man. "The appropriation of the female body by nationalism is contested relentlessly throughout . . . [and] raises poignant questions about what it means to be Chinese/peasant/woman" (Liu 1994, 45).

In most modern nations, the family has been valorized as embodying national morality. The obligation to educate and "emancipate" women derived from the imperative to produce more efficient mothers who, in turn, would reproduce, biologically and culturally, "superior" citizens (Yuval-Davis and Anthias 1989, 7–9). Tani Barlow (1985) and Wendy Larson have revealed that in China there existed another strategy among the May 4th generation of cultural iconoclasts whereby women were incorporated into the modern nation. These radicals sought to absorb women directly as citizens of the nation (*guo*) and thus caused them to reject their kin-based gender roles in the family or *jia*. The vitriolic May 4th attack on the family as site of the reproduction of hierarchy in society may have been the reason why the radical intelligentsia found it almost impossible to "identify women's role within the *jia* as a position from which to initiate a positive re-theorization of 'woman'" (Larsen 1991, 11). In doing so, they de-gendered women (who were to be just like male citizens of the nation), and many important women writers like Ding Ling ultimately abandoned writing about the problem of gender. Nonetheless, Larson observes a kind of resistance among some women writers to this mode of incorporation as they began to reject "'nation' as an overarching concept within which to frame 'woman'" (Larson 1991, 13).

Class and nation have often been viewed in scholarship as competing identities; the two having vied for the role of historical subject, class has emerged as the clear loser in recent times. Historically, I believe it is equally important to see class as a trope that constructs a particular and powerful representation of the nation—a nation-view. In China, Li Dazhao imagined the nation in the language of a class on the international stage: the Chinese people were a national proletariat (within an international proletariat) oppressed by the Western capitalists (Meisner 1967, 188). Certainly, this is not unique to China. Abdullah Laroui speaks of a phase of nationalism which he calls "class nationalism":

> Where, in confrontation with Europe, the fundamentalists oppose a culture (Chinese, Indian, Islamic) and the liberal opposed a nation (Chinese, Turkish, Egyptian, Iranian), the revolutionary opposes a class—one that is often extended to include all or part of the human race exploited by the European bourgeoisie. One may refer to it as class nationalism that nevertheless retains many of the motifs of political and cultural nationalisms; hence the difficulties experienced by many of the analysts who have attempted to define it.
> (quoted in Fitzgerald 1988, 10)

The class-nation of the international arena also has a domestic expression. In this conception, the alleged attributes of a class are extended to the nation, and the measure to which an individual or group fulfilled this criterion ideally governed admissibility to the national community. This is true in the case of Chinese communism, especially during the Cultural Revolution, when the goal was to purge or disenfranchise undesirable classes in the nation and strive to shape the nation in the image of the idealized proletariat. Here the idea of the nation becomes the site of a tension between a revolutionary language with its transnational aspirations and the reality of national boundedness. Yet another means whereby the language of revolutionary class struggle comes to define the nation is the process of placing the "universal" theory of class struggle into a national context. The elevation of Mao Zedong to the role of supreme theorist (together with Lenin and Stalin) and the creation of the "Chinese model" of revolutionary transformation in the late 1930s marks the Sinification of Marxism, in which national distinctiveness became embodied in the particular model of class struggle pioneered by the Chinese. One scarcely needs to mention how radically this "nation-view" differed from that of the KMT's quasi-Confucian representation of the nation.

While it may be difficult for some to conceive today of the return of class-based representations of the nation, it will be interesting to see whether the growing power of feminist movements all over the world will reshape the gendered representation of the nation. Certainly, national identities are historically changeable, reflecting as they do, changes in society. Even the societies of "mature" nations continue to produce new nationalisms or new nation-views where one might least expect to find them. Of the history of the relationship of the Ulster Irish, the Welsh, and the Scots to Britishness, historically the Scots may have had the weakest cultural bases for a separatist identity. Yet the circumstances of the 1960s and 1970s gave rise to a resurgent Scottish nationalism (Breuilly 1982, 280–90; Agnew 1987, 143–59). Separatist movements in India have flourished in recent years. What is little known, however, is that the nationalist movement under Congress leadership against the British Raj was among the strongest in some of these same areas, such as Assam. Subsequent chapters will show how the identities of groups in China, such as the Manchus and Hakka Chinese, and their relationship to Chineseness, fluctuated over the last two centuries.

National identities are unstable not only because they are susceptible to splits, whether by alternative criteria of identity formation (for example, religion rather than language) or by the transference of loyalty to a subgroup (even where the identity of this subgroup is new), but also because all good nationalisms have a transnational vision—witness pan-Africanism, pan-Asianism, pan-Europeanism, pan-Islamism, Shiism, Judaism. To be sure, the manner in which territorial nationalism negotiates its relations with the wider identification takes many forms. Some arguments for national identification find their legitimation in the ultimate achievement of a transcendent order. For instance, the reformist nationalism of Kang Youwei, at the turn of the century in China, justified nationalism as a necessary stage in the ultimate achievement of the "great unity" of all peoples of the world (*datong*). *Datong* was also an ideal that Sun Yat-sen would later celebrate when he linked the destiny of China to that of the oppressed peoples of the world.

In Iran, the criterion that came to determine political community historically had been the Persian language, first in the post-Hellenic Persian revival of Ardashir Sasani in 224 A.D. and then in the flowering of Persian literature under the Arab conquests. The great achievement of the latter period was the Shahnamah of Firdawsi (941–1020 A.D.), in which the poet created an idealized history of pre-Islamic Iran by deliberately avoiding Arabic words as far as possible. Subsequently, in the sixteenth century under the Safavis, Iranian distinctiveness came to be expressed through Shiism rather than language, as Iran became a "bastion of militant Shiism surrounded by hostile Sunni neighbors. . . . A fortress mentality, a we and they dichotomy, gradually developed" (Weryho 1986, 52).

Modern nationalism in Iran is formed by both Persian and Shiite myths, but it is clear that Shiism, while promoting national greatness, also obliges it to a transnational ideal (Benard and Khalilzad 1984). As Fischer and Abedi point out, the chief problem of Iranian thinkers like the Shiite cleric and student of Khomeini, Murtada Mutahhari, was to productively maintain this tension between the universal and the ethnocentric. Mutahhari argued against both Arabism and the pre-Islamic heritage, thereby claiming *Iranian* Shiism as central to the creation of Islamic civilization (Fischer and Abedi 1990, 176, 191). At the same time, Fischer and Abedi's ethnography shows with what swiftness the shape of Iranian nationalism in the streets could change from an anti-Arabism to solidarity as Muslims versus Jews in the aftermath of the Arab-Israeli war of 1967 (1990, 178).

Even in Japan, where one might most expect a perfect congruence between loyalty and territory and least expect any external sanctions for nationalist ideology, pan-Asianism and the idea that Japan derived its special position by protecting other Asian nations from the corrupting influence of Western capitalism bolstered Japanese national identity. For Japanese nationalism, the construction of an East Asian history (*toyoshi*) was necessary for it to reconcile the tension between pursuing the Western model of the "civilized" nation and retaining an autonomy from it (Tanaka 1993). To be sure, pan-Asianism, which grew from this historical construct, also worked nicely to promote Japanese imperialism in Asia, but it would be wrong to see only this dimension. Marius Jansen has written of the pan-Asianism of Miyazaki Torazō, Ōi Kentarō and others who inspired Sun Yat-sen and others with their zeal to destroy Western imperialism. "A re-birth for oppressed peasantries elsewhere in Asia was, for them, a necessary adjunct and stimulus to ameliorating the peasants' lot in Japan" (Jansen 1967, 219).

In Europe today, the contradictoriness of political identifications is in full flower. Resurgent nationalism has surfaced in tandem with the near-realization of a transnational dream—often in a single country, such as Germany. What remains unclear is whether the shape of the new European community will develop into a super-nation-state or whether the form of the nation-state will itself be superseded. Whatever its shape, it is likely that it will have to incorporate some of the functions and symbols of the nation-state. Etienne Balibar wonders whether in the building of the fictive ethnicity of Europe the tendency will be predominantly toward developing a European colingualism or in idealizing a "European demographic identity" conceived mainly in opposition to Turks, Arabs, blacks, and other "southern populations" (1991, 105). Depending on how these boundaries are drawn, the consequences for the "other" will be significantly different in each case.

The multiplicity of nation-views and the idea that political identity is not fixed but shifts between different loci introduces the idea that nationalism is best seen as a relational identity. In other words, the nation, even where it is manifestly not a recent invention, is hardly the realization of an original essence, but a historical configuration designed to include certain groups and exclude or marginalize others—often violently. (Linguistic definitions obviously exclude and marginalize different groups from those who seek to define nations by religious or racial criteria or the criterion of common historical experience.) As a relationship among constituents, the national "self" is defined at any point in time by the Other. Depending on the nature and scale of the oppositional term, the national self contains various smaller "others"—historical others that have effected an often uneasy reconciliation among themselves and potential others that are beginning to form their differences. And it is these potential others that are most deserving of our attention because they reveal the principle that creates nations—the willing into existence of a nation which will choose to privilege its difference and obscure all of the cultural bonds that had tied it to its sociological kin (see chapter 2).

The most easily identifiable expressions of nationalism as a *relationship* are the anti-imperialist movements the world over. Sun Yat-sen and other Chinese nationalists believed that it was in the self-interest of Chinese minorities to join with the Han majority against the imperialists during the war-ravaged republic because of the security in numbers. When the imperialist threat faded, it became easy for these minorities to perceive the threat from precisely the numbers of the Han majority. The pulling apart of East European nation-states in recent times presents the most dramatic indication that the conditions holding one type of nation together no longer prevail. What is just as important to note are the subnationalisms within Lithuania or Georgia as expressions of the great unraveling of our times. Canada is noteworthy not only because of Quebecois nationalism, but also because of the way in which the nation of Quebec might be challenged by a hidden other, such as the Mohawks. The hidden other consists not only of other groups but of alternative principles of grouping as well. Consider the chameleonlike identities in West Asia, where a different configuration is invoked depending on whether the threat is directed against Arab, religious, or territorial nationalism.

My aim is not simply to celebrate "difference." Rather, that individuals and groups simultaneously recognize themselves in and respond to different ideological and cultural representations suggests a critical power in society that is potentially resistant to totalizing ideologies. Historians have been generally concerned with the process whereby national identities are formed and evolve and have neglected to see that it is the same process whereby other identifications and alternative, often incipient, narratives of the nation are repressed and obscured. While the nation has been shown to be an unstable and contingent relationship, History, on the other hand, has often worked to secure the mystique of the nation, or in other words, its dubious claim to an evolving, monistic subjecthood. Social historians and others, while sometimes defying this claim in practice, have not constructed a theoretical challenge to history as the History of the nation-state.

In the following chapters, I will propose an alternative history which emphasizes the dynamic, multiple, and contested nature of historical identities. In place of an evolutionary History, I emphasize how historical actors mobilize particular representations of nation or community against other representations and, while doing so, appropriate dispersed meanings and pasts as their own. In this way, we may view the histories of nations as contingently as nations are themselves contingent. My task is to chart a way which exposes the repressive teleology of the History of the nation and rescues from this History the ways in which the past is meaningful to the present.

1

LINEAR HISTORY AND THE NATION-STATE

IF THE NEXT century is going to be the Pacific century, then the Pacific region will also write the history of the world. What kind of history might that be? The last two centuries have established History as we know it—a linear, progressive history—not only as the dominant mode of experiencing time, but as the dominant mode of being (Young 1990; de Certeau 1988; Soja 1989). That is to say, time overcomes space—a condition in which the Other in geographical space will, *in time*, come to look like earlier versions of us. Perhaps more than any other non-Western society, East Asian societies have successfully adopted this mode of Enlightenment History. While this History has quite possibly played a part in the attainment of certain modernist goals, it has also involved totalization and closure in order to destroy or domesticate the Other. The role of this chapter is to study the strategies of closure that have been developed in writing the linear History of the Chinese nation. At the same time, I will also explore the cracks and fissures through which we, like some of the historical figures we study, might read against the grain of this History.

Hegel's *Philosophy of History* (1956) remains to our day the most important foundation for understanding linear, and necessarily teleological, progressive History. For Hegel, the telos of History—the structure governing its progress—is the unfolding self-awareness of Spirit which is Reason. There are two moments in this self-awareness: that of Spirit itself embodied objectively in the rationality of religion, laws, and the State and that of the individual subject. Progressive self-awareness of the individual involves not only the recognition of the freedom of the self from the hold of nature and ascriptive orders, but most supremely, the realization of his simultaneous oneness with Spirit. This is true freedom, the end of History, and culminates, as is well-known, in the Prussian state where the real is the rational and the rational is the real. The histories that we (including Asian historians) write of Asia continue to be enmeshed in this Hegelian conception, although shorn of much of his metaphysics and his brutal racism. It is prefigured in our language through three overlapping Hegelian inheritances: Marxism, Weberian sociology of religion, and nationalist ideology.

Hegel evokes the unfolding of Spirit in an exquisite allegory of movement from darkness to light: of a blind man

> suddenly becoming possessed of sight, beholding the
> bright glimmering of the dawn, the growing light and the
> flaming glory of the ascending Sun. The boundless forget-
> fulness of his own individuality in this pure splendor, is
> his first feeling—utter astonishment. But when the Sun is
> risen, this astonishment is diminished; objects around are
> perceived, and from them the individual proceeds to the
> contemplation of his own inner being, and thereby the ad-
> vance is made to the perception of the relation between
> the two. Then inactive contemplation is quitted for activity;
> by the close of the day, man has erected a building con-
> structed from his own inner Sun; and when in the evening
> he contemplates this, he esteems it more highly than the
> original external Sun. For now he stands in a *conscious rela-
> tion* to his Spirit, and therefore a *free* relation. If we hold
> this image fast in mind, we shall find it symbolizing the
> course of History, the great Day's work of Spirit. (Hegel
> 1956, 103)

Within this framework, Hegel examines the extent of Spirit's self-awareness in the non-Western world. Africa (Africans are considered a grade above American Indians) is "the land of childhood, which lying beyond the day of self-conscious history, is enveloped in the dark mantle of Night" (Hegel 1956, 91). Spirit is somewhat better embodied in China and India but can scarcely gain self-awareness and hence remains "unhistorical History." China possesses objective rationality in the State, but the state rules the individuals who obey like mindless people. In India, the contemplation of inner subjectivity leads to the Negation of Reality, and thus the State, as the embodi-ment of Rationality, and true subjective freedom are both denied (Hegel 1956, 140). Interwoven into the philosophic, historical, and sociological discourse are unrestrained outpourings on the nature of Chinese and Hindoo character. The distinguishing feature of these peoples is that everything that belongs to Spirit—such as Heart, Religion, Morality, Science and Art—is alien to them. Both peoples are endowed with servile and brutish consciousness and without a triumphant assertion of the inner man (Hegel 1956, 138, 167).

It has perhaps not gone unnoticed that Hegel's *History*—delivered from 1822 to 1825—possesses a philosophical structure that is eerily appropriate for a conquering power poised for world domination. At least fifteen years before the Opium War, Hegel mentions in passing that the conquest of China by the British was an inevitable and necessary fact. History enables not simply the justification of world mastery by the West, but as Robert Young has pointed out, the appropriation of the Other as a form of knowledge. Thus the universalization of History subjects other social and epistemic forms into its own overarching framework and finds them severely wanting. Emmanuel Levinas has seen this as a characteristic of the concept of totality in Western philosophy which produces all knowledge by appropriating and sublating the Other within itself. The primary mode of such a totalization is History, which incorporates the Other into the time of universal history and under the name of abstract reason. Levinas contends that this is cruel and unjust and advocates that the only way for the Other to resist sublation is by deriving its meaning from a time separate from History (Levinas 1969, 52, 55).

Specifically, privileging History over other forms of experiencing time and over space is a double closure that denies intelligibility to people without History. There is neither time, space nor, one hopes, need here to rehearse the many different arguments by Lévi-Strauss (1962), Paul Ricoeur (1984), Hadyn White (1987), Michel de Certeau (1988) and, most recently, Sheldon Pollock (1989) and Paul Cohen (1992) in Asian studies, who show that historicality is constitutive of human existence and the experience of temporality is recorded through many different narrative and non-narrative modes. Examples of this include literature, mythology, genealogies, art, ritual, language, and the like. Moreover, they have also shown that the narrative form of History has itself a metaphysical dimension. Thus, in both cases, access to the past must be a qualified enterprise, a hermeneutic of both understanding and explanation.

History as the mode of being, whatever its provenance, became associated with the expansion of Western power, but it is important to note that these powers emerged simultaneously as nation-states and empires—a phenomenon that has yet to be adequately under-

stood. My argument is that if History is the mode of being, the condition which enables modernity as possibility, the nation-state is the
agency, the subject of History which will realize modernity. Hegel
emphasizes that the particularity of Spirit is always manifest in the
nation; and nations attain "mature individuality" only when the dim
and hazy forms of historical apprehension—legends and poetic
dreams—are dispelled and a people are *fully conscious* of themselves
in History (1956, 2). It is only nations in the fullness of (their) History
that realize freedom. Those without History, those non-nations such
as tribal polities, empires, and others have no claims or rights; even
more, nations have the right to destroy non-nations and bring Enlightenment to them. Thus do nations become empires. This is how
we can understand Hegel's belief that the British conquest of China
was an inevitable and *necessary* fact.

In order to understand how such assumptions became realized in
the empires of the late nineteenth century, it is important to grasp
that Hegel's History was perhaps only the most sophisticated formulation of the discourse of evolutionism which dominated the nineteenth century. Evolutionism, which, in the words of George Stocking (1987, 183), was like a massive tree with many branches, blended
organically with the landscape of Darwinism in the later nineteenth
century. By the end of the century, when *social* Darwinism began to
make an impact on the non-Western world, it represented the underside of Enlightenment rationality or, more appropriately, its monster-
child, for it was in the name of enlightened civilization that the hierarchies of "advanced" and "backward" races were sustained and the
destructiveness of imperialist exploitation justified.[1]

While the numerous works on social Darwinism indicate that it
was understood and used within Western societies in various different ways (Stocking 1987; Hofstadter 1955), some of its assumptions
were pervasive. For example, at the turn of the century in America,
even critics of imperialism did not seek to dislocate expansion from
its Darwinian racialist framework. Indeed, the assumption of racial
superiority was often inverted and used as an argument against an-
nexation: thus, for America to assume government of the Filipinos
would be to introduce an uncongenial and inassimilable people incapable of acquiring the Anglo-Saxon virtues of self-governance (Hof-

1. Cast in terms of "natural selection" and "survival of the fittest," evolutionary
racialism was, "from the European viewpoint, a grimly optimistic, but morally ambiguous doctrine, which could be used to justify the worst excesses of expropriation and
colonial rule" (Stocking 1987, 237).

stadter 1955, 192). As a discourse through which the reality of the nineteenth century world was apprehended, social Darwinism sustained a set of recognizable features that was not lost on the colonized or those on the peripheries of the world system of nation-states, especially in East Asia, where it sounded the alarm of the "Yellow Peril" (Hofstadter 1955, 189). Not surprisingly, the most important of these was race.[2] Social Darwinism tended to fix upon race—that combination of biology, environment and culture—as the repository of those attributes which enabled (or prevented) a group to evolve toward civilization. Stocking writes that there can be no doubt that evolutionary thought "offered strong ideological support for the whole colonial enterprise in the later nineteenth century . . . savages were not simply morally delinquent or spiritually deluded, but racially incapable" (1987, 237). We need only skim the writings of turn-of-the-century foreigners in China like Arthur Smith's on Chinese "characteristics" (1899) to see how cultural or racial stereotyping (later taken over by the colonized themselves as problems of "national character") tended to produce the need for enlightenment from outside.[3]

But race has to be understood within a wider discourse. Social Darwinism represented a closed, mutually defining discourse of History, nation, and race in which the only justification for nationhood was whether a race, as Hobsbawm (1990, 41) suggests, could be shown to fit in with or to advance Historical progress. We know that the birth of professional History in the universities of the West was deeply tied to national concerns, and the profession derived its authority from its role as the true spokesman of the nation. For instance, the historical profession was established in the French university system during the 1870s after defeat in the Franco-Prussian War. It regarded itself not merely as transmitter of the national heritage, but as "molders of opinion who had been entrusted with the task of employing the lessons of history to restore a sense of national pride among the citizens of a recently humiliated fatherland in search of

2. By race, I refer to a categorical difference of people engendered by perceived physical and attendant sociocultural differences. The perceived physical or biological differences include notions of "blood" or "species" and work to create an inassimilable categorical difference with the perceiving group. As a construct of difference, Michael Banton (1980) has shown us that different eras have employed different discursive concepts to explain and legitimate this difference, such as ancestry, blood, or genetics.

3. See, for instance, Arthur Smith's last chapter of *Village Life in China* (1899), in which the Christianity which will save China is founded on solid principles of social Darwinism, such as "natural selection."

regeneration and revenge" (Keylor 1975, 3). Professional historians in newly established history departments of universities in America of the 1880s took it upon themselves to replace a "factious" and "spurious" popular patriotism with an authentic and sound nationalism (Novick 1988, 71). The dominant view in the profession in late nineteenth-century America was that history should "heal the nation" after the bloody strife of the Civil War. But as Novick has pointed out, national reconciliation between Southern and Northern historians was based on a racialist nationalism of "Anglo-Saxonism" in which not only were blacks regarded as the "outcasts from evolution," but the purity of the race was sought to be preserved from the hordes of "Celts" and "Latins" pushing in from the margins of Europe (Novick 1988, 80–81; Hofstadter 1955, 172).

Evolutionary History had been the record of progress of the superior races and, by that standard, the stagnant, backward races could be said to have no History and, hence, no nationality. To be sure, the relationship between race and nation—still vague in Hegel—was a complex one that would, of course, unfold its own continuing history in the West. Several authors are, however, united in determining that, between 1870 and the end of World War I, a virtual blurring of the distinctions between race and nation took place (Hobsbawm 1990, 108; Hofstadter 1955, 172; Stocking 1987, 32, 66, 235). How and why European nations sought to view differences among themselves as racially based is a complicated matter beyond the scope of this chapter; the understanding that only certain advanced races possessed nationality and rights over races without nations and History was, as we shall see, resoundingly clear to the nearly colonized in East Asia. It was the reason why the only non-Western country to be able to break this closed circle in the era before World War II, Japan, needed to display not only its military and industrial prowess, but also the signs of racial/cultural superiority through such matters as beef-eating campaigns and the conquest of the recently barbarianized Chinese as the mark of civilized status (Gluck 1985, 88–90, 135; Pyle 1978, 75).

The circle of social Darwinist discourse not only enabled nations to be imperial powers, but also necessitated a cultural project to maintain the colonies as non-nations. Imperialism in the nineteenth century was justified as the battle of principles: of modern civilization against barbarism, of nations versus empires. Such was the basis of McCartney's assertion of his rights versus the Qianlong emperor. Yet, a half-century later, we see the British monarch herself as empress of India. Victoria was Queen of England, but as Bernard Cohn

(1983, 201) has pointed out, she was Empress of India. This dualism, this right to maintain empire while being a nation, was centrally dependent on the ability to demonstrate that the colonies continued to remain non-nations. In India, the state-sanctioned sociology of castes, tribes, and principalities was part of this great "colonializing" project. The numerous "invented traditions" undertaken by colonials in Africa to produce and fix the African "tribe" as a "traditional" community steeped in ritual and paternalistic ideology may also be viewed as part of this "colonializing" project (Ranger 1983, 230–36, 248). In China, as James Hevia (1990) has shown, the sack of Beijing in 1860 and in 1900 involved, among other things, a performative representation of the Chinese imperium as belonging to an order beyond civilization. After the Boxer sack, when it was once again necessary to do business with the imperial Chinese state, it became imperative for the imperial powers to reconstruct the Chinese emperor as a civilized emperor, a monarch in their own image. That modern empires could only rule non-nations was not just a descriptive statement; it had to be continuously reproduced to legitimate imperial rule by nations.

THE HEGELIAN LEGACY IN WESTERN SCHOLARSHIP

It is well known that the Hegelian world view is communicated, particularly about Asia, through Marx in his letters about China and in the discussion of the Asiatic mode of production. More keenly aware of the destructive underside of the Enlightenment, Marx faces up to the reality of this destruction. The brutalism of capitalism, which always accompanied the overseas journey of the Enlightenment, he described as a misery that was

> essentially different and infinitely more intensive than all
> Hindustan had to suffer before . . . England has broken
> down the entire framework of Indian society, without any
> symptoms of reconstitution yet appearing. This loss of his
> old world, with no gain of a new one, imparts a particular
> kind of melancholy to the present misery of the Hindu, and
> separates Hindustan, ruled by Britain, from all its ancient
> traditions, and from the whole of its past history. (Marx
> 6.25.1853, 95)

And yet this kind of sympathy against History, as it were, is less common than his tendency to privilege the forward movement of History. He felt that the destruction of these stagnant, nonhistorical societies was the price for affiliating with the telos of progress. He produced a striking image of the timelessness of these societies which must dissolve on contact with the British like "a mummy carefully preserved in a hermetically sealed coffin whenever it is brought into contact with the open air" (Marx 6.14.1853, 86).[4]

A less well-known mediator between Hegel and our own concepts is Max Weber, or at least the Parsonian reading of Max Weber, which makes him the founding father of modernization theory. Weber's studies of the religions of China and India represent, of course, much more erudite and balanced studies of these societies than is Hegel's *History*, but Weber too sought to investigate the nature of rationality in these societies and, in contrast to the Calvinist ethic, found them wanting. For Weber, these societies revealed highly sophisticated, rational systems, such as the Chinese bureaucracy or the Indian caste system, but they were "substantively rational" (lacking the "formal rationality" of modern subjects self-conscious of their freedom) and ultimately constrained by the unquestioned beliefs of the culture.

German authorities on Weber, such as Schlucter and Roth, minimize Weber's evolutionism and emphasize his effort to understand how rationalizations were tied to the metaphysical goals of these cultures. Weber was certainly alive to the danger of interpreting rationality monistically: the idea that only the rationality of the "disenchanted world" was valid (Roth and Schluchter 1979, 51). But Talcott Parsons' introduction to *The Sociology of Religions* (Weber 1969) locates Weber firmly in an evolutionary trend. He writes, "This book is clearly the strategically central part of a generally evolutionary view of the development of human society . . . [Weber] treated the development of the modern Western world, and particularly the sector of it influenced by ascetic Protestantism, as standing in the vanguard of the most important evolutionary trend." Sensing perhaps the affinity of his reading of Weber with Hegel's *History*, Parsons makes a passing effort to distance this reading from Hegel: "This factor [religious orientation] is, however, nowhere treated as automatically unfolding or 'actualizing itself' except through highly complex processes of interaction with other factors"; but the difference cited seems simply to give religious orientation a sociological foundation absent in Hegel's idealism (Parsons in Weber 1969, lx). However we regard Weber, there is an evolutionary strain in his writings which enabled

4. Marx was not always above the racist stereotypes of evolutionism either. Writing of the opium addiction of the Chinese, he opined, "It would seem as though history had first to make this whole people drunk before it could rouse them out of their hereditary stupidity" (Marx 1853 [14 June], 85).

the postwar resurgence of (to be sure, non–social Darwinian) evolutionism to appropriate him.

The subsequent section takes up the Chinese adoption of Enlightenment History as their own and pursues its inseparability from the project of creating a national subject evolving to modernity. This History involves not only reading in a dynamic of progress to modernity, but also a reverse project of recovering the primordial subject, of rejoining the present to the past through some essentializing strategy. For the remainder of this section, I wish to suggest that while foreign and particularly American historical scholarship on China is involved less with the creation of a specifically Chinese national subject—though there is something to Pamela Crossley's point (1990a) that Sinology remains wedded to the Confucian, assimilationist paradigm of Sinicization—it is still considerably involved with the nation as the vehicle of the historical passage to modernity. Whether the scholar sees China actually moving in that direction or forever arrested in the premodern, he or she participates in an evolutionism that is closely tied to the ideology of History. The central narratives of this scholarship remain tied to European, or rather, the Enlightenment model, whereas a wider, critical history, which reveals the repressive functions of this model of History, still remains mostly unwritten.

Few serious contemporary scholars still actively use the Parsonian modernization model. Moreover, my comments here do not reflect on the general quality and usefulness of the historical work done on China, much of which has evidently been very valuable for my own work both in this book and elsewhere. I do, however, feel that there has been insufficient attention to the structuring narratives in which many of these historical questions have been embedded and, in this respect, the assumptions of the Parsonian model have been hard to shake off.[5] In many social-historical accounts, these Weberian-Parsonian assumptions of the transition to modernity combine with a Marxist or neo-Marxist theory of stages to furnish the basic periods within which scholars engage in the activities of normal puzzle-solving. Thus, we speak of a "late imperial period" stretching from the Tang-Song transition through the impact of the West. This period is characterized by protocapitalist formations, proto-industrialism,

5. While some historians may believe that they do not write narrative histories at all, Paul Ricoeur shows how even the most resolute anti-narrativist movements in contemporary historiography, such as the Annalists, who seek to explode the concept of linear time, still cannot avoid the narrative model of emplotment (1984, 1: 208–25).

commercial capitalism, and emergent bourgeois values; the Weberian influence can be found in questions about the presence or absence of administrative rationality (the question of despotism), self-regulating urban complexes, gentry managerial society, and, most recently a civil society and a public sphere. The intellectual history of this composite paradigm emphasizes the presence or absence of the tension between worldly and transcendent values, of individualism and liberalism, and of autonomy from the state.

In his pioneering 1984 study, Paul Cohen drew attention to the Americo-centrism inherent in the different paradigms dominating Chinese studies, especially modernization and imperialism paradigms. He contrasted this with the bare emergence of what he calls the "China-centered approach" earlier figured in the work of Philip Kuhn, Evelyn Rawski, Frederic Wakeman, and others. By turning away from the centrality of "culture" and "tradition" and emphasizing history—presumably the shaping force of the past, these scholars were able to do more justice to the Chinese historical record. As admiring as I am of Cohen's critique, there are problems with the China-centered approach.

Do Chinese historical materials prefigure a certain narrative of their own which Western and Chinese historians have to listen closely to and then reproduce as best they can? Or are the historical materials simply "noise," heterophony, the meaning of which is disclosed by the narratives through which the historian "symbolizes" them? Cohen might present a weak version of the former, or an argument which combines the two, but our problems hardly end here. If there is a prefigured narrative to be recovered—with whatever our analytical categories add to it—how can we know whose history it is and what other voices it suppresses? The problem of essentialization remains.

The history of China can no longer be innocently a history of the West or the history of the true China. It must attend to the politics of narratives—whether these be the rhetorical schemas we deploy for our own understanding or those of the historical actors who give us their world. The first lesson we learn is that the history of China we confront has already been narrativized in the Enlightenment mode—and not simply by the Asian historical scholarship we read or through which we read our sources. From the first years of the twentieth century, many of the historical actors we study themselves sought to narrate their history in the linear, teleological mode and thus performatively propel Chinese history into the progress of universal History. This transformation of the Chinese past operates both as an order repressive of the heterophony of the Chinese past (and present, insofar as the representations of the past seek to shape the present) and as a Chineseness that is simultaneously Western and Chinese. The purpose of this book is not to recover an uncontaminated, originary history of China, but to locate the site where narratives, indeed layers of narrative, seek to appropriate or wrestle with the historical real, which, of course, cannot be meaningfully known except through narrative symbolizations.

THE APORIA OF LINEAR HISTORY AND THE POLITICS OF NATIONALISM

Western imperialism was, of course, unable to contain the momentum among non-nations to convert into nation-states. The story of national independence movements has mostly been told. The matter of History, however, remains obscure. History was the principal mode whereby non-nations were converted into nations. History was adopted as the mode of being of the nation not only in East Asia, of course, but all over the world. This affiliation with the civilized world permitted the defense of the nation (as a subject with History, of History), but, simultaneously, the commitment to History also necessitated modernity as its telos.

Thus nations emerge as the subjects of History just as History emerges as the ground, the mode of being, of the nation. To be sure, nations are not born full-blown out of nothing. In chapter 2, I argue against the ahistoricity of many recent studies of nationalism which ignore the complex transactions between premodern representations of political community and the modern nation. But for our purposes here, it is important to understand that modern nationalism seeks to appropriate these pre-existing representations into the mode of being of the modern nation—that is, the nation as existing in the time of History and embodied in the nation-state.

We have emphasized that History and the modern nation are inseparable. The nation—hence nationalist leaders and the nation-state who act in the name of the nation—attains its privilege and sovereignty as the subject of History; modern History is meaningless without a subject—that which remains even as it changes. Our own practice of history shows us that what endures through most of the changes in fashions of historical subjects of inquiry—such as monarchs, the state, classes, individuals, identity groups—is the silent space of reference: the nation. We take for granted that the histories we study are the histories of China, India, Japan, France. It is in this way that the nation insinuates itself as the master subject of History into the very assumptions of both professional and popular history. This nation-space is never innocently silent. It comes with claims to territories, peoples, and cultures for all of "its" history, and the historian is often already implicated with the project of an evolving subject simply by participating in the received strategies of periodization. That even the best social and local historians do not find themselves challenging this assumption or theorizing an alternative to the already-always nation-space is testimony to the complicity of History and the nation-state.

I would like to anchor the idea of the necessity of constructing a subject in linear History to the philosophical notions of Paul Ricoeur on historical time. They will also help clarify one of the most persistent splits in nationalist histories: between the atavism of the nation and its telos of modernity. The linear representation of phenomenological time, time as a succession of infinite "nows," generates a fundamental discordance in the experience of time. The fleeting presence of time, "the sorrow of the finite" in this representation cannot be overcome, according to Ricoeur, by philosophical attempts at resolution such as the Augustinian conception of *distentio animi* (Ricoeur 1984, 1:16–18) or Heidegger's hierarchy of temporality (1984, 1:60–62). Further, the discordance is heightened by the contrast between time as a series of indifferent instants and time as eternity, a recurrent, alternative perception of time (the time of God, the end of history). Thus we are faced with a paradox in which "on the cosmic scale our life span is insignificant, yet this brief period of time when we appear in the world is the moment during which all meaningful questions arise" (Ricoeur 1991, 343).

Historical time, according to Ricoeur, provides us with a sense of continuity that relieves the anxiety of temporal flux as a series of nows.[6] But this sense of historical continuity is enabled by the construction of an ideal unity that is by no means universal. Indeed, I would argue that traditional, cyclical conceptions of history which mark or emphasize return are not only alternative ways of constructing continuity, but also produce less anxiety than linear histories which expose the uncertainty of a voyage into the future without return. What then are the devices of coherence that linear History has had to construct to overcome anxiety or *distentio*? The most important

6. Following Heidegger, Ricoeur writes of historical time as a "stretching-along" of life, of a "becoming" between birth and death that is preserved from sheer dispersion (from Augustine's *distentio*) by the capacity to recapitulate—to repeat, to retrieve—our inherited potentialities (Ricoeur 1984, 1: 61–62; 1991, 102). It is this capacity to recapitulate which allows us to derive a sense of historical continuity from temporality as such.

device is the narrative of evolution, which anchors the future to a measure of certainty by means of the subject of History: that which evolves (whether as morally progressive or neutrally) is that which remains even as it changes. The subject of History is a metaphysical unity devised to address the aporias in the experience of linear time: the disjuncture between past and present as well as the non-meeting between time as flux and time as eternal.

However, Ricoeur reminds us that these narratives both hide these aporias under its ideal type of resolution as well as reveal them (1988, 3:139–40). Note, for instance, the way in which Hegel's History both records the evolution of Spirit in History but also marks the goal of History as the end of History. Hegel thus reproduces the aporia between flux and eternity. What interests me is the way in which the Historical effort to resolve the aporias of time produces rifts in the narrative which in turn become implicated with the politics of nationalism.

The nation as the subject of History is never able to completely bridge the aporia between the past and the present. At one level, the ideology of the nation-state even finds it politically serviceable. Little noticed by analysts, the nation actually both lives in History and also at the end of it. It simultaneously legitimates itself as an essence that continues through History (even while the particular dies), but as also free from its hold—modern self-consciousness is, after all in every way, the end of history. As the subject of History, it must daily reproduce the project of recovering its national essence—to secure its transparency as the already-always of the nation-space—especially in the face of internal and external challenges to this claim. At the same time, the Enlightenment discourse of modern civilization has made it imperative for all societies to affiliate themselves with modernity. Committing oneself to modernity and progress, however, is a commitment to the celebration of the new, the breaking of old shackles. Thus while on the one hand, nation-states glorify the ancient or eternal character of the nation, they also seek to emphasize the unprecedented nature of the nation-*state*, because it is only in this form that the people-nation has been able to *realize* itself as the self-conscious subject of History. That the nation-state *represents* this subjecthood, a topic discussed in chapter 2, is, of course, maintained parenthetically.

This split in the time of the nation is sometimes presented in terms of the dichotomy between the particular and universal or, in Asian studies, as the dualism between East and West. Thus Chinese "ti-yong" thinking (Chinese learning for essential principles, Western learning for practical use) and Indian dichotomies of (Vedantic) spirituality versus Western materialism have been interpreted as East versus West binary thought designed to address the identity crises of Westernized intellectuals who have given up their own culture for Western modernity. The need to speak of a separate but superior or equivalent traditional culture or history is psychologically comforting for non-Western intellectuals. Joseph Levenson, who posed the problem as a contest between history (the particularity of Chinese history) and value (universal modernity), is perhaps the most articulate advocate of this view (Levenson 1965, 109–16). It will be noted that this interpretation depends on burdening Chinese intellectuals with an intolerable sense of inferiority. Whether or not it is possible to sustain this kind of psychological generalization is not something I will engage here.[7] Suffice it to say that Levenson did not see that the dichotomy was itself a product of the affiliation with the new mode of History. Thus, I prefer to read these dualistic formulations as ways of addressing the gulf between the past and the present produced by the positioning of the nation as the subject of linear History.

As such, the temporal split may be found as much in American or French history as in the history of China, India, or Kenya. According to Peter Dimock (1992), George Bancroft's *History of America*, written in the 1820s and considered a founding narrative of American identity, reveals a paradoxical double dynamic of historicization and a simultaneous denial of history—the famous American exceptionalism. On the one hand is History in the Hegelian mode: the spirit of civilization mastering and ordering space, a history which in the name of progress (over non-History) destroyed peoples and cultures.[8] This is what allows Bancroft to say that "in the view of civilization, the immense domain (of America) was a solitude." It is a mode which allows him to dispassionately describe the massacre of Native Americans and the enslavement of blacks. On the other hand is the exceptionalism that Dimock writes about—the "new time" of the nation during which liberty gushes forth in copious and perennial

7. In an analysis of Mahatma Gandhi by Partha Chatterjee (1986) and in one of the older Liang Qichao by Tang Xiaobing (1991), the antimodernism of both historical figures is viewed not psychologistically, but as oppositionist. Though in very different ways, both authors see these figures as driving a wedge into, and creating a space of autonomy from, the totalizing History of modernity. In the end, however, this autonomous space is co-opted in both, and perhaps most, societies, by the nation-state, which converts it into an essentialized expression of "culture" (as opposed to "civilization," which comes to refer to Enlightenment History) and can use it to maintain traditional, often sexist, forms of domination (see chapter 7).

8. Peter Dimock, in personal communication (5 April 1992) says that Bancroft heard Hegel in 1819/1820.

fountains. This break with time is also the break with the rest of the world and establishes the uniqueness of the nation. Through these two narrative modes, the nation is both able to express its historicity at the same time that it will be able to declare its novelty, its freedom from History.

Sometimes the nation is unable to reconcile the temporal split, and narrative failure is expressed in the political conflict between those who would emphasize the ancient and pristine essence of the nation and those who stress the new and the modern. The conflict in Israel between the religious right, for whom the meaning of the nation is embodied in the sacred books, and the more secular nationalists who seek to project the nation along a progressive vision is a good example (as is the case of India, noted in chapter 2). The Handelmans have examined the conflict over the choice of the emblem on the Israeli flag during the founding of Israel in 1948.

> The emerging national culture of Israeli Jews tended to be secular, yet rooted in ancient Israel, and so again intertwined with religion. Therefore the symbolism had to include the symbolism of the ancient that would be understood clearly as a source of secular culture. (Handelman and Shamgar-Handelman 1990, 216)

But this was a heavy ambiguity for the emblem to bear and it flared into an open conflict between the Zionist religious parties and the primarily secular ones. The religious parties wished to use the menorah, which is identified with the birth of the Israelites as a nation, the Temple cult, and statehood blessed by the divine. The secularists wished to combine the symbolism of the menorah with that of the seven stars—the seven hours of the workday symbolizing the rationalization of labor and social benefits and, more widely, the values of the Enlightenment. This metaphor rapidly came under scathing attack by the religious parties and the resulting official emblem of Israel, the Titus menorah, "synthesized time (the last Jewish state), place (Jerusalem, Israel), the Jewish people, and the qualities of the primordial and eternal. But the ratified emblem contained no motif of the innovative aspirations of modern Zionism for the future" (Handelman and Shamgar-Handelman 1990, 219–20).

Perhaps the most significant political manifestation of this split inhabits the concept of the "people." As the basis of the nation's sovereignty, the people were old, and yet the people had to be reborn to partake of the new world. The foundation of the American Revolution is, of course, the people. During the revolution, the "people" could not be a source of legitimization of the new order when they were out on the streets engaging in popular politics. To serve as the source of authority, the people had to be authorized through a higher impersonal mechanism: the written constitution (Warner 1990). The people would have to be created to serve as the people. Similarly, one of the most important projects of intellectuals and the state in the new nations of China and India was and is to remake the "people." The pedagogy of the people was undertaken not only by the nation-state through the educational system, but also by intellectuals through the folklore movement, through literature and, most importantly, through the campaigns against religion (see chapter 3). The nation emerged in the name of the people, but the people who mandated the nation would have to be remade to serve as their own sovereign. The making/remaking of the people is the political expression of the temporal problem: the metaphysics of History as the evolution of the same.

The problem of the people inhabiting the aporetic time of the nation is most clear in the writings of Sun Yat-sen. His writings also reveal how this aporia presents a site of contestation of the narratives of the nation. Sun argues that China, which for him is the Han nation, was the world's most perfectly formed nation because the people were bound together by all five of the criteria that it took to form a nation: blood/race, language, custom, religion, and livelihood. At the same time, Sun is unclear on whether the nation is already fully awakened or whether national consciousness needs to be further aroused. He is torn between these options because, on the one hand, nationalists like himself could fulfill their mission only if the Han people still suffered from a "slave mentality" with no national consciousness. On the other hand, the pre-existing fullness of China as a nation was necessary for the legitimacy of any nationalist rhetoric. In other words, if the people-nation had always been present historically, then on what grounds could the present nation-state make a special claim to legitimacy as the first embodiment of the people-nation?

Initially, Sun maintained both positions by arguing that the awakening was also a re-awakening. There had been difficult historical periods when the Han people had risen to the occasion and revealed the fullness of their national being, as during the Han resistance to the Jurchens or the Mongols. Ultimately, however, Sun concealed this ambiguity by transforming it into a problem caused by Confucian cosmopolitanism: the original spirit of Han independence had been weakened by the cosmopolitanism which accepted alien rulers like the present Manchu regime as rulers of the Chinese people. This was, of course, precisely the cosmopolitanism advocated by his reformer enemies, who advocated a China composed of the Han as well as the other ethnic groups in the old empire. Sun and the republican revolutionaries sought to mobilize a particular history not only to serve as the foundation of the new nation-state, but to delegitimate the ideological core of the alternative territorial and historical conception of the nation (Sun Yat-sen 1986, 41–42; see also 1924, 645–48).

What appears as the delineation of an evolution of a nation is a complex project of repressions and recreations, the sublation of the other in the self. To us, in our subject positions as modern historians, the assumed transparency of linear History blinds us to its rhetorical strategies for containing these repressions, for preventing a rupture in the body of the nation. We need to reflect theoretically on such basic features as periodization and special eras as being not simply convenient ways to organize data, nor simply as the teleological path to modernity, but as rhetorical strategies to conceal the aporias and repressions necessitated by the imposition of a master narrative. When we do so, we can see how the everyday work of historians writing within these categories may reproduce the ideology of the nation-state.

THE NATION STATE AND CHINESE HISTORY IN THE ENLIGHTENMENT MODE

By the early twentieth century, Chinese history came to be written in the Enlightenment mode. The historian Liang Qichao was perhaps the first to write the history of China in the narrative of the Enlightenment. He made it clear that a people could not become a nation without a History in the linear mode. Indeed, his version of world history, written in 1902, perhaps among the first in Chinese, is not only written as an account of the European, and especially, Aryan, conquest of the world, it is also written from the European perspective of conquest and the bringing of enlightenment to the world (Liang Qichao 1902a [wenji v.4]: 1–30; see also Tang Xiaobing 1991, 133). Whereas his one-time mentor Kang Youwei had appropriated the idea of progress within the categories of Confucian historiography, Liang's narrative represents a total repudiation of traditional Chinese historiography as being unable to give meaning to the Chinese national experience.

From this time onward, much of the Chinese intelligentsia rapidly developed a linear, progressive history of China that was modeled on the European experience of liberation from medieval/autocratic domination. Liang had achieved this by reproducing the threefold division of Western history into the ancient, medieval, and modern periods in the Chinese context. Subsequent periodizations of Chinese history often elaborated Liang's basic scheme (Fu Sinian 1928, 176). Liang criticized traditional Chinese historiography for dividing history by monarchical reigns and ignoring the history of the people-nation (*guomin*, also translated as citizens). So closely was his conception of History linked to the nation-state that he employed a territorial metaphor likening the division of periods in linear History to a treaty between nation-states marking their respective jurisdictions (Liang Qichao 1901 [*wenji* v.3]: 10–11).

Besides the threefold periodization scheme, another device often resorted to in historical periodization—such as to be found in post–May 4th historiography of China—is that of the Renaissance. Both the threefold periodization and the idea of the Renaissance are of great significance in "re-dressing" the problems of the nation-state rhetorically. In the simple version, the ancient age is the age of the creation of a people and culture. It is a foundational trope of purity and originariness. The medieval age is one of decay—inner ills and outer barbarians vitiate the purity of the people or culture. Efforts to renew the spirit or purity work only temporarily. The modern period is one of renewal—often through struggle—and change, change—it is hoped—toward progress. The modern period may or may not come with a renaissance; certainly the idea of the renaissance dramatizes the general disposition of the modern era to recover a lost past— the problem of reconnecting with the past even as one sheds the accretions of a middle age, whether this be Confucianism, barbarian rule, or superstition—as one forges into a new world. The entire apparatus then works to recover the continuity of culture and people even while it permits the historian to reject that against which one will fashion the future.

The schemas of History work to re-dress the temporal split and thus "forge" the homogenous and continuous national subject. On the other hand, the cracks in these schemas are apparent when historians address the inevitable question of with whom the present is to be sutured. What or who constitutes the national subject? Which groups, which races, which regions, which classes make the nation and which do not? At a more subtle level, the narratives of different historians also reveal different degrees and modalities of closure or openness in defining the national subject, thereby disclosing the fragility of the enterprise itself. In the non-Marxist historiographical tradition of modern China, the project of defining the national subject has preoccupied the most sophisticated historians, especially in the context of the problem of periodization. Both the global discourse of social Darwinism and the anti-Manchu politics of the Republican Revolution forced a conception of the national community that was made up exclusively of the Han race (*zhongzu*).

Even Liang Qichao, who had opposed the narrow racism of the revolutionaries by calling their nationalism of the Han a petty nationalism (*xiaominzuzhuyi*) in opposition to his own conception of a great nationalism (*daminzuzhuyi*), could not fully avoid the racialist underpinnings of the discourse he had adopted. His History is shot through and through with the evolutionist notions of the time. This is particularly clear in his logic that a people without a linear History will soon be forced off the stage of History because they have no means of forming groups and uniting against others who will aggress upon them. Moreover, Liang had little doubt that only the white, Aryan race and the yellow race (at least potentially) possessed History (Liang Qichao 1902a [*wenji* v.4]: 15–20). But where Liang stopped short was in determining that a nation should be the polity of a single race.

In Liang's periodization, ancient Chinese history extended from the sage emperors till the Qin unification (221 B.C.). "This was a China of China. This was the period when the Chinese people(s) developed themselves, competed among themselves and organized among themselves. They were victorious over the barbarian races" (Liang Qichao 1901 [*wenji* v.3]: 10–11). The medieval period was the history of a China of Asia which would extend until the Qianlong era (1796). This was a time when China had interactions with other Asian peoples and developed its centralized autocracy. While the Han people were often actually overwhelmed by central Asian races, spiritually, the Han overcame them and, by the end of the period, the races of Asia (I believe he means the Han and China's Central Asian neighbors) came together to form a great race facing the outsiders. The modern period was one of China in the world where the Chinese would, together with other Asian peoples, rid themselves of autocracy and compete with the Western nations (Liang Qichao 1901 [*wenji* v.3]: 12). In this model, there is an antiquity which saw the birth of the true China—a China of China, as well as a middle period dominated by autocracy and political defeat. But Liang's politics of "great nationalism" obliged him to incorporate the non-Han into the nation (see chapter 4 for further elaboration of this position and chapter 5 for his anxieties regarding periodization). This was not the case for the revolutionary theorist Wang Jingwei.

In one of the foundational essays of modern Chinese nationalism, written in 1905, "Minzudi Guomin" (Citizens of a Nation), Wang Jingwei[9] defined a nation in terms taken from Bluntschli: common blood, language, territory, customs, religion, spiritual and physical nature, and history. For Wang it was necessary to conceive of the nation both as a legal entity, a nation-state (*guojia*) formed by its citizens, and as a racial (*zulei*) group, which is how he used the term *minzu*.[10] Wang's goal is to reveal that a state made up of a single race is infinitely superior to that made of a number of races. There are two reasons for this: first, equality. Common race implies that a people are brothers and "when they are brothers, they are naturally equal" (Wang Jingwei 1905, 84). They also have freedom because (reciting a much quoted line from the *Zuozhuan*) he says, since the hearts of those not of our race (*zulei*) are different, so a conquered race will be kept unfree and different races will always fight. In addition, he notes that the civilized countries of the West have no race of foreign rulers (Wang Jingwei 1905, 97).

In much of the real world, however, races have not been coextensive with the nation-state and have had to "assimilate" (*tonghua*) other races. In this context, he develops a fourfold typological scheme (Wang Jingwei 1905, 85) to include historical situations where:

1. races of equal strength merge to form a new nation;

2. a majority conquering race absorbs the conquered minority;

3. a minority conquering race assimilates a majority race; and

4. a conquering minority is assimilated by a conquered majority.

This scheme can be seen to represent the methodology for comprehending the different lines of evolution (or nonevolution) of races into nations the world over. As such, it was a creative application of the lessons of social Darwinism learned by Wang not only to grasp

9. The irony of the author of this foundational text of nationalism becoming the head of the Japanese puppet regime in China in 1940 should not be lost.

10. We need to clarify here once again, as every author on the subject has done, that *minzu* indexes a surplus of meaning and refers to both nation and to race. As such, it reflects the same meaningful indistinctness between race and nation in Western discourses of the time. Here, however, Wang explicitly uses it to mean race.

the race-nation linkage at a global level (for the typology and the essay in general is studded with numerous historical examples from all over the world), but also specifically for China. Except for two relatively short periods (the Yuan and the Jin to Sui), China had occupied the second type until the Manchu conquest, whereby the Han conquering majority absorbed the defeated minorities. Since the Manchu conquest, however, China had slipped to the third type and the Han were in danger of being absorbed by a conquering minority (Wang Jingwei 1905, 86–87). Yet, now since the Han had advanced in their nationalism and recognized the supreme principle of the necessity of preserving the race in the struggle for existence, the Manchus would either be absorbed or wiped out, thereby demonstrating the triumph of the fourth type (Wang Jingwei 1905, 95).

Wang's essay has a foundational quality not only because it was so influential, but because it recuperated the three terms of the circular discourse of social Darwinism—race, nation, and History—into a systematic nationalist doctrine. A nation could progress—or could have progressed in History—only if it reflected the qualities of a civilized race. Hence Wang's concern for racial purity in the nation. As for History, with the exceptions he cites, the Han have had a glorious History of absorbing others and would rise again to absorb the Manchu rulers. Wang's essay reveals social Darwinism as a discourse for Chinese intellectuals in the strongest sense of the word. It did not merely legitimate their conception of the nation; it structured their very perception of the world.

Against the background of these two founding narratives of the Chinese nation, let us consider some of the most important Chinese historians writing during the Republic. One can see how complex temporal schemes of periodization become, at the same time, strategies to overcome or negotiate gaps in the project of creating a continuous racial/national subject. In 1918, the historian Fu Sinian once again addressed the problem of periodization. Like Liang, Fu declared that history was meaningless without periodization. Western history gained its meaning by tracing change through the three periods of ancient, medieval, and modern. In China, recent historical texts have sought to follow the Western-style periodization set up by the Japanese historian Kuwabara Jitsuzō in his *Brief History of China*, which, significantly, had earlier been titled the *Brief History of East Asia*. Kuwabara, a graduate of Tokyo Imperial University in 1896, represented the pride of modern scientific History in Japan and combined this high-minded History with an extraordinary contempt for China and its antiquated "barbarisms" (Fogel 1984, 120–21).

Fu sought to draw attention to the limitations of this Japanese model and to provide an alternative scheme. Kuwabara had divided Chinese history into four periods:

1. High Antiquity, from the prehistoric period until the Qin unification, a period of the creation of the Han race (*zhongzu*, a word which Fu glosses in English as race).

2. Middle Antiquity, which ran from the Qin until the end of the Tang and which he regarded as the pinnacle of the Han race.

3. Recent Antiquity, from the Tang until the end of the Ming, a period characterized by the decline of the Han and by the vigor of the Mongols.

4. The Modern Age, dominated by the Manchus and the eastward advance of the Western powers. (Fu Sinian 1928, 176–77)

Fu objects to this periodization because it refers not simply to China as such but to East Asia in general. Kuwabara initially takes the rise and fall of the Han race as the basis for periodization but then inconsistently switches to the Mongols and East-West relations in his later periods. It does not take much to see that what Fu finds objectionable is Kuwabara's suggestion of the incompleteness or the early loss of Chinese national subjecthood. Indeed, in Kuwabara's scheme, there are no leads in the modern era to trace back to the authentic national subject. It also does not take much to imagine what kind of Japanese dreams could be projected on a history of China as the history, not of a continuous national subject, but of a territory dominated by different world powers. Fu proposes instead a periodization that will better account for the history of the Han race. In other words, not only must the history of China be the History of the national subject, but this subject is specifically the Han race. And it is the fate of this race that should shape our understanding of the different historical periods. Of course, within these basic divisions, historians will need to further subdivide periods, which may be based on developments in politics and culture or customs.

In Fu's basic divisions, the first relevant break in Chinese history occurs, not with the centralized state of the Qin, but in the age following the Wei-Jin period, when, with the end of the Western Jin in the fourth century A.D., the central plain became overrun by the barbarians. For the two thousand years of history until this time, Fu claims that the Han race had maintained its purity. There was, of course, some assimilation, but there was no admixture. The Han remained as such—without addition or subtraction. We can see in Fu's account what Ricoeur has called the power of the narrative to symbolize: here the symbolization of the purity of a people is achieved simply by bounding time. He calls this two-thousand-year period the first China. He seals it with a striking metaphor, one which contains important clues as to how this period will leak into the others. After the fall of the Western Jin, a small "Chinese" state was maintained by the Eastern Jin in the Jiangnan region. Weak and small though it was, it was preoccupied with the idea of reconquering the central plain, and for Fu and other historians it remained a slender but sure thread linking the second China to the first. Of this role, Fu writes that the Eastern Jin bears a relationship to the central plain, similar, not to the relationship between the eldest son and the lineage, but to a cadet son who is permitted to grace an ancestral temple. In this genealogical metaphor, there is a fall from glory of the ritually correct transmission of the line, but the continuity of the bloodline itself is not surrendered (Fu Sinian 1928, 179).

The subsequent period from the Sui to the Song was characterized by a mix of Han and barbarian (Hu) blood, cultures and, of course, politics. It is one, however, in which the barbarian influence diminishes over time and there is a resurgence of Han power. This is once again reversed in the Southern Song and thereafter when the Han are overwhelmed by foreign forces. This entire period Fu refers to as the second China. He suggests a third China emerging with the Republic, but he remains vague about it. Fu is by no means a simple nationalist historian. For instance, his second objection to Kuwabara's periodization charges that Kuwabara blunders by regarding the Han race of the Han period and the Tang period as the same people. If the Tang belongs to the second China, then the Han race of the Han dynasty and the Han race of the Tang dynasty cannot be considered the same. In his conclusion, he acknowledges that he might be criticized for diminishing the glory of the Han people by claiming that the Han and the Tang did not belong to the same people but declares his principled opposition to sacrificing the truth of history. This declaration must be considered in the context of his earlier metaphor of the continuity of the bloodline—one which makes it possible to see the periodic re-emergence of the power of the Han race. The very categories of a developmental history seem to tie it to the construction of a national subject.

Almost twenty years later, in 1936, when the entire historiographical world of China was preoccupied with the Japanese invasion and the particular claims it was to make on the narratives of Chinese history, we see many of the same concerns that occupied Fu elaborated in the work of Lei Haizong. Lei objects to the popular threefold Westernized periodization of China into an ancient, medieval, and modern periods. He recognizes that such a periodization responds to the desire to universalize Chinese history, but he believes that the difference of Chinese culture necessitates a serious rethinking, beginning with nothing short of a rectification of names. In what sense can we speak of a *Chinese* history, an English history, a European history? There follows a most interesting deconstruction of the categories of European history whereby Lei demonstrates how European historiography makes claims on periods and areas which have little relationship to the present location of the claimants of this history. Western Europe regards Greece and Rome as the source of its classical heritage, but in its own time, the cultural world of ancient Greece was actually Asia minor and Egypt. Yet, it is curious as to why Greece is considered the West and Egypt the East. Moreover, when Egypt was flourishing, Europe was undergoing its Stone Age, yet in European histories, the European Stone Age is studied prior to the history of Egypt (Lei Haizong 1936, 276–81). Lei clearly seeks to challenge the narrativization of European history as a hegemonic activity.

Lei takes as given that culture and territory must be continuously related to each other in order to account for a history. Thus a given territory may have two temporally distanced cultures, but unless a relationship can be demonstrated between the two, they do not amount to a history. Now the West Europeans claim a close historical relationship to the ancient histories of Greece and Rome; yet neither in racial stock nor in terms of their cultural centers do they have much in common. All of the Latin peoples—the French, the Spanish, the Italians—who claim a historical connection with the ancient Roman tradition are thoroughly mixed with German blood. Can they claim this history as theirs? Lei, who earned a Ph.D. from the University of Chicago, uses the positive and materialist historical categories of Western historiography itself to challenge its claims to the glory of others. In the same act, though not in his words, he also challenges nationalist historiographies which oblige us to forget the mixed and bloody origins of nations which are now written as fratricides between fellow nationals (Anderson 1991, 200). Lei provides us with a searing account of the repressions and narratalogical techniques involved in the production of History as the unfolding of the national subject into modernity.

But if Lei's intent is to show up the hegemonic devices of European historiography, it is only to reveal to his fellow Chinese that Chinese history, properly written and properly periodized, demonstrates the world's only truly continuous historical nation. What began as the deconstruction of History, turns into the familiar project of recovering the nation: the Prussian monarchy of Hegel is replaced by the Chinese republic. Stepping back from his radical critique, Lei suggests that although in a strict sense we may criticize Western categories, in a broad sense the history of ancient civilizations of Babylon, Egypt, Greece and Rome and the Islamic world have been shaped by and do belong to a history of the West. This leaves two independent culture areas: India and China. Since India can be considered to be part of the Indo-European tradition, that leaves only China as the true alternative to Western historical culture (Lei Haizong 1936, 301). Only thus can we know that the history of the world is not unitary and appreciate a historical periodization for China that does not slavishly follow the Western model. Here one can recognize Lei's participation in the same historiographical world of Fu Sinian. For Lei, the history of China is divided into two cycles (*zhou*): from antiquity till the Eastern Jin (383 A.D.)—a cycle of the formation of the pure culture of the Huaxia (or Han) people and the classical age of China; and a second cycle from the fourth century until the present—a period of repeated invasions by northern barbarians and Buddhism and one in which a new society of both blood and culture, a mixed China, was produced.

In delineating the phases of the first period, Lei sought to demonstrate the continuity between the neolithic age and the Bronze Age of the Shang and Zhou and demonstrate that the neolithic people were the ancestors of the Huaxia people. As did Fu, Lei too regarded the ability of the Eastern Jin to hold off the northern barbarians from taking over Jiangnan and the south of China in the battle of Fei Shui (383 A.D.) for a few more generations as a critical dividing line. Had the barbarians overrun eastern and southern China at the time, there may well have been no history of China because at that time these regions were as yet thinly populated by the Han people. By holding off the barbarians, the Eastern Jin were able to spread the population and culture of the Han sufficiently so that it could never be obliterated. When, in the second phase, the mixed Chinese culture spread, it was only able to produce a recognizably Han person because of the legacy of the Eastern Jin. In this second phase, the Han people were often threatened and were not as vigorous as in the first cycle, but they were still able to preserve the unique cultural tradition (of the first period). Thus, in the end, it is only the Han people who are able to recall an authentic history (Lei Haizong 1936, 301).

Gu Jiegang, arguably the most brilliant historian of the 1920s and 1930s, is well known for exploding nationalist historical myths and getting into trouble with the KMT. As Lawrence Schneider's splendid intellectual biography of Gu reveals, few scholars were so deeply aware of the many suppressions necessitated in the creation of the Confucian cannon through Chinese history. Gu was able to show how orthodoxy concealed a number of alternative, oppositionist tendencies and traditions in Chinese historical culture, such as, for instance, astronomy, alchemy, Mohist egalitarianism, and the like in the "penumbra of Confucianism" (Schneider 1971, 248). More than any other scholar, Gu saw that the study of the past was important not only in order to attack it as a burden (that the now rampant attack on Confucianism amounted to), but to release the true past, the repressed narratives, from under this accumulated burden.

Gu comes closest to challenging the project of History as recovering the pristine national subject—certainly the Han as the pristine national subject. At one stage, Gu even sought to demonstrate that the great Han legend of Yu was of non-Han origin. The manner in which Gu subverted the myth of Han purity was to transform the very narrative of Chinese history. Instead of a story of the fall from purity and the shedding of an unwanted middle period, Gu posited decay within the Han polity itself. The periods of flux, chaos, and competition were for Gu the most creative periods of Chinese history; political unification by the centralized empire and the institutionalization of Confucianism led to constriction and, ultimately, decay. It was only the contributions of the non-Chinese peoples and cultures— such as the Five Barbarians (*wuhu*), the Khitan, the Jurched, and the Buddhists—that was able to sustain Chinese civilization (Schneider 1971, 264, 293). In this way, Gu prefigured the historical trope of a culture periodically rejuvenated by its outsiders and its marginals—by the Other itself that could be found in the writing of the novelist Shen Congwen and others.

But for all of his radicalism, Gu's history remained in some ways very much part of the national project. This was, as might be expected, clearest in his writings of historical geography during the Japanese invasion. In the 1938 text entitled *A History of the Changes in China's Frontier Regions*, Gu indicated that the purpose of compiling such a work was not only to demonstrate without a doubt to the

Japanese imperialists ("our covetous, powerful neighbors"), but also to enlighten the Chinese people that the Han peoples had spread to Manchuria, Mongolia, and even into Korea during the Tang and earlier dynasties and thus had historical claims there which Japan refused to acknowledge (Gu Jiegang 1938, 4). However, a closer reading reveals that another unstated goal of the text is to demonstrate how the Han race had historically been able to preserve itself in the face of destructive barbarian onslaughts upon them. The opening lines of the text depict the Han race as the first people (*xianmin*) who occupied the central plain surrounded and served by others (*yilei*). They were able "to exhaust their minds and blood, fully utilize their vitality and stamina to diligently manage their circumstances until this day" (Gu Jiegang 1938, 1).

Gu traces the full development of the identity of the Han race to the Qin unification in the third century B.C. He attributes it to the formalization of its administrative system, in particular the commanderies (*jun*) which controlled the frontiers. Thus did emerge the culture of the Chinese, properly speaking (Gu Jiegang 1938, 106). The empirical thrust of the work concerns the policies devised by the successive dynasties to manage and control the barbarians. As with the historians discussed above, Gu finds the invasion of the *wuhu* barbarians during the Jin when the people were "violently scattered for over 130 years" and the establishment of the Eastern Jin as a preserve for the Han people to be a cataclysmic event and a turning point (Gu Jiegang 1938, 147–48). It forever transformed barbarian management policy from the orderly administrative schemes of the previous era to the "loose rein" (*jimi*) and more varied policies of the later dynasties (Gu Jiegang 1938, 167–68). In this work, the interactions between the Chinese (or Huaxia civilization, see Gu Jiegang 1938, 66) and the barbarians are treated not so much as the evolution of a composite Chinese culture or as contributing to the rejuvenation of Chinese culture, but more as the effort of the Han to struggle to preserve Chinese culture.

Schneider suggests that Gu actually employed a polar concept of the barbarian; for propaganda purposes he often exploited the stereotypes of traditional Chinese history—presumably to depict the emergent national subject as triumphant over the barbarian. In the process, however, he succeeded in confining the national subject to the Han and perhaps undoing his own great efforts to bring the other "races" into the nation (see Schneider 1971, 258–93; see also this ambiguity in his autobiography [Gu Jiegang 1966, 166, 167–68]).

Moreover, despite his great self-awareness of the uses and ruses of historical narrative, he remained convinced of the supreme objectivity and accuracy of his own historical findings and method.

In my studies, the figure whose historical writing comes closest to challenging the totalizing disposition of History is the great writer, and sometime literary historian, Lu Xun. Several scholars (Huters 1984; Anderson 1985; Chow 1991; Huang 1990) have noted Lu's extreme discomfiture in his stories with the role of omniscient narrator, whether in the first or third person—especially when the narrator is confronted with the predicament of having to represent the voice and subjectivity of the oppressed. Standing at the intersection of fiction and history, Lu's *The True Story of Ah Q* turns out to have been the most compelling narrative of Chinese history to his generation and beyond. Although it is fictionalized, I have found few that can better his analysis of several events of modern Chinese history, not least of all, the Republican Revolution of 1911. *True Story* narrates the history of modern China as an allegory of failed national character, a project which in itself does not stray far from the path of History. But the fictional form allows Lu to work with a range of techniques of satire, distantiation, and self-parody which constantly undermine the totalizing monologic of the Historical voice. For instance, the extended introduction to *True Story*, well-known for its barbs against certain types of histories, has been read by Martin Huang as reflecting Lu's anxiety about his ability as an intellectual to give voice to a peasant (Huang 1990, 434). Whether self-consciously or not, Lu develops techniques that undermine the authority of the narrator/author, techniques of which professional History conceived as an evidentiary science is relatively innocent. It is therefore interesting to consider Lu in his role as historian.

Consider the essay entitled "The Relationship of Letters and Lifestyle in the Wei-Jin period to Drugs and Alcohol" (1927). To what extent does Lu Xun's sensitivity to the techniques of anti-closure reveal itself in his historical writings? Lu explores the cultural sensibility of the Six Dynasties, and specifically the very Wei-Jin period that is so critical in the historians considered earlier. Rather than see the period as preserving the qualities of the originary, pure culture of Fu's first China, Lu finds it nonconformist in most respects. According to Leo Ou-fan Lee, Lu was specially drawn to the literati of such a transitional period which resembled his own in its anguished quest for meaning in a time of chaos (Lee 1987, 39). The writer who set the tone for the period was also the founder of the Wei dynasty,

Cao Cao.[11] Cao Cao was an absolutist, particularly known for his harsh laws. But Lu is more concerned with the impact of the times on his literary style, which is honest and uncompromisingly defiant of conventions. It is also characterized by a certain spontaneity (*tongtuo*)—a style in which one said what one wished. These same qualities were reflected in Cao Cao's policy toward recruitment of talent in his declaration that he did not care if a man was filial or loyal (in the Confucian sense) as long as he had the talent. As these tendencies developed, they unloosed the constraints of the old Confucianist thought and opened up the mind to foreign and heterodox ideas (Lu Xun 1927, 488–90).

In the literature of the period as a whole, Lu discovered a literary self-consciousness that was remarkably modern and an independence which resisted the moralizing politics that had subordinated art to history in Confucianism. Lu discusses the writers of this period who had been ignored or castigated by the Confucian tradition. These scholars, including the renowned Seven Sages of the Bamboo Grove, experimented with drugs and alcohol and intensified their opposition to a culture dominated by the ritualistic order of the imperial Confucian system (Lu Xun 1927, 500). Lu's insight into the independence of the writing appears to be confirmed by Ronald Dewoskin, who describes the Wei-Jin era as the time when the writing of history and fiction first diverged. However, the acceptability of narrative without need to be justified as true historical record was, and remained, partial. What the genres of this era, such as the *zhiguai* ("records of the strange") made possible was fiction in the garb of history, or what Dewoskin calls "mock history" (Dewoskin 1977, 51).

We may speculate about the master of irony, Lu's, attraction to the style of mock histories. Indeed, he himself wrote the essay in a counter-Historical, parodic style. As in the introduction to *True Story*, it opens with a satiric commentary on "proper" history: particularly the historical fate of short-lived dynasties. Long-lived dynasties have many good people whereas short-lived ones have hardly any. This is because a long-lived dynasty can produce a historical tradition of many people singing its praises whereas a short-lived one is subjected to the historical judgments of another dynasty. This was the

11. Strictly speaking, accession to the imperial throne by the Cao Wei dynasty was proclaimed in 220 A.D., on the death of Cao Cao, by his son Cao Pei. In fact, of course, Cao Cao was virtually responsible for the founding of this dynasty (see Gernet 1972, 178).

case with the "notorious" Qin and the Wei founded by Cao Cao (Lu Xun 1927, 487). Having thus relativized History, Lu proceeds to give us his own revisionist account of Cao Cao. We know that Lu Xun was a careful historian (Lee 1987, 28–29), but it does not stop him from mocking the certainties of evidentiary History, as for instance, in the episode of the execution of the scholar, Kong Rong by Cao Cao. Lu challenges the historical record, which suggests that the cause of the execution was Kong's expression of unfiliality.[12] Lu believes that Cao Cao used the charge of unfiliality as a pretext to get Kong. Had he himself not declared that he did not care for filiality when he sought men of talent! But, of course, Lu says, Cao Cao is dead and there is no way we can find out what he really intended. Besides even if he could have asked him would he have not had him executed! (Lu Xun 1927, 492–93).

How can we situate Lu's reading of this period in relation to the histories of the Chinese nation discussed above? In the discussion of professional Chinese historians committed to a linear History of the nation, I examined how they went about constructing the subject of this History, which in order to be authentically national had to reveal a strong measure of continuity and homogeneity (chapters 2 and 4 examine the implications of this conception for minorities and the vast territories that they historically dominated). All of them have, to varying degrees, been attentive to the discontinuities of the past, but the effort has been to demonstrate the historical origin and reconstitute the continuity of the Han race. Critical to each historian has been the period from the third to the sixth centuries A.D., the era of the Six Dynasties or the "period of disunion." In the violent scattering of the fully, if recently, formed national subject, the Eastern Jin was identified as the carrier of Han national culture, even by Gu Jiegang. One may, from a different angle, however, view the period and the Eastern Jin in particular, as remarkable for the way in which the literati, to whom Lu Xun was so drawn, absorbed the radically different cultures of the autochthonous peoples of the south, upon which the post-Han states were established. Indeed, Dewoskin believes that the literati were able to channel these cultures into the

---

12. Exemplary of his era, Kong Rong challenged Cao Cao on the latter's effort to impose a ban on wine, which Cao felt would lead to the decline of the kingdom, by urging him to ban marriage as well since women also led to the weakening of the kingdom. However, the record shows that Cao Cao executed Kong on the charge that Kong had been unfilial: Kong had apparently compared the mother-child relationship to that between a pitcher and its contents—once the pitcher was emptied the two were quite separate and had nothing to do with each other (Lu Xun 1927, 492–93).

newly emergent literary genres and retain their heterogeneity and autonomy, if only by transforming them into "mock histories" (1977, 35–36). I believe that it is this autonomy and difference that Lu finds so refreshing.

The principal point I want to make, however, is that Lu differs from the other scholars, not by overtly challenging the nationalist Historical project, but by constantly questioning its narrative form. There are three features of his essay that suggest this. First is his view of the writing of traditional Confucian history as repressive, and the effort to recover repressed histories. In this, Lu is, of course, not alone and a whole generation of scholars, most notably, Hu Shi and Gu Jiegang, found the entire Chinese past to be a rich archaeological site where they recovered counterhistories buried under the canonical histories of the Confucian establishment. But what distinguished Lu from most of his contemporaries was his acknowledgment of the contemporariness of history, his practice of history as genealogy. To acknowledge history as genealogy is not only to see it laterally in its "proper dispersion" (see chapter 2), but to see history as projecting back from one's present location. This we see in the repeated comparisons between the Wei Jin period and the Republic as periods of anarchy, competitiveness, and creativity. He also makes an explicit comparison between arbitrary political power and the amorality of the intellectual in an age when morality served as a front for unspeakable political crimes. Lu suggests that for the seemingly amoral or immoral Wei Jin literati to have declared their morality publicly would be similar to the present experience of an intellectual of integrity responding to a warlord's invitation to speak about the pieties of the Three People's Principles. To do so would be to implicate oneself in the abuse of morality, then and now (Lu Xun 1927, 502–3). In this self-consciousness of the situatedness of any reading of the past, Lu differed fundamentally from Gu and Lei, whose works involved demonstrating with considerable brilliance how others used the past but who remained convinced that their own researches represented objective, dispassionate History. Finally, we sense this difference also in the tactical devices that Lu brings from literary writing to parody the microtechniques of Historical closure.

For all of his archaeology, genealogy, and parody, does Lu Xun offer us the true voices of the period? Can we really recover the repressed voices from the totalizing discourse of History? Deconstructionists who have turned their interests to history, such as Gayatri Spivak (1988, 3–5), have described the writing of history as an "exchange in the functions of signs." This is an important insight that allows us to see the way in which linear History, by understanding the past through the linguistic signs of the present, reduces or sublates the past to the present. In this way, the language of the present conceals the meanings of another time and another space. But I would rather not think that the exchange of signs is both the beginning and the end of history; that under the semiotic rubble which we call history, lies irretrievably buried, the meanings of the past. Through the course of these essays, I try to show how changes in narrative and linguistic values are often the trap-doors through which we can understand history. If we do our work right, we should be able to recover something of what our subjects did or said even if the effort to reproduce "the subaltern consciousness" or "women's consciousness," as in "the national consciousness," is an essentialist mirage.

Thus, while my purpose is not to abandon objectivity, I believe the objectivist model of History has been profoundly flawed because it has been inattentive to the linguistic and, more specifically, narrative forms of History—a History which those with power such as the nation-state un-self-consciously dominate. Facts yield their meaning only in a pattern, and while an important part of our job is to collect and ascertain the facts, it is just as important to work our way through the different levels of narrative involved. As I will try to show in these chapters, we need to reach out to the words and deeds of our historical subjects, even as we reach into our own narrative structures and across to our Asian colleagues' narrativization of their own histories. The exploration of history is always a movement between language and the historical real.

CONCLUSION

The Hegelian narrative of Enlightenment History has been difficult to disentangle from the evolutionism that dominated the nineteenth century. By the early twentieth century a discourse, loosely identified as social Darwinism and guided by a circular reasoning involving the three terms of race, nation, and History had taken root among the Chinese intelligentsia. Social Darwinism did not simply present this reasoning as a difficult but possible way for the Chinese nation to struggle out or up from its dependent position in the global capitalist system; in the hands of Chinese intellectuals, social Darwinism began to produce the very categories through which the world could be seen and acted upon in its terms: race, nation, and History.

The three terms were unified by the narrative construction of a

Historical subject: an agent constituted by a homogenous community (race) within a territorial state (nation) that had evolved into the present so that it was now poised to launch into a modern future (History) of rationality and self-consciousness in which contingency or history itself would be eliminated (end of History). Such a Historical subject was, however, an ideal unity that could never fully resolve the break between the past and the present in linear time by claiming to be both of the past and the present. Indeed, precisely because the subject of national History is torn between components representing the past and the present can we see the nation presented simultaneously as essentially atavistic and unprecedentedly novel (as self-conscious collective subject).

The third part of this chapter revealed how, in their efforts to forge a continuous national subject to address the temporal split, the various historians combined the three constitutive terms of this subject somewhat differently and with greater or lesser degrees of openness. Thus, Liang had difficulty equating race and nation and Gu developed a regenerative view of the relationship of races to History, whereas Wang pressed the theme of Historical assimilation much more strongly. But the lineaments of the basic narrative remain in place and the construction of the national subject as the continuously evolving racial entity in the academic histories of the first half of the twentieth century would have implications for territories, cultures, and peoples which will be discussed in later chapters. By associating History with atavistic, racial categories, this national History would reproduce the assumptions and attitudes of evolutionary History.

At the same time, the preoccupation with the utopia of modernity in the Chinese narrative of History, its role as the only standard of value, closed off, as we shall see in Part Two, much that its older histories, narratives, and popular cultures had to offer. Chinese intellectuals, by and large, have not challenged the Enlightenment project to the same extent as postmodern and postcolonial intellectuals. For the record, I should note that I myself am committed to the goal of achieving and retaining what is of value in the discourse of modernity. But the absence of a critical attitude toward the discourse of Enlightenment rationality, with its instrumental hierarchies of forms of knowledge and modes of living, has implications which shape the attitudes of many Chinese not only to these forms within their society, but toward the world without. For instance, both during and after the Maoist period, Third World histories in world history textbooks for children in the PRC, are all lumped together in a single chapter and continue to be virtual caricatures featuring anti-imperialist, antifeudal struggles (Martin 1990, 102). Indeed, since the decline of communist ideology which had included a transcendent or universalist dimension, my experience in China indicates that there has been a tendency to focus on a nationalism with recognizably social Darwinian overtones.

I began the essay by looking to the next century as the Pacific century. The role of History in the constitution of nations evolving through competition into modernity has been truly monumental, at least in China. But the price of History has also been very dear, not because the narrative has actually succeeded in extinguishing different modes of being and time (in Michel de Certeau's words, the repressed past will return to haunt the present [1988]); but because, with significant exceptions—such as Lu Xun and periodically, Gu Jiegang—the closures of modernity and History have not enabled a language that can recognize and negotiate with that which has been dispersed and repressed. We still do not know what histories will look like beyond the era of the nation-state. But we should seize the moment of the decoupling of History and the nation to think of how to write histories that open as they close.

2

BIFURCATING LINEAR HISTORIES
IN CHINA AND INDIA

THIS CHAPTER challenges the idea of a single national History by considering multiple narratives of community in the regions of China and India. At the same time, I will critique the increasingly popular characterization of the nation as representing a radical discontinuity with the past. This view, in which histories are nothing but retrospective constructions to serve present needs, presumptuously privileges the present over the past and itself succumbs to a Hegelian metaphysics of the self-conscious, modern subject. Thus, in order to chart our path between the evolutionary and the reductionist models of history, I will suggest a bifurcated history which seeks to grasp both the dispersal of the past and its transmission over time in the same moment.

Since at least Ellie Kedourie there has developed a tradition in the scholarship of nationalism which rightly debunks nationalist histories for their mythologies and suppressions of uncomfortable events. Alerting us to the self-consciousness of this exercise, Benedict Anderson has recently pointed out the unproblematic way in which Joseph Ernest Renan could write about being "obliged to having already forgotten" wars between different polities; and how these wars subsequently came to be written as "fratricides" among fellow Frenchmen (Anderson 1991, 200). While I am obviously sympathetic with the critique of teleology in this literature, I am suspicious of the proposition which often accompanies it: that nationalism is a radically novel mode of consciousness. I am suspicious because this position ignores the complexity of the nature of historical memory and causality and because it remains tied to the idea of self-consciousness as a uniquely modern phenomenon. In neither modern nor premodern society is it possible to sustain the notion of a unified consciousness presumed by the concept of nationalism.

Two of the most influential recent works on nationalism, by Ernest Gellner (1983) and Benedict Anderson (1991), emphasize the radically novel and modern nature of nationalist consciousness. Both are extremely fine studies and, while I agree with many of their insights regarding the reproduction of nationalist ideology, I would like to challenge their interpretation of the nature and history of nationalist consciousness. Both analysts identify national consciousness conventionally as the coextensiveness of politics and culture: an overriding identification of the individual with a culture that is protected by the state. Both also provide a sociological account of how it was only in the modern era that such a type of consciousness—where people from diverse locales could "imagine" themselves as part of a single community—was made possible.

Gellner presents the following account of this discontinuity. Preindustrial society is formed of segmentary communities, each isolated from the other, with an inaccessible high culture jealously guarded by a clerisy—Gellner's general term for literati ruling elites. With the growth of industrialism, society requires a skilled, literate, and mobile workforce. The segmentary form of communities is no longer adequate to create a homogeneously educated workforce in which the individual members are interchangeable. The state comes to be in charge of the nation and, through control of education, creates the requisite interchangeability of individuals. The primary identification with segmentary communities is thus transferred to the nation-state as the producer of culture (1983). Thus a new type of consciousness, born of a homogenous culture and tied to the state, emerges in an industrial society.

In Anderson's view, nationalist consciousness was made possible with the breakdown of three defining characteristics of premodern society: sacred scripts, divine kingship, and the conflation of history with cosmology. Together, these had made for an unself-conscious coherence in society which broke down with the spread of print media in the capitalist market. Print capitalism permitted an unprecedented mode of apprehending time that was "empty" and "homogenous"—expressed in an ability to imagine the simultaneous existence of one's conationals. Travel and the territorialization of the faith relativized this community by defining it as limited, and the decline of monarchy transferred sovereignty to the community. To be sure, many of the characteristics of nationalism evolve historically through a succession of modular types of nationalist movements. But he believes, nonetheless, that nationalisms have a defining systemic unity embodied in the unique type of self-consciousness of the people imagining themselves as one (1991).[1]

First, consider the argument empirically. The long history of complex civilizations, such as that of China, does not fit the picture of isolated communities and a vertically separate but unified clerisy. Considerable research about complex networks of trade, pilgrimage, migration, and sojourning shows that villages were linked to wider communities and political structures. We also have a sense of how, through central place theory, these linkages worked to transmit resources and information throughout the society, as well as a differentiated picture of what areas, and when these areas, were more or less integrated with the central places of the empire (Skinner 1964–65; 1977). This was the case as well in eighteenth-century India (Bayly 1983; Habib 1963). Moreover, even if the reach of the bureaucratic state was limited, notions of the culture-state indicate the widespread presence of common cultural ideas which linked the state to communities and sustained the polity.[2]

It was not only, or perhaps even primarily, the print media that enabled Han Chinese to develop a sharp sense of the Other, and hence of themselves as a community, when they confronted other communities. The exclusive emphasis on print capitalism as enabling the imagining of a common destiny and the concept of simultaneity ignores the complex relationship between the written and spoken word. In agrarian civilizations, this interrelationship furnishes an extremely rich and subtle context for communication across the culture. For instance, in pan-Chinese myths, such as that of gods Mazu and Guandi, not only were oral and written traditions thoroughly intertwined, but the myth provided a medium whereby different groups could announce their participation in a national culture even as they inscribed their own interpretation of the myth (through the written and other cultural media, such as folk drama and iconography) (Watson 1985; Duara 1988b). As such, these groups were articulating their understanding of the wider cultural and political order from their

1. In the 1991 edition of *Imagined Communities*, Anderson adds two new chapters which draw on scholarship that has emerged since the first edition of 1983. These chapters, which contain some brilliant insights and analyses, depict nationalist ideology as a hegemonic activity. They thereby compensate for the earlier tendency to depict nationalism as a transparent unity.

2. See, for instance, Burton Stein's concept of the segmentary state in India (1980) and Stanley Tambiah's galactic polity in the Thai kingdom of Ayutthaya (1985).

own particular perspective. There were large numbers of people in agrarian societies who were conscious of their culture and identity at multiple levels and, in that sense, were perhaps not nearly so different from their modern counterparts.

The point is not so much that national identity existed in premodern times; rather, it is that the manner in which we have conceptualized political "identities" is fundamentally problematic. In privileging modern society as the only social form capable of generating political self-awareness, Gellner and Anderson regard national identity as a distinctly modern mode of consciousness: the nation as a whole imagining itself to be the cohesive subject of history. The empirical record does not furnish the basis for such a strong statement about the polarity between the modern and the premodern. Individuals and groups in both modern and agrarian societies identify simultaneously with several communities, all of which are imagined;[3] these identifications are historically changeable and often conflicted internally and with each other. Whether in India or China, people historically identified with different representations of communities, and when these identifications became politicized, they came to resemble what is called modern "national identities."

Behind this modern versus premodern polarity lies the assumption of modern consciousness as a *unified* episteme marked by an epistemological break with past forms of consciousness. As the embodiment of modern subjectivity, the nation is *ipso facto* denied any credible links with the past. At the heart of this break is a deep confusion between the novelty and, indeed, revolutionary character of institutional arrangements in the modern world and the radical novelty of consciousness, specifically of a cohesive and self-aware collective subject. Indeed, the self-consciousness of modern subjectivity in the writings of these analysts bears an unexpected resemblance to Hegelian epistemology. Recall that for Hegel the unfolding of Spirit (reason) through History culminates as man "stands in a conscious relation to his Spirit" (Hegel 1956, 103) and that a nation-state, unlike other communities, possesses a self-consciousness because it involves the production of History in its very progress. But, having

---

3. Etienne Balibar, discussing "imaginary" communities, remarks that *"Every social community reproduced by the functioning of institutions is imaginary,* that is, it is based on the projection of individual existence into the weft of a collective narrative, on the recognition of a collective *name* and on traditions lived as the trace of an immemorial past (even when they have been created and inculcated in the recent past). But this comes down to accepting that, in certain conditions, *only imaginary communities are real"* (Balibar 1991, 93).

attained self-consciousness, it also stands at the end of History.[4] Quite apart from the validity of such a characterization of "modern consciousness," we may also remind ourselves of the destructive side of this epistemology, one which justified domination of "unselfconscious" societies and polities as the Other of the modern, rational self.

These modern analysts assume the cohesive collective subject of History as, first of all, possible and, second, possible only in the modern era. My alternative obliges me to reject both positions. In the strong sense, a cohesive self-conscious subject is an abstraction: as the introduction has shown, the meaning of the nation for the pluralities which inhabit and may identify with it—whether it is an inner-city African American, a Californian farm worker, or a suburban homemaker—are as different as they are themselves from each other. In a restricted and temporary sense, however, the nation may exist as a unified subjectivity: a provisional *relationship*, a historical configuration in which the national "self" is defined in relation to the Other. Depending on the nature and scale of the oppositional term, the national self contains various smaller "others"—historical others that have effected an often uneasy reconciliation among themselves and potential others that are beginning to form their differences. Thus I must reject the second position in both the strong and the restricted senses and the first position in the strong, though not in the weaker, relational sense. But, if a unified subjectivity can be salvaged only in this weak sense, this subjectivity is by no means uniquely a product of modern society.

I will argue that there were totalizing representations and narratives of community with which people identified historically and with which they may continue to identify into the modern nation. Of course, premodern political identifications do not necessarily or teleologically develop into the national identifications of modern times and there are significant ruptures with the past. A new vocabulary

4. As I will try to show in chapter 3, the understanding of modernity in the social sciences as a unique type of subjectivity which is self-conscious and thus rational is a deeply held assumption. While I reject this, it is also important for to me to reiterate that I do believe that there are certain institutional and technological complexes—like the nation-state system—and discourses linked to these complexes that we may call modern in the sense that we do not see them operate historically and globally until the nineteenth century. Thus, I use the term "modern" to refer to these complexes and discourses. My critique applies to the use of "modernity" to differentiate a whole era or system from another by a single epistemological principle such as self-consciousness.

and a new political system—the world system of nation-states—selects, adapts, reorganizes and even recreates these older representations. But the historical memory of archaic totalizations does not always disappear, and as this memory is periodically re-enacted, it often provides potent material along which to mobilize the new community.

HISTORICAL MODELS OF POLITICAL COMMUNITY

In India and China, representations of community as a social totality are not new. Historical conceptions of political community have lived off a process of radical "Othering" and were periodically re-enacted, thus keeping them alive in historical memory. Of course, at different times, different social forces have seized this memory and turned it to their own needs, but the very process of its pursuit has enhanced the power of this historical memory. At the same time, it was an awareness of social totality that coexisted historically with other representations, including competing visions of community.

Consider first the case of imperial China. Before the advent of the modern nation-state, there were several models of political community in China. One of these has been called "culturalism" and has been counterposed to modern nationalism. Joseph Levenson was the most articulate expositor of the idea of culturalism, which he saw as a mode of consciousness distinct from nationalism. Levenson observed a radical discontinuity between a nationalistic identity, which he believed came to Chinese intellectuals around the turn of the twentieth century, and earlier forms of Chinese identity. The high culture, ideology, and identification of the literati, he believed, were principally forms of cultural consciousness, an identification with the moral goals and values of a universalizing civilization. Thus the significant transition here is from a "culturalism" to a nationalism, to the awareness of the nation-state as the ultimate goal of the community (Levenson 1965). Culturalism referred to a natural conviction of cultural superiority that sought no legitimation or defense outside of the culture itself. Only when, according to Levenson, cultural values sought legitimation in the face of the challenge posed by the Other in the late nineteenth century, do we begin to see "decaying culturalism" and its rapid transformation to nationalism—or to a culture protected by the state (politicization of culture).

Levenson's notion of culturalism has enabled us to identify a particular conception or representation of political community that may have emanated from the literati (although, identification with this representation was not necessarily restricted to the literati). Where he is mistaken, I believe, is in distinguishing culturalism as a radically different mode of identification from ethnic or national identification. In order for it to exist as a pure expression of cultural superiority, culturalism would have to feel no threat from an Other seeking to obliterate these values. In fact, this threat arose historically on several occasions and produced several reactions from the Chinese literati and populace. First, there was a rejection of the universalist pretensions of Chinese culture and of the principle that separated culture from politics and the state. This manifested itself in a form of ethnocentrism to be considered momentarily. A second, more subtle, response involved the transformation of cultural universalism from a set of substantive moral claims into a relatively abstract official doctrine. This doctrine was often used to conceal the compromises that the elite and imperial state had to make in their ability to practice these values or to conceal their inability to make people who should have been participating in the cultural-moral order actually do so. The universalistic claims of Chinese imperial culture constantly bumped up against, and adapted to, alternative views of the world order which it tended to cover with the rhetoric of universalism: this was its defensive strategy.

Consider this second reaction first. The Jin and Mongol invasions of northern China during the twelfth century and their scant respect for Chinese culture produced an ideological defensiveness in the face of the relativization of the conception of the universal empire (*tianxia*). In the twelfth and thirteenth centuries, Confucian universalists could only maintain their universalism by performing two sleights of hand: connecting individuals to the infinite—rather than to a regime espousing universal values, thus severing theory from fact; and internalizing the determination of personal values—rather than making it contingent upon the traditional Confucian concern with an objective moral order (Trauzettel 1975). During the Ming dynasty, a Han dynasty that succeeded the Mongols, Chinese historians dealt with the lack of fit between much of the known world and the Chinese worldview simply by maintaining a silence (Wang Gungwu 1968, 45–46). When one looks at the tribute trade system, which is often cited as the paradigmatic expression of its universalistic claims to moral superiority, the imperial state adapted readily to the practical power politics of the day. For instance, in the early nineteenth century, the tiny northwestern khanate of Kokand successfully challenged the Qing tribute system (like the Jesuits, the Russians, and several others before) and had established all but the formal declaration of equality with the Chinese empire. The Qing was forced into a negotiated settlement, but it continued to use the language of universalism—civilizing values radiating from the son of heaven—to conceal the altered power relations between the two (Fletcher 1978b).

It seems evident that when the universalistic claims of this culture were repeatedly compromised and efforts were made to conceal these compromises, advocates of this universalism were operating within the tacit idea of a *Chinese* universalism—which is, of course, none other than a hidden form of relativism. We have tended to accept Chinese declarations of universalism at face value far more readily than we do other official doctrines. Is it perhaps because it plays a crucial role as the Other in interpretations of the encounter with the nation-states of the west?[5]

Viewing "culturalism" (or universalism) as a "Chinese culturalism" is to see it not as a form of cultural consciousness per se, but rather to see culture—a specific culture of the imperial state and Confucian orthodoxy—as a criterion defining a community. Membership in this community was defined by participation in a ritual order that embodied allegiance to Chinese ideas and ethics, which revolved around the Chinese emperor. While this representation of political community may seem rather distant from nationalism, one should consider that the territorial boundaries and peoples of the contemporary Chinese nation correspond roughly to the Qing empire, which was held together ideologically precisely by these ritual practices.

Just as significantly, during the Jin invasion of the twelfth century, segments of the literati completely abandoned the concentric, radiant concept of universal empire for a circumscribed notion of the Han community and fatherland (*guo*) in which the barbarians had no place. This ethnocentric notion of Chineseness was, of course, not new. Chinese authors typically trace it to a quotation from the ancient classic, the *Zuozhuan:* "the hearts of those who are not of our race must be different" (Li Guoqi 1970, 20; Dow 1982, 353). Others (Langlois 1980, 362) find it still earlier in the concentric realm of inner and outer barbarians found in the *Shangshu:* pacific cultural activi-

5. We are perhaps beginning to see the complex status of "culturalism" as a concept, or more appropriately, as a representation of Chinese culture. While it obviously occupies an important role in constructing nineteenth-century China as the Other, it also plays a major part—perhaps as the centerpiece—in the intellectual apparatus of Sinology. In this respect, like the closely related concept of "Sinicization," culturalism also may have reflected an "unskeptical approach to the civil ideal in Chinese elite culture" (see Crossley 1990a).

ties were to prevail in the inner part, whose inhabitants were not characterized as ethnically different, with militancy toward the outer barbarians who appeared to be inassimilable. Trauzettel believes that in the Song, this ethnocentrism brought together state and "the people." The state sought to cultivate the notion of loyalty to the fatherland in the peasant communities, from among whom arose resistance against the Jin in the name of Han Chinese culture and the Song dynasty (1975).

While the representation of the ethnic nation is most evident in the Song, it reappeared after the Manchu conquest in 1644. Its most explicit advocate in the late imperial period was Wang Fuzhi. Wang likened the differences between Manchus and Han to that between jade and snow, which are both white but different in nature, or, more ominously, between a horse and a man of the same color, whose natures are obviously different (Li Guoqi 1970, 22). To be sure, it was the possession of civilization (*wen*) by the Han that distinguished them from the barbarians, but it did not stop him from the view that "it is not inhumane to annihilate (the barbarians) . . . because faithfulness and righteousness are the ways of human intercourse and are not to be extended to alien kinds (*i-lei* [*yilei*]) (in Langlois 1980, 364). Although Wang may have espoused the most extreme view of his generation, several prominent scholars of the Ming-Qing transition era held onto the idea of the fundamental inassimilability of the *yi* (barbarian) by the *Hua* (Chinese) (see Onogawa [1970] and Wu Weiruo [1970]).

Despite the undoubted success with which the Qing made themselves acceptable as the legitimate sons of heaven, they were unable to completely suppress the ethnocentric opposition to their rule either at a popular level or among the scholarly elite. The anti-Manchu writings of Wang Fuzhi, Huang Zongxi, and Gu Yanwu during the early period of Qing rule, together with collections of stories of Manchu atrocities during the time, *Mingji Yeshi* (*Unofficial History of the Late Ming*), staged a reappearance around the middle of the nineteenth century (Wu Weiruo 1970, 263). Zhang Taiyan, for instance, claims to having been nourished by a tradition both in his family and in wider Zhejiang society which held that the defense of the Han against the barbarians was as important as the righteousness of a ruler (Onogawa 1970, 216). Certainly Han exclusivism seems to have reached a height by the late eighteenth century, when the dominant Han majority confronted the non-Han minorities of China in greater numbers than ever before over competition for increasingly scarce resources (Naquin and Rawski 1987). Thus, it is hardly surprising to find that, from at least the time of resistance to the increased foreign presence in southern China after the Opium Wars through to the Boxer Rebellion of 1898 to 1900, there existed a general expectation, not only among the elite, but also among the populace, that the state would protect the culture and the people of the empire (Wakeman 1966; Esherick 1987). Although not all segments of the population were affected by it, this representation of political community was sufficiently rooted to make it a powerful mobilizing force in the nineteenth and twentieth centuries.

Thus, at least two representations of political community in imperial Chinese society are discernible: the exclusive Han-based one founded on an ascriptive principle and the another based on the cultural values and doctrines of a Chinese elite. What has been described as culturalism was a statement of Chinese values as superior but, significantly, not exclusive. Through a process of education and imitation, barbarians could also become part of a community sharing common values and distinguishing themselves from yet other barbarians who did not share these values. Thus the cultural conception resembled the ethnic conception in that both periodically defined the distinguishing marks and boundaries of a politicized community; only the criterion of admissibility into the community differed.[6]

In history, the two representations were *both* separate and related. At any point in time, the efforts to realize the one or the other could have very different effects—indeed, life and death effects—regarding who was to be considered as inside or outside of the community. But as John Fincher has pointed out, "culturalism" and "racism" were also intertwined in such a way that the "historian's vocabulary has no very satisfactory definition of the strong sense of political community in 'traditional' China" (Fincher 1972, 69). Fincher looks at the writings of the anti-Mongol thinker, Fang Xiaoru (1357–1402) who, in the face of general literati support of the Mongol dynasty, made a clear racialist distinction between the Mongols, whom he likened to animals and Han Chinese. Yet, if the border between the Chinese and the barbarians was impermeable and based on biological fact, Fang was still only "half a racist" (Fincher 1972, 59), because he also believed that Chinese who enabled barbarians to rule could themselves become barbarians. He thus invoked the culturalist prin-

6. David Pong's analysis of what he calls Confucian patriotism presents a good example of how the culturalist representation of political community struggled for ascendancy in the late nineteenth century. The Confucian patriot was preoccupied with the problem of moral virtue, not as an end in itself, but as a means to achieve the social and political integration of society (1973, 662).

ciple, although in reverse: that birth among the Han did not ensure inclusion in the community. We will encounter several such examples of separateness and interpenetration and we may invoke the concept of the "supplement" to grasp the relationship between "culture" and "race" here. The supplement embeds the paradox of being separate from, yet necessary to, the completion of a phenomenon. It thus complicates the binary opposition between "race" and "culture" which some of the historiography discussed above has found useful in its explanation of modern nationalism.[7]

For Hegel, the ancient cultures of China and India each represented a lack in relation to the full development of Spirit which complemented the other. Spirit had made its progress through these cultures but found them wanting in the unity of the freedom of individual and state, of Unity and Difference, which made for true self-consciousness. China possessed objective rationality in the State, but the state and its laws belonged to the One Individual (the Emperor). These laws ruled the individuals as being "from outside" and the individuals were like children obeying their parents without will or insight. In India, the contemplation of inner subjectivity led to the Negation of Reality—the Hindu nature is Spirit in a state of Dream (Hegel 1956, 140)—and thus awareness of State as the embodiment of Rationality was denied. Thus, "if China may be regarded as nothing but a State, Hindoo political existence presents us with a people, but no State" (Hegel 1956, 161). This complementarity of lack, as it were, plays the role of something like an archetype in the comparative historical sociology of India and China.

The notion of a lack of a state in India, or conversely, the overpowering role of society (read caste) is so deeply ingrained in both Indology and general understandings of India that there is a tendency to be especially suspicious about characterizations of totalizing political communities in precolonial India. Consider the cosmic ideology of Brahmanism because, in many ways, Brahmanic universalism (an obviously more specific and serviceable term than Hinduism) is interpreted similarly to Chinese culturalism. Ainslee Embree has summed up its core features: it includes the concept of the cosmic order and the role of the Brahmin in maintaining and interpreting this order;

7. Jacques Derrida has discussed the concept of supplement in the context of a larger category of related notions that belong within a "*general strategy of de-construction* . . . [which] avoid both simply *neutralizing* the binary oppositions of metaphysics and simply *residing* within the closed field of these oppositions, thereby confirming it. . . . [T]he *supplement* is neither a plus nor a minus, neither an outside nor the complement of an inside, neither accident nor essence" (1981, 40–43).

the concept of multileveled truth, of a hierarchical but rational order of society, of karma, of reincarnation, and of the concept of dharma (religious or moral duty) (Embree 1985, 23–24). As in Confucianism, Brahmanic universalism is not dependent on the wielding of state power but, rather, exercises its control from outside of and upon the state.

To be sure, a scholar like Embree believes that in some ways Brahmanism did provide a historical basis of a unifying ideology. Brahmanic texts became the source of political and social legitimacy for Hindu rulers since the first century B.C. Moreover, these texts showed some familiarity with the natural boundaries of the subcontinent and an awareness of Aryavarta (land of the Hindus/Aryans) as a cultural region with a common heritage of language and value with others of their class throughout the subcontinent (Embree 1985, 27). But he believes that it is precisely this Brahmanism which prevented actual states from achieving a conflation of polity and community within the state because its universalism constantly directed the attention of Hindu rulers away from this goal and toward a deterritorialized, cosmic order (Embree 1985, 32). Thus the sum of Embree's argument appears to be that while Brahmanism provided the framework for a cultural community, it did not and could not produce that conflation of culture and polity so necessary to the emergence of nations.

More recent work, however, indicates that such a judgment of culturalist determinism may be premature. Just as cultural universalism was relativized (even while retaining its doctrine officially) as a result of the great Central Asian invasions in China, Brahmanic India was also so affected by the Central Asian invasions from the eleventh to the fourteenth centuries. In a nuanced and detailed analysis of the *Ramayana* epic before and during this period, Sheldon Pollock finds that this epic became the principal means of creating a representation of the politicized community in medieval Hindu India. Such was not the case with the other famous Indian epic, the *Mahabharata*, in which the problem of political power—"man is slave to power, but power is slave to no man"—cannot be strictly said to be resolved because the *fratricidal* struggle is accompanied by a profound moral ambiguity. As Pollock puts it, not only is the antagonist not "othered" in the *Mahabharata*, but rather, they can never forget that they are indeed "brothered" (Pollock 1993, 281–83).

In contrast, the *Ramayana* responds to the problem of political power by a straightforward divinization of the king, Rama. According to Pollock, the divine king is the only being on earth capable of combatting evil, and evil itself is clearly "othered," or more exactly, demonized. The period from the eleventh to fourteenth centuries witnessed the Turkic invasions of India, and Muslim political control came to be more or less established by the end of the period. This was also precisely the time when the divine political order of the *Ramayana* became historically grounded as numerous dynastic histories began to read the political world through the *Ramayana* narrative (Pollock 1993, 273–77). Although Pollock furnishes many examples, particularly clear is the explicit identification of the historical ruler, Prithvi Raj II (twelfth century), with the divine Rama and the explicit demonization of the enemy, the Turkic forces from Central Asia. The *Ramayana* enabled a totalizing conception of society built on a radical distinction between self versus Other.

Thus, once again, relativization finds its way into a cosmic ideology and creates a representation of political community—in this case, a Hindu political community—where culture and polity are conflated. Pollock also emphasizes that the *Ramayana* was repeatedly instrumentalized by Hindu elites of the medieval period to provide a "theology of politics and a symbology of otherness" (Pollock 1993, 286). This certainly is not a reference to a real identification with this community among all who considered themselves Hindu, nor was it territorially coextensive with all of India. Rather, it was a representation of political community with which it was possible to identify and around which to mobilize. Migration, sojourning, and pilgrimage, which often followed trading networks and which probably intensified during the medieval period, brought these ideas and rituals to a large community of believers. Pilgrimage is perhaps the privileged means by which a religious community is both ritually and spatially delimited. In India, pilgrimage centers marked an interlinked, subcontinent-wide territory not simply as a sacred space, but in the face of a demonized Other living in this territory, as the sacred space of Hindus.

While no Hindu power was able to successfully construct the politicized religious community across the subcontinent, one should not ignore that it existed as a representation and that several rulers, from Prithvi Raj II in the twelfth century to the Marathas or Jai Singh of Jaipur in eighteenth century, did try to actualize it. At the same time, the drive toward the Brahmanical goal of a Hindu community, Bharatvarsha or Aryavarta, was countered by the urge to create the regional political community. The literature on regional states is most abundant for the eighteenth-century successor states to the Mughal empire, such as the Sikh and Maratha kingdoms. At one level, these eighteenth-century polities were a product of state-building processes developing around emergent capital markets, professional service classes, modern European military technology and standing armies (Bayly 1983).

At another level, they were built around medieval devotional cults (Bhakti) which had integrated the regions linguistically. The syncretic impulses of these cults, which created a popular literature of regional identification, coexisted in some tension with the pan-Hindu model of political community outlined above.[8] In the eighteenth-century Maratha state, for instance, N. K. Wagle (1989) reveals how Maharashtrian Hindu chroniclers, Muslim saints, and local judges sought ways to create a syncretic, regional tradition of adaptation and compromise even while the distinction between Hindus and Muslims was all too clear.

Finally, there existed a concept of political community which the Rudolphs have called the subcontinental empire. This appears to have been a regulative ideal among those who sought to rule South Asia as an empire. According to the Rudolphs, the subcontinental empire was a polity of ancient origins which recognized "ordered heterogeneity"—a polity which legitimated distinct cultural and functional communities, but who "lived as races apart" in their relations with each other (Rudolphs 1985, 43). In this conception, state power was limited by society's autonomous claims to self-regulation. Although this ideal was sanctioned by classic Brahmanical texts, it informed the ideals of the Moghuls and the British as well. The nature of this political conception is such that it is difficult to imagine it as the object of identification among ordinary people or collectivities. Nonetheless, to the extent that this tradition was articulated and kept alive in historical memory, it was perhaps an important influence upon the modern Indian nationalistic rhetoric of "unity in diversity."

To characterize premodern India and China simply as universal empires whose elites (Mandarin or Brahmin) were concerned with

8. Because of this tension with the pan-Hindu model, it is difficult to imagine these regimes as moving toward the model of territorial nation-states. But if nation-states were not about to emerge in the subcontinent, one might imagine a plausible counterfactual scenario: had the French continued to engage the British for control of India until the mid-nineteenth century, a range of semi-independent (or semi-colonial) states with a fair degree of linguistic and cultural homogeneity within themselves might have evolved. The basis of the nation-state in India might have been the regional states of the eighteenth century. As it was, the establishment of the British empire brought forth the Indian nation in the image of the Raj much as the modern Chinese nation was made in the image of the Qing empire.

cosmic values while the peasants lived with their noses to the soil misses the complex and dynamic nature of these societies. Individuals, strata, or groups identified not only with one or more of the different representations of communities outlined here, but with others as well: provincial, linguistic, and sectarian, for example. Also noted were the unstable, intersecting, and supplementary characters of these representations and, correspondingly, the identifications of people with them. The next section considers the underlying process by which certain representations are mobilized to create an overarching, closed community. Even while such a self-aware historical community may later disappear socially, the trace of it often lives on in historical memory and can return to haunt the present.

THE ANALYTICS OF COMMUNITY CLOSURE AND NARRATIVES OF *DISCENT*

How do historical groups try to transform a society with multiple representations of political community into a single social totality? This process involves the hardening of social and cultural boundaries around a particular configuration of self in relation to an Other. Its analysis is important for my larger argument about history because this process of closure is relevant to both historical and modern communities; moreover, instead of dwelling on the invention of history, it reveals how historical and cultural resources are mobilized in the transformation.

Sociologically, communities may be thought of not as well-bounded entities but as possessing various different and mobile boundaries that demarcate different dimensions of life. These boundaries may be either soft or hard. One or more of the cultural practices of a group, such as rituals, language, dialect, music, kinship rules or culinary habits, may be considered soft boundaries if they identify a group but do not prevent the group from sharing and even adopting, self-consciously or not, the practices of another. Groups with soft boundaries between each other are sometimes so unself-conscious about their differences that they do not view mutual boundary breach as a threat and could eventually even amalgamate into one community. Thus, differences in dietary and religious practices may not prevent the sharing of a range of practices between local Hui Muslim and Han communities. The important point is that they tolerate the sharing of some and the non-sharing of other boundaries.

An incipient nationality is formed when the perception of the boundaries of community are transformed, namely, when soft boundaries are transformed into hard ones. This happens when a group succeeds in imposing a historical narrative of descent and/or dissent on both heterogeneous and related cultural practices. I will permit myself a deconstructive excess and coin the word, *discent* to suggest the porosity of these two signifiers. It reveals how the tracing of a history is frequently linked to differentiating the self from an Other. The narrative of *discent* serves as a template by which the cultural cloth will be cut and given shape and meaning. When this narrative is imposed upon cultural materials, the relevant community is formed not primarily by the creation of new cultural forms—or even the invention of tradition—but by transforming the perception of the boundaries of the community. The narrative of *discent* is used to define and mobilize a community, often by privileging a particular cultural practice (or a set of such practices) as the constitutive principle of the community—such as language, religion, or common historical experience—thereby heightening the self-consciousness of this community in relation to those around it. Not only do communities with rigidified boundaries privilege their differences, they tend to develop an intolerance and suspicion toward the adoption of the other's practices and strive to distinguish, in some way or the other, practices that they share. In this sense, communities with hard boundaries will the differences between them.

Because the narrative succeeds in privileging certain cultural meanings as the constitutive principle of a community, it shapes the composition of the community: who belongs and who does not, who is privileged and who is not. Thus if common history (or Confucian ritual) is privileged over language and race, language and race always lie as potential counternarratives: mobilizers of an alternative nation that will distribute its marginals differently. Thus, within the community defined by hard boundaries, there will always be other soft boundaries which may potentially transform into hard boundaries, or new soft boundaries may emerge and transform into hard ones. A bifurcated history (discussed below) will be particularly attentive to these emergent narratives, which are often effaced or appropriated by the dominant narrative.

This mode of analysis challenges the notion of a stable community that gradually develops a national self-awareness like the evolution of a species (History). Rather, it asserts a deliberate mobilization within a network of cultural representations toward a particular object of identification. The following chapters examine the role of various social actors—often different groups of intellectuals and politicians—who develop and deploy narratives to redefine the boundaries and identities of a collectivity with multiple identifications. But even when this closure is successful, it will unravel in time; the privileged practices that organize this identification will also change.

Consider the history of Manchu identity. The Qing dynasty (1644–1911) originated from a Manchu ethnic community which maintained an ambivalent attitude toward the dominant Han culture that it ruled. In the early stages of its rule, it actively sought to maintain Manchu distinctiveness through a variety of means, including a ban on intermarriage and Han migration to Manchuria and the fostering of different customs. In time, however, not only was the ban on migration and intermarriage ignored, but Manchu embracing of Chinese political institutions caused it to blur the distinctions between it and the communities it ruled. More important, and unlike the Mongols, the Manchus recognized early the roots of politics in culture and rapidly became the patrons not only of elite culture, but also of popular Han gods like Guandi and Mazu. Thus by the eighteenth century, in terms of their social and cultural relations, the Manchu communities resident in the hundreds of garrisons outside of their homeland in the northeast were losing their literacy in Manchu as well as contact with their folk traditions and melding into the general Han populace (Crossley 1990b, 3, 30; Kuhn 1990, 68–70).

At the same time, however, powerful countertendencies worked to shore up—or reconstruct—a Manchu identity. Most noteworthy was the effort of the Qianlong emperor (1736–1795) to introduce a classic narrative of *discent* of the Manchus—the *Researches of Manchu Origins* discussed by Crossley (1987). *Researches* traced the *descent* of the Manchu clans to the first attestable peoples of the northeast, thereby demonstrating a "racial" distinctiveness which Crossley defines as "immutable identity based on ancestral descent" (1987, 762). Moreover, it celebrated the Manchus as inheritors of the imperial tradition of the region that was independent of (dissented from) the Han Chinese imperial tradition and most closely associated with the Jin empire of the twelfth century. To be sure, this narrative of *discent* played a part within a wider representation of power necessitated by the imperatives of ruling an empire that encompassed both Han Chinese and Central Asian polities (Crossley 1987; Kuhn 1990, 69). Confucian universalism was offset by racial exclusivism because, as Crossley remarks, every "racial" group—Manchus, Mongols, Tibetans, Han, and others—had their proper status according to their race. These races bore a relationship to the emperor set by the historical role of their ancestors in the creation and development of the state (Crossley 1987, 780). But this narrative, which endorsed a conception of "race" as a constitutive principle of community, was also motivated by the fear on the part of the emperor of total cultural extinction of the Manchus. Thus, the Qianlong emperor took it upon himself to champion the Manchu language and values and to punish those who forgot their roots (Kuhn 1990, 66–68).

Manchu identity flowered tragically in the late nineteenth century, both in response to Qianlong's efforts and also as a reaction to a Han ethnic exclusivism that became most evident during the years of the Taiping Rebellion. As early as 1840, in the days before the British attack on the lower Yangzi city of Zhenjiang during the Opium War, the tension in the city led to hostility between the Manchu soldiers in the garrisons and the civilian Han populace. Countless Han were slaughtered by Manchu soldiers on the allegation that they were traitors. Elliot shows that the entire event was interpreted as ethnic conflict both by survivors and by local historians (Elliot 1990, 64). This simmering tension culminated in the horrifying massacre of Manchu bannermen and their families during the Taiping Rebellion and again in the Republican Revolution of 1911 (Crossley 1990b, 130, 196–97). Manchus in the Republican era sustained their identity only by hiding it from public view and by quietly teaching the oral traditions to their children and grandchildren within their homes. Today, Manchu identity finds expression not only in their status as a national minority in the PRC, but as Crossley observes, in such forms as the Manchu Association formed in Taipei in 1981 (Crossley 1990b, 216).

The Manchu search for a separate identity may be traced back to a narrative which privileged "race" as the definer of community. The tragedy of it was that this rhetoric forced a highly, if incompletely, assimilated people to turn their back on what had, after all, become their culture. And yet it would be wrong and untrue to the mode of analysis I have tried to establish here to posit an essentializing evolutionary trend in the growth of Manchu identity and the worsening of Han-Manchu relations. Crossley is sensitive to the ambivalences of Manchus toward this identity, and important leaders of the Confucian intelligentsia were committed to a cosmopolitanism within their nationalism that included the Manchus as Chinese. Perhaps least understood in this regard are the Boxer "rebels" and various secret society groups in the last decades of the nineteenth century, who actually sought to support the Qing court—as the representative of Chinese culture—in the effort to expel the hated Westerner. As chapter 4 demonstrates, the presence of these tendencies in popular culture—which ran counter to Han–Manchu rivalries—contained the seeds of an incipient counternarrative that was nipped in the bud by the republican revolutionaries.

My effort to link narratives of *discent* to the self-definition of a group is relevant not only for ethnic nationalisms such as those of the Manchu or Mongols, but also for those less visible communities within. These include regional and provincial groupings within the Han, such as the Cantonese, the so-called "subethnic" groups, such as the Tanka boat people, the Hui and Subei people. For example, the mid-nineteenth century Taiping Rebellion was built up by the Hakka minority of south China, who discovered a narrative of *discent* in a version of Christianity which depicted them as a "chosen people." This narrative gave them a mission as "god-worshippers" in their protracted, dreary battle against the earlier settlers in south China, whom they now saw as idolatrous, and caused them to celebrate their own distinctive traditions over those of the larger Han community of which they were a highly ambiguous part. As the movement developed imperial ambitions, the Hakka coupled their anti-idolatrous message with appeals to an older rhetoric of the struggle of the Han against the Manchu (Kuhn 1977). The Taiping movement is instructive in showing how a community which had been successfully hardened by a redemptive narrative of *discent* was, in another political context, obliged to re-open the question of its identity, or rather, identities.

Several points should be noted in this analysis of community closure. First, while it has been analyzed principally for a period before the establishment of modern nationalism, this process is also relevant for modern nationalism. Moreover, the conceptualization of a narrative of *discent*, also relevant for the modern period, suggests that an exclusive or overriding identity is not usually constructed *de novo*, but built from existing representations of community, although much is lost and transformed in the process. Finally, in both premodern and modern societies, a plurality of representations, narratives, and identities continues to persist, even though the technical and institutional means of both closure and resistance differ in the two societies.

THE MODERN NATION-STATE SYSTEM AND THE QUESTION OF HISTORY

It is now clear that what is novel about modern nationalism is not political self-consciousness, but the world system of nation-states. Over the last century, this system, which sanctions the nation-state as the only legitimate form of polity, has expanded to cover the globe.

Externally, the nation-state claims sovereignty within distinct, but not undisputed, territorial boundaries. Internally, the state claims to represent the people of the nation and, through this claim, has steadily expanded its role in society, often at the expense of local authority structures. For instance, "children" have come increasingly under the jurisdiction of the state as the institutional rules governing childhood were diffused to all types of nation-states over the last hundred years (Boli-Bennet and Meyer 1978). It is important to grasp that the form of the nation-state is sanctioned by a battery of discourses generated from the system as a whole. We have seen how social Darwinism joined race and History to the nation-state. Later, anti-imperialism and even socialism and Marxism would come to sanction the nation-state. At the same time, these nation-states also have to confront other alternative or historical representations from within the societies they govern.

The territorial conception of the nation also has a history which may be traced to what William McNeill has characterized as the system of competitive European states. From as far back as 1000 A.D., each of these states was driven by the urge to increase its resources, population, and military technology over the others. In their competition, these states gradually became dependent on capital markets, both externally and internally, which further propelled the development of their economy and the competition between them (McNeill 1982). In time, the Roman Catholic Church came to sanction some of these emergent regional states by endowing them with a theory of sovereignty without at the same time obliging them to achieve a universalizing empire. This was possible because of the separation of temporal and spiritual authority or, in other words, the source of legitimacy from actual exercise of power (Armstrong 1982). The culmination of this conception of the nation was first seen in the French Revolution and exemplified in the idea of citizenship for all within the territory (Eley 1981).

However, no contemporary nation-state is a nation exclusively in this territorial sense. Even among the early modern European states, European dynasts had to combine the theory of territorial sovereignty with ethnicity to create modern nation-states (Armstrong 1982). While most historical nations, defined as self-aware and even politicized communities, may have lacked the conception of themselves as part of a system of territorially sovereign nation-states, at the same time, modern nations seek the sources of their cohesion not in the territorial conception but from a narrative of the nation that privileges a particular principle defining community, such as, say, language, race, religion, etc. (and repressing the others).[9] It is true, as Balibar (1991) and others point out, that territorial boundaries can themselves acquire a salience and develop powerful attachments for their citizens. Yet, even these territorial identifications have to be founded on an inherited, if contested, narrative of the "homeland" such as the "central plain" (*zhongyuan*) or Aryavarta.

The shape and content of national identities in the modern era are a product of negotiation between remembered historical narratives of community and the institutionalized discourses of the modern nation-state system. The question remains as to the nature of historical influence, of the role of the past in the present. Michel Foucault, following in the footsteps of Nietzsche and Walter Benjamin, makes a persuasive critique of history as continuity. It is important for my analysis to firmly grasp his reworking of 'genealogy' as a way to disrupt the continuum of traditional history.

> Genealogy does not pretend to go back in time to restore an unbroken continuity that operates beyond the dispersion of forgotten things; its duty is not to demonstrate that the past actively exists in the present . . . having imposed a predetermined form to all its vicissitudes . . . On the contrary, to follow the complex course of descent is to maintain passing events in their proper dispersion. (Foucault 1977, 146)

Dispersal is the moment in which the genealogical historian must try to recover a "counter-memory." But while we seek to grasp with one hand the dispersal of the past, we must, with the other, grasp the reality of the transmission of the past.

To my mind, the critical questions lie less in the realness of the transmission, and more, as we shall see, in its modality, which obliges us to understand history as a simultaneously dual or bifurcated movement of transmission and dispersion. The recent preoccupation with the invention or construction or imagining of the past obscures the fact that any transmission is also a reinvention. Every community, in order to recognize itself as a community, has to produce a believable self-image of its past in the present; that is, in the new and changed reality in which it finds itself. This difference is particularly noticeable to us when the present is dominated by a totally alien discourse, but it should not conceal that the engagement of the past with the present is ongoing and real.

---

9. In reality, of course, territorial boundaries of even the most modern nation-states are extremely porous and culturally hybrid. Just consider the border between the United States and Mexico.

Of course, skeptics may argue that if every transmission is a reinvention, then the past has no reality whatsoever. Once again I will turn to Paul Ricoeur. Ricoeur finds a complementarity, but also a difference, between fiction and history, or rather historiography. Both are represented by narratives that emplot (or re-figure) events into a humanly comprehensible order, specifically to mediate the aporia or discordance between the restricted time of mortals and the unlimited time of the cosmos (Ricoeur 1988, 3: 104–26). Historical refiguration addresses this aporia by means of specific, observable connectors to the past, such as seasonal cycles, the biological overlapping of generations, and especially the "trace" of the past in such things as documents and monuments. Fiction invents "imaginary variations with respect to the cosmic reinscription effected by history" (Ricoeur 1991, 351). Thus, the historian is differentiated by his or her ability, through entering the world of traces, to speak about something observable in the past.

In the notion of the connecters, especially the trace, Ricoeur anchors a (underdetermined) notion of the reality of the past.[10] As the material presence of the past, the trace is both nature and culture: it is an object susceptible to the laws of causation, but it is also interpretable as a sign, a meaning. Ricoeur calls it a "sign-effect." Thus the document or monument is the material basis of the figurative emplotment of the past, "of a special relation *to* an actual past in the relating *of* that past" (Rosen 1993, 68). As a sign, the trace is interpreted, but the trace signifies beyond "any intention of giving a sign" (Ricoeur 1988, 3: 125). It is a sign of the past whose materiality is revealed in that it is not exhausted by successive interpretations.

The notion of the trace has also emerged as an important way to understand how the past is transmitted or relayed. Writing about Derrida's views on trace, Marian Hobson likens history to a network of return telephone calls. She quotes Derrida on Husserl:

> From a received and already readable *document*, the possibility is offered me of asking again and *in return* about the originary and full intentions of what has been handed to

10. This brief summary cannot do justice to the three-volume meditation on the problem of time and its narrative figurations, but chapter 6 of volume 3 presents perhaps the most lucid and, to my mind, persuasive effort to construct an argument for the underdetermined concept of the reality of the past. By isolating the usable parts of Collingwood, Hadyn White, and Michel de Certeau, Ricoeur reconnects them to construct his argument of history as the Analogue of the past, which he then secures to the materiality of the "trace."

me by tradition. The latter, which is only mediacy itself, and openness to telecommunication in general, is then as Husserl says, *open to continued inquiry.* (Hobson 1987, 110).

I see the working of trace here as similar to Ricoeur's sign-effect: history comes to us like a telephone call to which we are obliged to respond, presumably, within its initiating framework. Thus, we in the present together with our caller from the past, are coproducers of the past. How we respond to the call and how differently we may respond from each other reflects both our present circumstances and our creativity.[11] Tejaswini Niranjana's model of "translation" to understand the process of historical transmission is related and relevant. She argues that, in his later writings, Walter Benjamin saw the task of the historian as the same as the task of the translator: the past is a foreign language, but one which presents us with a translatability. Translation cannot recover some pure originariness, but it must be aware, through the kinship of languages, of "the critical constellation" in which precisely this fragment of the text/past is found with precisely this translation/present (Niranjana 1992, 114, 117). Thus, while there is no simple break with the past, neither is transmission simply causal. It is more in the nature of a relay, a translation or a "return call."

Understanding transmission as a translation or return call or a reconstitution of the meanings of the past involves a crucial relationship with the dispersed past, the past as radically heterogenous. Transmission of the meaning of a trace or an event is premised upon repression or appropriation of (and sometimes negotiation with) other, dispersed meanings of the trace or event by the structures and signifiers of a narrative. It is of great importance to grasp the *particular process* whereby transmission seeks to appropriate, conceal, or repress dispersed meanings because it is often through this conflictual relationship that we can glimpse history outside of the categories of the nation-state: at the instant when the transmissive act seeks to appropriate the dispersed event. Moreover, we are privileged to view this appropriating instant precisely because there is more than one force which seeks to appropriate it—given that there is more than one way to conceive of the nation. It is in the contest over the meanings of

---

11. Chapter 2, volume 3, of Ricoeur's *Time and Narrative* also contains a detailed exposition of Husserl's conception of phenomenological time and his discovery of "retention" and "secondary remembrance." While Ricoeur may be the most subtle and complex critic of history as a totalizing discourse, he is less helpful when it comes to the contests of historical narratives.

historical events that we are alerted to how the dispersed meanings of the past are appropriated to construct a linear narrative.

Let us consider how modern representations of the nation engaged with historical narratives in China during the years before the Republican Revolution of 1911, when modern nationalism took hold among the Chinese intelligentsia. The constitutional monarchists, represented by Kang Youwei, inherited the Confucian culturalist notion of community. Although Kang was influenced by modern ideas, the conception of political community that he retained drew on culturalist Confucian notions. This is evident in his lifelong devotion to the emperor (Protect the Emperor Society), which in the political context of the time meant more than a nostalgia for monarchy. Since the monarchs were Manchu and not Han, it implied that he was convinced that community was composed of people with shared culture and not restricted to a race or ethnic group (imputed or otherwise).

In his debates with the anti-Manchu revolutionary Zhang Taiyan, Kang cited Confucius to argue that although Confucius had spoken of barbarians, barbarism was expressed as a lack of ritual and civilization. If indeed they possessed culture, then they must be regarded as Chinese. Invoking the memory of the cultural community, Kang declared that during the Warring States, Wu and Chu had been different countries but had become part of China by the time of the Han. Similarly, although the Manchus were barbarians in the Ming, by now they had acquired Chinese culture and so had become Chinese. Kang asked whether it was necessary for China to get rid of the Manchus in order to build a new nation or whether the nation could embrace all ethnic groups on a harmonious basis, including the Manchus, Hans, Miaos and Moslems, as well as the Tibetans[12] (Onogawa 1970, 245, 249).

The revolutionaries, such as Zhang Taiyan and Wang Jingwei, articulated their opposition to this conception by drawing on the old ethnocentric tradition that acquired new meaning in the highly charged atmosphere of the 1900s. To be sure, Zhang was a complex figure whose thought can scarcely be reduced to any single strain, but he and Wang Jingwei succeeded in articulating an image of the new community that was persuasive to many in his generation. At the base of this reformulation of the old ethnocentrism was a dialec-

12. Liang Qichao, Kang's one-time disciple, developed this argument further, alleging that the revolutionaries deliberately confused bad government with racism. What was important was that the government was badly run; whether it was run by Manchus or Han was beside the point. There was no reason why China could not be rebuilt on a multiracial basis.

tical reading of Wang Fuzhi's notions of evolutionism interwoven with a new social Darwinist conception of the survival of the fittest races. Thus, each group was engaged in dialogue with disputed legacies that were, nonetheless, real and by no means completely reducible to modern discourses.

We can better understand the complex transactions between past and present by examining the representational and linguistic structures of revolutionary ideology. For instance, several scholars (Dikötter 1992; Price 1992) have pointed out the way in which the values of the Chinese lineage or descent line, perhaps one of the most important social institutions in late imperial China, were "translated" (in Niranjana's sense) to develop the modern concept of race. The transition from lineage to this conception of race as a community united by blood ties was enabled by the common semantic source, the signifier *zu*, which referred to the descent group and also to race or kind (a term also of greatest importance to Wang Fuzhi in the seventeenth century [Dikötter 1992, 29]). Republican revolutionaries like Chen Tianhua, Zou Rong, and Song Jiaoren were able to maneuver within the play of this signifier and, hence, with the emotions it evoked, such as filiality. Thus Chen Tianhua pronounced: "The Han race is one big family. The [mythic] Yellow Emperor is the great ancestor, all those who are not of the Han race are not the descendants of the Yellow Emperor, they are exterior families. One should definitely not assist them" (cited in Dikötter 1992, 117). According to Dikötter, "race" became the symbol of fictive biological cohesion that could link lineage loyalties in the face of foreign aggression (p. 71). Donald Price believes that the representation of the nation embedded in the new conception of common descent from the Yellow Emperor was enabled by an extended and redefined filial piety (*xiao*). Racial vengeance against the Manchus was now an obligation one owed to one's ancestors whether or not they were of one's immediate lineage (Price 1992, 1052–53).

These notable contributions to our understanding of early twentieth-century anti-Manchuism have emphasized the manner in which historical ideas have enabled the transition to the new evolutionist conception of the racial-nation. By linking race to the more tangible cultural institution of lineage, the revolutionaries were able to deploy an unfamiliar narrative—which, as we have seen in chapter 1, emphasized the strife between Historical and non-Historical races—as their narrative of *discent*. In this way, they could mobilize existing cultural symbols to build the walls of a community without the Manchus. At the same time, the new evolutionist narrative of History also tried to recast and so to appropriate the dispersed meanings of existing symbols and practices. Ancestor worship, filial piety, and kinship terminology (see in particular the concept of "brotherhood" in chapter 4) which tended to be focused within the lineage (*zongzu*) were now sought also to be turned outward to the race and nation (*zhongzu, minzu*). Thus, the mythic Yellow Emperor, whose status as national symbol came to dominate nationalist discourse throughout the first few decades of the twentieth century, continued to be officially revered as the originator of the race and the founder of the nation until 1941. In 1957, the religion of the Yellow Emperor was established in Taiwan with government approval (Dikötter 1992, 116–17). Neither the notion of simple continuity nor that of invention can do justice to the subtle transactions between the past and the present. The past does not shape the present simply by persisting in it. It enables the transformation of the present and in that transformation, is itself much transformed. Attention to the manner in which dominant narratives seek to inflect and mobilize the meanings of existing symbols and practices offers a more promising beginning to understanding history.

The revolutionary position also retained the capacity to invoke the oppositional culturalist model of community as its supplement. The revolutionary invocation of racialist memory at the turn of the century could not confine the othering process to the Manchus alone. The construction of the Han Chinese self as the national subject necessarily threatened other non-Han groups, as Kang Youwei had warned it would. Most of the large minority communities had viewed their incorporation into the Qing empire as being on a par with the enforced incorporation of the Han; they did not equate the Qing empire with Zhongguo (China). The overthrow of the Qing in 1911 created for them the possibility of independence; the rhetoric of racialist nationalism made it urgent. Given their own equation of nation and race, the revolutionaries could hardly counter the growing Mongol independence movement, the establishment of an independent Mongolia in 1911 (Nakami 1984), and the threatening situation in Tibet and Xinjiang. It was in these circumstances that Sun Yat-sen and the leaders of the new Republic sought to supplement their racialist narrative with the culturalist narrative of the nation espoused by their enemies—the reformers and the Qing court itself. The Chinese nation was now to be made up of the "five races" (Manchu, Mongol, Tibetan, Muslim, and Han) and so it happened that the boundaries of the Chinese nation came to follow the outline of the old Qing empire just as the Indian nation was sought to be made in the image of the British empire. Later, the narrative of race as constitutive of the nation would itself be dispersed or, perhaps, absorbed inside a larger nationalist narrative of the common historical experience against imperialism.

In India, several models of political community furnished the framework within which the modern nation was contested. We can find these historical conceptions within the motley body of the Indian National Congress, which emerged in the late nineteenth century as the representative of Indian nationalism. Thus for instance, the secularist model of Jawaharlal Nehru and Rabindranath Tagore drew on the idealized conception of the subcontinental empire. The Rudolphs (1985) point out that each of the empires in South Asia built on the symbols of the classical idea of a universal ruler: Akbar restoring the Hindu idea of a *chakravartin* in the Persian idea of *shahanshah;* the British using Mughal ceremonies and language to revitalize the imperial state. Thus colonizers and conquerors reinforced a process of political formation whereby communities and regional kingdoms were incorporated (and not subsumed or obliterated) into an ordered heterogeneity.

Nehru may have been the first to narrativize a history of the subcontinental empire into what comes to be known as the secular History of India. In his view, what he considered India was the secular unity of different communities and religions, each of which had made distinctive historical contributions. For him, Hinduism and its achievements were merely one of the sources of India's greatness, together with those of Buddhism, the Turkic emperors, traditional science, among other sources. For Nehru, the History of India was the most authentic testimony to the capacity (read necessity) of Indians to maintain a "unity among diversity." The high points of Indian history were the reigns of Asoka, the Guptas, Akbar, and the great Mughals, all of whom attempted to develop a political framework to unite the cultural diversity of the subcontinent. While in contemporary India this idealized version is countered by a forceful process of state-building, nonetheless, the memory of ordered heterogeneity is perhaps visible in the notion of Indian secularism, which is not so much a strict separation of state and society as it is the equal support of the state for all religions (Nehru 1960, 121–28).

The memory of Brahmanic universalism as the foundation of the new political community, filtered through Orientalist discourses of the nineteenth century, was appropriated in its split form as universalism and its supplement of closure. Its universal form was articulated by Sri Aurobindo (1872–1950) and others and influenced

Mohandas Gandhi. Aurobindo emphasized Advaita Hinduism, a radically monistic faith which believes in the unity of all being and denies the reality of the many particular entities in the universe. In this highly abstract system, a communal framework was created to absorb or tolerate heterogenous elements domestically within an essentially Brahmanic universalism. Thinkers like Aurobindo and Gandhi, of course, had to develop strategies to square the circle: to contain their universalism within their terminal political community of the nation. One such strategy was to devise the Spiritual East/Material West duality whereby India remained the privileged locus as the origin and repository of true (Hindu?) Spirituality.

The supplement to Brahmanic universalism, which in recent times has threatened to overcome this universalism, is the historical memory of the nation-space as Aryavarta, whose charter is traced to the medieval political readings of the *Ramayana*. A recent expression of this Hindu nationalism has drawn much attention by its violent mobilization campaigns to recover the site of the alleged birthplace of Rama in Ayodhya from a Muslim shrine which existed there until Hindu nationalists destroyed it in December 1992. The Ayodhya destruction is only the most recent expression of a series of campaigns launched by Hindu nationalists since the end of the nineteenth century, such as the protection of the cow, the promotion of religious ceremonies to capture public spaces, and the takeover of other Muslim shrines. These nationalists, like the anti-Manchu revolutionaries, foreground atavistic revenge in their narrative of *discent*. Through this narrative of vengeance, they seek to reinvest local gods, local issues, and local conflicts with national meaning. Hindu nationalism has no use for universalism and declares a homogenized Hinduness (Hindutva) to be the sole or privileged criterion for inclusion in the political community of the nation. They thus seek to transform the relatively porous boundaries of local communities into an overarching hard boundary between a national community and its Muslim Other. It is a project that recalls the radical othering we found in representations of medieval Hindu community. Although on the face of it, the lofty universalism of Aurobindo and Gandhi seems far removed from such a thoroughgoing communalism, the supplement of Hindu nationalism could easily exploit the ambivalence toward outsiders within their thought.

How can the conception of bifurcation illumine these complex exchanges between the present and its multiple, contending pasts? Bifurcation attends to the moment and mode of appropriation of a dispersed history and its reconstitution when possible. In Zhang Tai-

yan's narrative of the racial community in the early twentieth century, he may have stressed the influence of seventeenth-century
thinkers, but we can also see that his ideas are coherent within the
discourses of his time: social Darwinism, social psychology, and other
disciplines employed in the construction of a national subject. While
in the seventeenth century the Manchus were seen as usurping, un-
cultured barbarians, in 1900 this image was appropriated by a discourse which saw them as primitive peoples bent on keeping China
low in the ranked hierarchy of nations (see chapter 4). Similarly,
when Aurobindo or Bankim Chandra (see chapter 7) raised the East/
Spirit versus West/Matter duality, their claim of transmitting an ancient universalism represented an appropriation of this universalism
to build an Orientalist discourse of the colonized. To recognize this is
to locate the past in what Foucault has called its "proper dispersion."

Moreover, this appropriation into a particular narrative often obscures or represses other competing historical narratives of the time.
Since the ascendancy of secular nationalism in India, the narrative of
religious nationalism has been suppressed in the Westernized sectors
of society which have monopolized the national image. Thus, until
recently, Indian historiography from school textbooks to research
monographs has not been able to understand the gathering power
of the narrative of vengeance despite the violent partition of India
at independence and the recurring violence between Hindus and
Muslims. In the same way, the social Darwinist narrative of race in
China was partially concealed by the subsequent invocation of the
oppositional Confucian representation of community and finally marginalized by the rhetoric of anti-imperialism.

If bifurcation unmasks appropriations and concealments in historical transmission, it can also lead us to other ways to approach the
historical, specifically to the historical conditions enabling narrative
transmission and to the effects of this transmission. In trying to capture the dispersed event, social forces return it to the memory of
an evolving narrative. The event which is returned, is re-cognized
through a metaphoric or metonymic association with the memory of
past events. As such, although it recasts both event and memory and
reconstitutes the linearity of the process, the appropriation process
is not entirely arbitrary. Not all events can equally be made to enhance the narrative. The selection is conditioned by a logic of historical and cultural affinity, as in the example of the Republicans' extension of lineage to develop the modern concept of race. Deconstructing
a semantic transformation, such as in the signifier *zu*, allows us to
recover a causal or, at least, a conditional relationship.

Moreover, every "addition" or "evolutionary phase" accompanying each reconstitution yields a certain effectiveness to the narrative which should not be underestimated. The power of some narratives to persist itself depends on the fact of their pursuit among successive historical forces. The *Ramayana* has today become the vehicle of the self-understanding of Hindu nationalism because its power to serve as a model of political community derives from its very pursuit by different historical groups. Even though its periodic replay reflects the actual dispersal of its meaning, Hindu nationalists and others have sought to return its meaning to an apparently coherent historical memory that is available as a significant political resource to a new generation.[13]

Thus, the reality and power of narrative transmission should not be doubted just because it is formed of repressions and reconstitutions. By linking new events back to an animating story, this story is extended into the present which it seeks to shape. This, then, is none other than narrative *as* history. And it is the effects of this history which permit us to grasp the specific character of political community in the societies I have compared: why "religion" furnishes an idiom for defining political community in India and "race" for China before and after the emergence of the modern nation-state.[14]

Analytically, one may think of this narrative transmission as a second-order history, a history constantly at risk of being falsified by the localized, dispersed and truer meanings of events which it seeks to appropriate. But, in practice, the distinction between the localization of meaning and the way in which narrative shapes the real is sometimes hard to sustain because the same historical actor who disperses the meaning of an event may also return it to a centralizing historical narrative (for example, see Liang's statism in chapter 5 and Mao's federalism in chapter 6). More important, the above characterization of narrative scarcely warrants its rejection as a mode of histori-

13. The *Ramayana* today can hardly be said to refer to the same Hindu self. Indeed, Hindu nationalism today is a reconstituted self which faces a configuration of the Other different from even a hundred years ago: it can ignore old enemies like Christian missionaries and has to deal with new elements such as assertive low castes and the Sikhs; even Muslims represent a very different political meaning now that they are a much smaller, underclass minority.

14. Indeed, in China, the old narrative of race, assumed to have been suppressed by the new communist narrative of class as the constitutive principle of citizenship, raises its head from within this narrative in, among other things, the discourse on eugenics in contemporary society (see, for instance, *South China Morning Post*, 22 December 1993).

cal writing. Since we have few other means to understand the past, I am less inclined to reject all narrative than to enhance its enabling potential by clarifying the particular ways, and to what ends, the ties of the narrative to the present confront its past.

CONCLUSION

I have described a multiplicity of historical representations of political community in China and India which may be seen as examples of complex agrarian polities. This multiplicity includes the representation of totalizing communities that both resemble modern nations and continue to be relevant to them. As such, even in recent theories of nationalism, notions of differences between the modern nation and traditional empire turn out to be highly exaggerated. Moreover, these notions reflect and reproduce a highly suspect presumption of an epistemological gap between national consciousness as cohesive and self-aware and premodern consciousness as dominated either by universal cosmologies or parochial identities. The modern nation is formed through a process similar to that of its totalizing predecessors which deploys a narrative of *discent*—the tracing of a history which legitimates its difference from the Other—to fix and privilege a single identity from among the contesting multiplicity of identifications. In neither society can this closure prevent alternative narratives from challenging the hegemonic representation of political community.

The territorially sovereign form of the modern nation is shaped by the global system of nation-states and its discourses. The representations of political community in the modern nation continues, however, to be shaped by the transactions between historical narratives and the discourses of the modern nation-state. I have tried to grasp these transactions through the notion of a bifurcated history. Bifurcation reveals that the apparent transparency or continuity of historical language often conceals the appropriation of a different meaning. Foucault writes about such meanings being appropriated by "substitutions, displacements, disguised conquests, and systematic reversals" (Foucault 1977, 151). At the same time, however, dis-covering the appropriation process itself allows us to see the historical conditions that enabled it and the historical effects of the appropriating narrative. Bifurcation is also well-suited to the conception of identities as fluid and contestatory since ascendant identifications tend to narrate histories of *discent* that suppress or conceal alternate identities. Conversely, the voices of a suppressed identity may seek to articulate counter-representations and even counter-narratives (see chapters 5 and 6) which a bifurcated history should be poised to grasp.

While this chapter continues the critique of linear, causal History begun in chapter 1, it is equally directed at those who deny history altogether. In so doing, these modern analysts deny the dual movement of history and privilege the contemporary, the modern, as a temporal system with clear beginnings (and an end?), a unified consciousness which absorbs and annuls the past. This is the metaphysics of "the end of history," a metaphysics which, ironically, the modern nation-state also requires to secure its ultimate claim of the unity and transparency of the national body itself.

PART TWO

3

THE CAMPAIGNS AGAINST RELIGION
AND THE RETURN OF THE REPRESSED

THE NARRATIVE of History, we have seen, hosts a contradictory tendency among its advocates, who desire both to belong to the past and to break with it. The Hegelian formulation of the "end of history" exemplifies the urge to break with the past and institute the modern self-conscious subject as the telos of History. In the Chinese narrative of History, the "end of history" syndrome is particularly well-developed. It became especially pronounced among the most vocal segments of the Chinese intelligentsia in the period during and after the May 4th movement, and has resurfaced periodically, perhaps most infamously, during the Cultural Revolution.

I will highlight not these most dramatic outbursts of the syndrome, but its appearance in more ordinary times, in the 1900s and the late 1920s, and among a group of modernizing nationalists seemingly less committed to such an eschatalogical vision as the communists. I will explore how these intellectuals and reformers employed the "end of history" rhetoric in their campaign to destroy a world of popular religion which they condemned as superstitious and backward. Thus, this chapter, and likewise the next, focuses more on the appropriating moment of History, whereas the subsequent two chapters focus on counternarratives of history.

Examining the campaign against popular religion gives me a chance to write a bifurcated history from two angles. First, whereas in the narrative of History, the campaigns merit attention as a minor episode in the modernization of a nation; in a bifurcated history, they appear as the effort to appropriate an entire world of dispersed meanings, practices, and ideals embedded in popular religion under the sign of the modern: the era of self-consciousness and end of contingency. The realm of popular religion turns out, however, to be a reef upon which the Enlightenment project in China repeatedly crashes; and the resistances it offers are critical moments in a bifurcated history. I will return to popular religion again in chapters 5 and 7.

Second, I am able to write a bifurcated history by grasping the changing meaning of the modern itself. Even while the representation of the modern continued to emphasize the advent of utopian self-consciousness, the content of the modern underwent subtle, but significant changes. The rhetoric of the campaign against religion concealed the dispersed meanings of its own struggles as the goals and views of its initiators were gradually appropriated by a different struggle involving the modern state. It is by reading both, the gaps and conflicts within the rhetoric of the campaign as well as the resistance offered to the campaign by those most affected by it, that we are able to restore the hidden meanings of the campaign against religion.

SELF-CONSCIOUSNESS AND THE END-OF-HISTORY

The absolute conviction of the radical reformers that they possessed the Truth derived from the logic of History the telos of which is self-consciousness. In 1915, six years before he and his comrades set out to found the Chinese Communist Party, Chen Duxiu sought to establish the importance of self-consciousness (*zijue*), which was based on true knowledge and reasoning rather than upon irrational emotions (Chen Duxiu 1915, 69). In the late 1920s, the radical KMT (Kuomintang) reformer who called himself Zeng Jue (Already Awakened) confidently pronounced that since the present era belonged to science, which had proven the nonexistence of god, religion was an unnecessary anachronism (1930a, 120–21). Within these dozen years, the triumph of what has been called "scientism"—the view which places all reality within the natural order and deems it knowable by the methods of science—became firmly lodged among the most vocal and active segments of the Chinese intelligentsia. Scientism was the specific manifestation of the end-of-history syndrome in China. Since this syndrome prompted the intelligentsia to rid their world of such retrograde anachronisms as religion, it behooves us to explore the doctrine of self-consciousness not only among the modern Chinese intelligentsia, but also its kinship with our own historical narratives.

For Hegel, the History of the world represented successive stages in the progress of the spirit of self-consciousness which constitutes freedom. The successive stages were not simply a chronological sequence, but a progress of unfolding, of making this spirit explicit. In this way, that history which is not relevant to the realization of spirit is excised and the succession of historical time is sublated into the eternal present. The difference is between the dead past and the living past, the latter being related to what is "essential." Thus the advent of the modern era of self-consciousness marks its break with history by abolishing what is different from itself in history. In this era, the unnecessary, the contingent—the stuff of history—will be overcome by the self-conscious subject.

David Kolb has shown that the unified subject, self-conscious of *his* or *her* freedom, is one of the most important premises in the conception of modernity. In Max Weber, this premise is exemplified most clearly in his notion of "methodological individualism," which presumes a distanced self formally defined in terms of its power to choose. According to Weber, one of the distinguishing hallmarks of modernity is its recognition that the beliefs and attitudes in society are based on choice—a constrained choice doubtless, but choice nonetheless—on the part of the individual. Thus, modern thought recognizes what traditional societies had failed to recognize, namely that values are self-chosen and not grounded in a larger cosmic scheme. For Weber, traditional societies may reveal highly sophisticated, rational systems, such as the Chinese bureaucracy or the Indian caste system, but they are ultimately constrained by the unquestioned beliefs of the culture. In contrast to this "substantive rationality," the modern self, empty and formal, making efficient decisions to maximize self-chosen values, engages in "formal rationality." Modern subjectivity has grasped the fundamental truth of its own emptiness and is thus unconstrained in its power to know (Weber 1958; Kolb 1986, 9–12).[1]

Chapter 2 explored this epistemic break between conceptions of the modern and premodern in Chinese studies, particularly through Levenson's paradigmatic distinction between culturalism and nationalism. On the other side of culturalism—a set of substantive beliefs guiding people's actions—Levenson saw the nation as an indubitably

1. To be sure, Weber himself was well aware of the danger of interpreting science monistically: the conviction that scientific rationality in the disenchanted world is the only possible form of rationally interpreting the world. But the degree of Weber's ties to the classical model of rationality—both in his methodology and his ethic—is a subject of some disagreement among Weber scholars (see Roth and Schluchter [1979, 51]).

modern form in which actors are possessed of a self-consciousness not to be found in traditional societies. For the modern Chinese nationalist, "tradition," or the presence of the past, was a second order of knowledge, a psychological comfort at best, a cynical manipulation at worst. While "tradition" in a nationalist discourse is useful to reach through to the masses or to respond to the cultural dilemmas of Westernized intellectuals, this tradition is a reconstructed image and one that is selected and reorganized by the modern nationalist for certain ends.

To be sure, Levenson's ideas of the uses of tradition have much value. It is undoubtedly true that traditional or what I would rather call "historical" ideas and values are used for purposes other than that which they themselves proclaim. The conception of a bifurcated history suggests that the past is never replayed in the same register. Thus, for instance, Chiang Kai-shek's New Life movement sought to restore Confucian moral values in everyday life; they were intended not only to shore up the social and moral order as they might in the empire, but also, or perhaps, principally, to define what was Chinese. Levenson has said of this effort, "Nationalistic eulogies of the Chinese essence were only a counterfeit of culturalistic confidence in it. The nationalist-traditionalist impulse was for China to be Confucian because Confucius was Chinese, not because he told the simple truth" (1965, 153–54). Modern nationalists did not have "a primary belief in Confucianism, but a belief in the need to profess belief" (1965, 142).

What I find objectionable here is the identification of each era with its own epistemology in the characterization of the ideas of one era as "believed" and another era as "needed to be believed": as fulfilling something other than what they claim. Self-consciousness—in Levenson's understanding of modern actors—as the freedom to choose, marks precisely the break with allegedly traditional substantive beliefs such as in "culturalism." In premodern as much as in modern societies, knowledge becomes tied to networks of interests and goals which are other than what they profess. "Traditional" goals, beliefs, ideas and values, lead a life in the social world that fulfill or negotiate their status with other objectives and interests in the old empire as much as in modern society.[2] The notion of substantive traditional

2. It goes without saying that this critique can be extended—as it has been above—to those who would depict the world solely in terms of a traditionalist worldview, as for instance by fundamentalists the world over. They seek to obscure many modernist assumptions even as they utilize them to depict the world in the traditionalist image.

life does little justice to the gaps, the differences, the play, and the concealments that are at the heart of what has been called a tradition.

Similarly, we tend not to explore the possibility that the notions of the empty, formal self in possession of rational method may blind us to the existence of other beliefs, interests, and indeed other selves lurking within us, a glimpse of which we may occasionally catch in our contradictions, inconsistencies, and in our actions. Like traditional beliefs, modern ideas and values can hardly be taken only at face value—in terms of their own self-definition. They too are implicated in ambiguities and contradictions, in power struggles, and in the masking of other objectives. Both the modern self and its interests are as much constituted by representations and powers beyond its full control as is the historical self. At the same time, people in all societies can also manipulate these representations to attain other goals. Substantive values and formal means exist in elusive combinations in both "traditional" and "modern" societies. Although modernization theory has long been discredited, the assumption of traditional and modern as two coherent and exclusive eras or systems continues, as Paul Cohen (1984, 91–96) points out, to persist in Chinese studies as much as in studies of nationalism (see chapter 2). At a fundamental level, this contrast—like the end of history problematic—is secured by the concept of the self-conscious modern subject.

Traditional and modern elements are not so isolatable from each other nor so invariant that they determine our lives as "modern" or "traditional" or even in identifiable combinations thereof. Our lives interweave historical and new elements inextricably. What is seemingly traditional, like having extended families or believing in the gods, can be seen as a rational way of behaving from the particular and even modern circumstances of people's lives. Take the example of Confucianism. Confucianism used to be seen as traditional and retrograde, cultivating subservience to authority chiefly through the family. Nowadays, there is a growing tendency to view Confucianism as "traditional," but compatible and conducive to modern development. The argument has been turned around to say that Confucian family authority cultivates self-sacrifice, educational values, and upward mobility through which a modern society has been achieved in East Asia. How do we make sense of this turnabout? I think it would be wrong to see Confucianism as still a basically traditional institution that was earlier misunderstood to be incompatible with modernity. Practices and institutions are often inherited from the past, but they do not remain of the past in some essential way—which is what the term traditional implies. What we call Confucianism in the early twentieth century was not an inert inheritance from the past, but equally a range of responses to this very inheritance in the contemporary scene. As such, it was given new meaning and value—as for instance in the New Life movement discussed above—on contact with modern discourses such as History and social Darwinism. It became as much a modern as a traditional phenomenon—or more simply, made nonsense of that distinction.

Because the dichotomy of tradition and modern is too fixed to reflect a dynamic reality does not mean that these categories are not useful. Their value, however, emerges from understanding them as discursive representations: as ways people understand and talk about themselves and others; as ways, for instance, in which some intellectuals deploy their self-perception as self-conscious subjects and the Other as mired in superstitious beliefs. They are, most certainly, representations which have powerful reality effects, but as structures of signification their meaning is never so fixed that they simply reveal a transparent reality. Rather, we need to pursue their unceasing entanglements with other goals and powers to reveal their fuller meanings in a bifurcated history.[3]

MAKING THE PEOPLE FOR THE END OF HISTORY

The May 4th movement demanded, as did the Cultural Revolution in a different context, the break with the past in order to achieve Enlightenment self-consciousness. From another perspective, these

---

3. When one ceases to regard the modern subject as the fixed foundation of knowledge or History as simply the documentation of lived reality, but rather also as constitutive representations, one is often charged with nihilism. I do not find this charge meaningful or useful. The choice before us is not between a simple, *a priori* theory of rationality and a self-invalidating doctrine of naive relativism. People can have comparatively good arguments, but often enough these arguments are universalized and moralized in order to invalidate competing or alternate viewpoints. The problem of cultural imperialism arises, it seems to me, when the standards of justice are embedded in a discourse that is unable or unwilling to recognize the particular location from which it views reality. (For a detailed statement of my position, see Duara 1991, 71–73).

I am somewhat more sympathetic to the charge that the loss of a coherent modern or national subject makes it difficult to advocate a political program because of the variability or flux of political agency. Yet, as Joan Scott has pointed out, there are also evident examples of a politics empowered by this approach, politics that are not only critical of existing social hierarchies but able to point out the premises of their operations. She points, for example, to legal theorists and feminist theorists who formulate and act on ethical positions even while they acknowledge complexity and contradiction (Scott 1988, 9). See also the notable effort by Laclau and Mouffe to enable a politics that acknowledges difference (1985).

events may be regarded as among the most spectacular instances of the failure of History to redress the aporia of time: where the urgency to realize utopian timelessness occasions the destruction of all association with time or history. How did this temporal break fall out on the question of the nation? For all of his ambivalence toward it, Sun Yat-sen had not relinquished the past. The discussion in chapter 1 indicates how he had worked on a strategy of reawakening the people of the nation. The people had demonstrated the quality of patriotism before and he sought to recover this quality. Indeed, even as late as in his lectures on the Three People's Principles, he expressed a greater faith in more traditional organizational forms upon which to build the nation, such as native place associations and the family, over the much more politically restive modern associational forms (Strand 1993). As we shall see, his preference on this issue was a point of contention between the radical nationalists, who saw no value in the past, and their critics.

But by rejecting all of the past, the May 4th activists problematized the concept of the nation; the problem would continue to dog the polemicists of the antireligious campaign as well. In an essay written in 1915, entitled "Patriotism and Self-consciousness" and alluded to above, Chen Duxiu wrote about emotion and knowledge as two opposed forces contending for control over people's minds. Knowledge and reasoning were the basis of true self-consciousness (zijue), whereas emotion led to irrational thinking. Patriotism (aiguozhuyi) was, in Chen's view, associated with irrational emotions and would thus have to be rejected so that a new order founded on self-conscious individuals could be constructed (Chen 1915, 69–70). In this early essay, Chen pursues to its extreme the logic of the break with both history and nation that is implied by total commitment to the doctrine of self-consciousness. Few would accept such an extreme position. Li Dazhao, for instance, refused to separate patriotism from self-consciousness: he took self-consciousness to refer to a process in which purposeful people sought to change the world and thus could bring forth a new China (Meisner 1967, 21–25).[4]

Even when the break with the nation was minimized, the break with history especially dramatized the need to *make* the people as the foundation of the nation. The nation had already emerged in the

4. Levenson has written eloquently about the psychological impossibility of sustaining the break with history. He suggested the ways in which the radicals, and especially the communists, were ultimately able to resolve this crisis by rewriting national history as the history of the "people" rather than of the ruling classes.

name of the people, but the people who mandated the nation would have to be remade to serve as their own sovereign. It was no longer a question of reawakening the nation and the people, but rather, making them from scratch. *Who* would be responsible for making the people? Confronted by the crisis of the Chinese state and drawn to the emergent global revolutionary discourse at the end of the second decade of the twentieth century, the successors of the Chinese literati generated the representation of the "intellectual" at around the same time as they made the image of the "people." Creator and creature became dialectically related, interdependent representations, each of which authorized the other.

I shall be looking specifically at a group of radical nationalist intellectuals in the late 1920s who worked with a well-developed sense of the end of history and the need to remake the people through the antireligious campaign. To be sure, I do not wish to tar the entire May 4th generation by my characterization of this group. Modern intellectuals in China crystallized as a group first around the May 4th movement as the *qiming xuezhe* (literally, scholars of the Enlightenment), the "already-enlightened thinkers" who would liberate the "still-to-be-awakened" populace (Schwarcz 1984, 9). However, Vera Schwarcz writes that the shocks of political life in the mid-1920s taught them to humble themselves and accept a more restricted role as fellow-travelers among the revolutionary masses. They shed their self-image as the pioneer prophets of the Enlightenment and called themselves more simply, *zhishi fenzi*, or knowledgeable elements (1984, 149, 170). Humility and self-searching characterized perhaps a great majority of the intellectuals in this period of both chaotic and systematic bloodshed. Nonetheless, the interdependent representations of intellectual and the people, a legacy of the May 4th movement, continued to weight the intellectuals with an acute sense of responsibility for the people-nation and their awakening into the modern era.

Thus even moderate intellectuals who felt the need to recreate links with history did so within a framework of understanding that to remake the people as the foundation of national sovereignty was the most urgent task of their day. Gu Jiegang represented one such intellectual who sought to reconstruct the historical image both of the intellectual and the people in light of the May 4th denunciation of history. Gu was part of the movement of National Studies of the 1920s, which, as Lawrence Schneider says, allowed one to get away from one part of the past in order to affiliate the present with another (Schneider 1971, 58). Gu sought to find the folk history of the people in the *Book of Odes* (*Shijing*) as the ancient repository of the folk cultural tradition (Schneider 1971, 174). The model of the intellectual seems to be located in Gu's historical studies of anti-authoritarian and protoscientific, if frustrated, characters (Schneider 1971, 86–120). They are in some ways reminiscent of Lu Xun's nonconformist and tragic scholar-hero of the Wei-Jin period.

Gu realized and fused these "historical" aspirations in the folklore movement that he launched in the early 1920s. Schneider reveals that Gu's attitude to the folk was definitely ambivalent. The people represented a creative force, but were in need of education by the intellectual, who was to be the "helper of the growing garden" (1971, 149). On the one hand, Gu was motivated by a spirit of self-sacrifice and strongly opposed the extremist methods of the campaigns against popular religion. On the other, he recorded the customs of the people in order to purge them of the "evil" ones (Schneider 1971, 129, 169). Popular culture, as an alternative to the Confucian tradition, could be the foundation of the nation, but only when mediated through the intelligentsia. Gu succeeded in restoring a history to both intellectuals and the people, but it was a people who would have to be remade to fit the new representation of them.

I am suggesting here that while the intelligentsia as a whole should not be identified with the extremist abuses, nonetheless, even the moderate segments of this class seemingly subscribed to the "end of history" problematic: where those in possession of the Truth of self-consciousness would make the perfect world. This is most evident in the victory of what has come to be called the "debate over scientism." Danny Kwok has documented the ascendancy of scientism among the intelligentsia through various phases beyond the May 4th movement. By the end of the 1920s, not only was the victory of positive scientism over metaphysics and other more cautious versions of empiricism complete in the realm of what may be called "philosophy of life," but the polemic extended to the realm of society and history whose laws of motion were now deemed fully knowable (Kwok 1965, 142–63; Chan 1953, 232).

Such was the power of the new ideology that even conservative Kuomintang thought felt compelled to justify its ideas in terms of their scientificity. Chiang Kai-shek wrote:

> I believe that the book, *Great Learning*, is not only China's orthodox philosophy but also the forebear of scientific thought, undoubtedly the source of Chinese science. If we bind together the *Great Learning* and the *Doctrine of the Mean*, we shall have the most complete text on the har-

mony of philosophy and science and the unity of spirit and matter. Thus I call it the "Scientific Nature of the Great Learning and the Doctrine of the Mean." (Cited in Kwok 1965, 185)

Less well documented and analyzed is the commitment of the twentieth-century state to modernity. Ever since the call for modernizing reform in the early 1900s, but especially since the establishment of the Republic in 1911, the Chinese state has been caught up in a logic of "modernizing legitimation"—where its raison d'etre has increasingly become the fulfillment of modern ideals (Duara 1988a). The nation-state's agenda for remaking popular culture certainly differed from that of the radical intelligentsia in its concern for political stability and resource extraction, among other things. Moreover, its espousal of the rhetoric of emancipation is inextricable from the expansion of its power in society. Thus, the penetration of the nation-state into all aspects of society in the twentieth century (see also Meyer 1980) was justified in the emancipatory language of "the end of history": it is found in the claim that it is a political form radically different from previous states in its ability to represent all of the people and, through the mastery of the true nature of reality, bring everlasting progress. Even the moderate Sun Yat-sen, with his faith in traditional organizations, was infected by this utopianism and revealed a naive faith in the emancipatory power of modern political technology:

Once China has acquired a powerful government, we need not fear, as did the European and American people, that this government will be too strong or out of control. . . . Once the people are fully sovereign, and their methods of controlling government are complete, then there is no need to fear that the government will become too powerful or out of control. Europe and America previously did not dare construct machines of over a hundred thousand horse-power because the construction of these machines was not perfect and the means of controlling them not fine enough, and so they were afraid of their runaway power. But now there has been great progress in the development of machinery, their construction and means of control are so fine that very powerful machines are being built. If we want to build a political machine and desire the development of this machine, we too need to follow this path . . . (Sun Yat-sen 1986, 203–4)

The growth of state power in modern times has involved a twofold process of expansion and penetration and justification of that expansion. The promise of scientific control and material progress has been central to the growth of state power in China. As moderns, we perceive this twofold process through a means-ends gestalt where expansion represents the means and modernity, the ends. But causal relationships are complex in history and, just as effects are also causes, so too ends can become means. In the campaigns against popular religion, intellectuals and state played different roles. Each conducted the campaign for its own version of a new people, but for both, the goals of the movement became caught in the strategies of power which each sought to wield.

THE CAMPAIGNS AGAINST RELIGION

The campaigns which sought to destroy popular religion did not merely seek to secure a representation of the people, but tried to remake real people so they could conform to the representation. It was a forced, violent remaking, the implications of which extended beyond religion. In rural China, religion did not merely refer to a compartmentalized sector of life, as it does to many in our society. Religious ideas, beliefs, practices were intertwined with every aspect of life. Religious associations often provided the ritual and organizational nodes sustaining a network of services and activities, a topic which will be explored more fully in chapters 5 and 7. Its importance in rural life is attested to by the repeated attacks by both state and intelligentsia throughout the twentieth century and by the repeated resistance to these attacks by the "people." Indeed, its resurgence, particularly in recent times in many parts of China, is evidence of the return of the repressed that haunts the representation of the real.

I will examine three phases of this movement: the campaigns beginning with the New Policy Reforms (*xinzheng*) and running through the Republican revolution (1900–1915), the KMT phase, from 1927 until 1930, and a third phase, the present, which I will consider in the conclusion. I will, however, focus on the rhetoric and politics of the second campaign immediately following the establishment of the KMT government in Nanking because the materials on this campaign are the most revealing. The regional locus of the first campaign was the north China plain where the modernizing regime was strongest; that of the second campaign was the lower Yangzi valley and Guangdong province where the Nationalist Party was strongest. In the first phase, the campaigns were led by enthusiastic administrators in cooperation with rural leaders; in the second phase the leadership was principally in the hands of the Nationalist Party activists. In these two campaigns, images of popular gods were desecrated or forcibly removed from rural temples and the temples themselves were refashioned into elementary schools and offices for local governments. The income from the properties of temples and associations now became the revenues of the village government and, ultimately, much of this income found its way to higher levels of the government as the tax burden of the village began to accelerate at a rapid rate (Duara 1988a, 148–52).

The modernization agenda of the Chinese government began with the reforms of the Qing dynasty (1644–1911) in the time span from 1902 to 1908 and continued through the Republican period (1911–1949) and beyond. New schools, new police, new government institutions were the most visible signs of this agenda in rural China. Modernizing reformers in the state and among the elite saw the realm of popular religion and culture as a principal obstacle to the establishment of a "disenchanted" world of reason and plenty. But their campaign to rationalize rural culture was also accompanied by other instrumental motives, which were sometimes acknowledged and sometimes not, but which ultimately came to dominate the campaign.

Since the reforms required financing, new strategies and institutions of revenue extraction quickly became a salient feature of the modernizing program. Modernizing reformers quickly began to see the realm of popular religion also as an important potential source of revenue that could be tapped without much effort. The villages and market towns of China were crowded with many different types of religious associations, voluntary and ascriptive, isolated and extended, that performed a variety of spiritual and secular activities for rural folk. Most of them were also propertied or endowed with other financial resources. These ranged from small religious societies that doubled up as credit societies to large villagewide or marketwide associations with extensive landholdings that financed the maintenance of several temples and the festivities of the temple fair (Gamble 1963).

The first phase is ironically associated with Yuan Shikai, a figure depicted by generations of historians as the reactionary and dictatorial president of the Republic who would be emperor. In fact, Yuan was the most active promoter of modernizing reform—by way of the Japanese model—in late imperial China. Ernest Young, the leading authority on the Yuan presidency, says that, even in his most conservative phase, Yuan "was still part of the modernizing movement that sought to fulfil nationalist aspirations" (Young 1983, 236). An entire generation of students trained in Japan served as his closest advisors and were placed by him in key positions, first in the provincial governments that he headed, and later, in the national administration of the Republic (Thompson 1988, 206–7).

Beginning with his governor-generalship of Zhili and Shandong at the turn of the century, Yuan advocated a series of radical reforms at the local level that established the institutions of local self-government, modern police, and Western-style education (MacKinnon 1980, 136–79). In its zeal to eradicate superstition and establish a modern society, the Yuan administration sought to systematically dismantle the institutional foundations of popular religion. Its success in appropriating temples and temple property in the first phase was not inconsiderable. For instance, in Ding county, Zhili, the number of temples declined by 316, from 432 in 1900 to 116 in 1915 (Li Jinghan 1933, 422–23). This initial success was due largely to co-operation by the rural elite. The local elite saw new avenues of social mobility in the new schools and the formal positions of village government. Education had, of course, always been a route to advancement in imperial China and now it seemed to be more readily accessible to the village elite (Duara 1988a, 156).

The commitment of the Yuan administration to secular and modern goals worked to justify the intrusive agenda that the state launched to acquire local resources. To be sure, the Confucian disdain toward some of the gods of popular culture reinforced the commitment to destroy this realm. However, it is to be noted that where the Confucian worldview spoke of elements of this realm as *xie*, commonly translated as heterodoxy and implying an undesirable but alternative set of beliefs, the pejorative and trivializing neologism *mixin* (superstition), by which the entire realm of popular religion was now characterized, brought with it a much more absolutizing distinction between the scientific and the primitive. While targeting some elements for eradication, the Confucian imperial state had sought to control and order this realm principally by trying to appropriate the symbolism of the great gods—by superscribing their meanings—in the popular tradition (Duara 1988b). In other words, it had utilized the very framework of religious symbolic expression to communicate and negotiate with rural society. The new administration sought to destroy the very institutional underpinnings of this framework.

But if the reformers were the zealots for a modern awakening, they were also the agents of a total reorganization of the power structure of rural society. Monks and priests who had depended on religious properties were cut off from their sources of livelihood; local religious societies that fulfilled social as much as spiritual needs were dispossessed and replaced by government offices that seemed mainly interested in extracting revenues and uncovering unregistered property. The new schools that were set up were of little use to ordinary villagers who could not afford to spare their children for such luxuries; they were attended principally by the children of the elite. And finally, in the process of eradicating superstition in the village the state had developed direct access to the collective property and resources of the village that it had never had before (Duara 1988a, 148–57).

This conspicuous displacement of power in the village did not go unresisted. Consider the example of Ding county, a model county in north China. Here in Zhaicheng village, the Mi family had launched a vigorous reform program and by the first decade of the twentieth century had established schools, self-defense, hygiene, and welfare institutions. The village had also had an exuberant religious associational life with such associations as the Drama Association and the Lantern Festival Association owning as much property as 120 *mou* of land. The leading reformer, Mi Digang, and his associates, who lacked enough resources for their modernizing efforts, argued that the resources of all of the religious associations were being unproductively employed and in 1905, the village government, which they controlled, appropriated the lands owned by these associations. This action provoked a violent protest and Zhaicheng villagers were joined by other villages in the area. There followed a protracted legal suit which was apparently longer than any other known in the area and ended by exhausting all parties. The result of the lawsuit was not known, but the protest subsided over the years (*Zhaicheng cunzhi* 1925, 45; supplement 18–19).

The experience in Zhaicheng village was not uncommon in the villages of north China, although the protest was not often so longdrawn (Duara 1988a, 151–52). While resistance within the village was often suppressed, it could and did reorganize at a transvillage level. Supravillage religious societies in the countryside, such as the White Lotus, the Red Spears, and the Big and Small Sword Societies in the lower Yangzi valley, were too extensive and militant for local organizations to dispossess and control. They represented the one part of popular religion that escaped both the symbolic and institutional controls of the modern state (Duara 1988a, 156). Their delegitimation would have to be conducted at a discursive level, at a level beyond debate.

In the second phase, the campaign was spearheaded by the left wing of the Nationalist Party, which during the 1920s saw itself as the inheritor of the iconoclastic May 4th movement. In his study of the Nationalist response to the May 4th movement, Lu Fangshang reveals how most of the important Nationalist leaders were fundamentally antireligious. Although Sun Yat-sen was himself a Christian, as Dai Jitao and other KMT leaders pointed out, Sun was committed to keeping religion outside of politics and maintaining the separation of church and state (Lu Fangshang 1989, 337–39). Most political leaders besides Sun, such as Li Shizeng, Wang Jingwei, Zou Lu, and Cai Yuanpei, were more active in extending their support to the burgeoning antireligious movement developing among the youth both within and outside of the party during the 1920s (Lu Fangshang 1989, 336–45; Yamamoto and Yamamoto 1953, 134, 138, 142). The party actively backed the anti-Christian movement—which tellingly combined the end of history syndrome with an intense nationalism—and it continued this support for the broader antireligious movement conducted by the Anti-Religious Federation and the Great Federation of Non-Religionists (Zhang 1927, 187–207).

In 1928 and 1929, the party organization launched a vigorous "antireligion" and "antisuperstition" (most radical nationalists refused to distinguish between the two) drive in Guangdong and the lower Yangzi provinces of Jiangsu, Zhejiang, and Anhui. State control over the revenues from religious properties was an important issue, as it had been in the earlier campaign, but the advent of party politics and the politics of mass mobilization had made the situation considerably more complex. After 1927, the left wing of the Nationalist Party, which had been active in mass mobilization for the Nationalist victory at the local level, was beginning to lose control to groups and organizations that were personally loyal to Chiang Kai-shek. For instance, the Fourth Plenum of the Second National Party Congress in January 1928 drastically reduced the importance of mass movements in the party's political program, and the relevant departments in the party's headquarters were abolished (Yamada 1979, 234–35; Wang K'e-wen 1986–87, 10–17). Among other things, this meant that the higher levels of the party and local administration had started to seize the initiative away from the local party in local affairs. The non-Communist left KMT now began to fight a desperate rearguard battle to re-establish its control over political power in the party and in local affairs that lasted until 1930 (Yamada 1979, 264–83). The antisuperstition campaign launched during these years, while representing the modernizing ideals of the radical KMT, thus also became inextricably involved with these political issues of the day.

Harking to the founding ideals of the Nationalist Party, Sun Yat-sen's Three People's Principles, the radical nationalists declared that in the period of political tutelage, the masses had to be shown the path to rational progress. Religious authority was an obstacle to the development of a progressive society based on the Three People's Principles (Zeng Jue 1930a, 118; 1930b, 120). These nationalists of the left wing of the KMT viewed their project of "disenchanting" the people of China within an evolutionist paradigm in which religion and superstition were obstacles to progress. The reformist weekly in Guangdong, *Fengsu Gaige* (*Reform of Customs*), ran many articles on the theme of combatting religion and superstition during 1929 and 1930. In an essay entitled "Discussion of the Religious Problem in the Trend of Human Evolution," Huang Shaodan revealed two streams within human evolution: the evolution from darkness and ignorance to enlightenment in the life of consciousness and the evolution from external control to autonomy (*zizhi*) in the organization of the means of competitive survival. Together they furnished the rationale for both the modern and the sovereign nation. Religion was a vestige from the ignorance of the stone ages which could not be permitted to exist because it impeded progress (Huang Shaodan 1930, 85–86). Within this evolutionary paradigm, the break with history was secured through the establishment of a distinct modern era redolent of the end of history syndrome. The writer Zeng Jue (Already Awakened) deemed the allegedly coherent and discrete nature of the modern era as the most important justification for the destruction of religion. Just as the monarchy was unsuited to the present age, so too was religion unnecessary in an age in which science had proved the nonexistence of God (Zeng Jue 1930b, 120–21).

The persistent critic of the campaign in Guangdong, Fang Cao, seeking to counter these charges, appealed to none other than the father of the nation, Sun Yat-sen. Sun, he said, had great faith in traditional organizations (*guyou tuanti*) such as the family and religion, and he regarded religion as one of the few important elements able to hold together a nation (Fang Cao 1930a, 158). Had Sun not suggested that it was religion that had permitted Jews, Arabs, and Indians to remain a nation despite the dissolution of a territory and state? Fang's implication that the radicals were insufficiently patriotic touched a raw nerve. A flurry of essays responding to Fang appeared, led by Zeng himself. Zeng continued to read Sun's writings from the same axiomatic principle that the modern era was a coherent totality that could not tolerate what did not belong in it. Had Sun not written that human society evolved through four stages in which religious authority was characteristic only of the second; was religion therefore not anachronistic in the present? Zeng claimed that the spirit of Sun's ideas of a new society mandated that all of the vestiges of the earlier eras which stood in the way of the establishment of the ideal society of the Three People's Principles would have to be eradicated. Contrary to the view that Sun favored traditional organizational forms in the building of the nation, Zeng asserted that it was the modern associational form of professional groups that was critical to the nation; Sun had referred to the older forms only as past sources of cohesion which must be discarded or eliminated in the present era (Zeng Jue 1930b, 120–21).

Nothing deserved to be eliminated more than religion, since it was a relic of an era of 200,000 years ago. After religion was destroyed, the nation could then display its artifacts and artistic products—which it would not permit foreigners to buy—in museums in the way that one does with products of a bygone era and in the way that, with the future attainment of The Great Unity (*Datong*), individual languages will only be the objects of antiquarian researches (Zeng Jue 1930a, 116–19). The past for the radical nationalist is then simply subsumed into the present, which is eternal and without a real history, since, as Ricoeur says of Hegel's History, it simply dissolves rather than resolves the problem of the relationship of the historical past to the present (1988, 3: 202). In this, as in many ideas today, we can recognize "the unacknowledged doublets of some Hegelian ghost, beginning with the concepts of the spirit of a nation, of a culture, of an age" (1988, 3: 204).

The intellectual foundations of the evolutionism of the radical nationalists had begun to change subtly, but significantly, from the social Darwinism of the pre-May 4th era. Certain social Darwinist presuppositions now appear interreferenced with Marxist conceptions. Marxism in its particular manifestation as anti-imperialism was beginning to dislodge social Darwinism as the most significant discourse of Chinese intellectuals in the 1920s. Yet the expression "dislodge" is perhaps only partially correct, because while it may have dislodged the ethics of social Darwinism, it reproduced the evolutionism and valorized what had been an ambiguous progressivism of the former within its own context. James Pusey, in his monumental study of social Darwinism in China, suggests that Marxism was enabled in China by the prior acceptance of social Darwinism (1983, 445–56). If Darwin had proved the truth of biological evolution, Marx had proved the truth of human evolution. But Marx was still more; he was seen as a "Super-Darwinist," one who had proved that "revolution was evolution's way for man" (Pusey 1983, 445). Marxism was, like the notion of "culture" (see chapter 7), able to operate certain transformations on social Darwinism which would give it a redemptive quality. The laws of the jungle could be mastered to redeem humanity.

If we can find within Marxism the effects of social Darwinism as a trace, the discourse of the radical nationalists was more hybrid—combining the different assumptions of both Marxism and social Darwinism and also ideas of *Datong*, or the Great Unity, as the telos of evolution. Huang Shaodan's essay had spoken of two streams of evolution: of consciousness and of the organization for competitive survival (*shengcun jingzheng*). Religion was not only a vestige of an earlier form of consciousness, but in the sphere of the organization for survival, religion impeded the development of a self-reliant attitude among the people. Thus far we are mostly in familiar social Darwinian territory. When accounting for the specific role of religion, however, the rhetoric takes on a Marxist tone: religion is an instrument of the despotic ruling classes (*tongzhi jieji*). Even after splits had taken place in orthodox religion (the reference here is unclear) and one wing of it had parted company with monarchical power (presumably popular Buddhism and Daoism), these heterodoxies continued to keep the masses enslaved to the passive and ignorant mentality of orthodox religion (Huang Shaodan 1930, 90).

But the transformation of the evolutionist discourse actually made it more difficult for the radical nationalists to sustain an argument for nationalism. Chen Duxiu had revealed the fate of the nation in the ultimate logic of History, and Fang Cao's criticisms revealed the vulnerability of their position. Whereas Chinese social Darwinism had successfully secured the nation as the most important entity in the competition for survival, the decline in its appeal after the May 4th movement meant that it would play a minor role in legitimating the nation. It is possible that both the Marxist emphasis on groups in the struggles of History as well as the telos of collectivist *Datong* helped the radicals to focus their attention on the nation, but it is also true that as universalist doctrines, both were highly ambivalent toward the nation and could only justify it as an intermediate stage to true liberation.

The radical nationalists confronted the classic aporia: how could they posit the existence of a cohesive nation—the nation in time—when the narrative of History they espoused necessitated not only a break with the past but also its dissolution in utopian models? The radical nationalists reveal two strategies for recovering the nation and the people without recourse to history. The first was to endow the break with the past itself with such affective force that it acquired a generative power capable of legitimating new representations. All revolutions have this generative power; it is usually secured by linking narratives or testimonies of the event—the moment of rupture— from within, usually by participants, with later or wider narratives that refer back to this founding event. Thus, Huang Shaodan writes that it was only in the modern era, after a number of revolutions had taken place and the idea of popular sovereignty had emerged, that the people could *fanshen* or turn over their old selves and become self-governing (Huang Shaodan 1930, 90). Here the moment of rupture, which is at the same time the moment of rebirth, is captured through the rites of revolutionary passage of *fanshen*. *Fanshen* is a signifier whose genealogy is yet to be undertaken. In William Hinton's classic documentary of the Chinese communist revolution with that title, readers are alerted to the central role of *fanshen* in the personal testimonies of the revolution. At least during certain stages of the revolution, this passionate ritual of rebirth, dramatized in speak bitterness sessions, appeared to generate powerful emotions which the Communist Party sought to manage and incorporate into its narrative of the revolution. To be sure, Huang's reference does not yet reflect the immense power of this idea of the rebirth of the people, but he appears to prefigure the role of *fanshen* in his own effort to invest the break with the past with a charismatic power that will authorize the remaking of the people and the nation.

A second strategy to secure the national community without historical ties involved sharpening the sense of its distinctiveness from the Other. Most important in this respect is the anti-Christian movement which preceded the antisuperstition campaign of the late 1920s by about ten years. In the summer and spring of 1922, a movement among students directed against Christianity in particular, and religion in general, and which seems to have been an extension of the May 4th movement, burst out briefly in the major cities. But two years later, from 1924 to 1928, a more highly structured movement among students and other urban groups was organized by the two major parties, the KMT and the CCP. The anti-Christian focus quickly became part of the nationalist struggle against the twin enemies of imperialism and militarism. The movement specifically targeted the loss of sovereignty in the realm of education, and it raised the demand of canceling the missionary privilege of establishing educational institutions (Lutz 1988, 94–98). The centers of the second phase of the movement were the cities of the central and lower Yangzi valleys and Canton. Guangdong University, later to become National

Zhongshan University (Sun Yat-sen University) in Canton, became a major center of activities for both the anti-Christian movement as well as the later campaign against superstition or popular religion (Lutz 1988, 136–39). Let us look more closely at a letter written by "the workers of the Committee to Reform Customs." The letter warns against the dangers of Christianity and appeared in the journal *Fengsu Gaige* in 1929, toward the end of the specifically anti-Christian movement and during the height of the campaign against popular religion.

The letter exhorts "our brothers" to oppose Christianity not only because it represents a bygone relic that is an obstacle to science and progress, but especially because it promotes the advancement of imperialism. However, the letter does not regard the two factors as separate, but succeeds in closely linking the imperialist dimension of Christianity with the debilitating and stupefying effects of religion in general. According to it, the Christian church spearheaded the efforts to weaken the people so that Western imperialism could advance in China. By setting up churches and their educational institutions, not only did China lose her educational sovereignty, but these institutions nourished a passive and obedient youth who lost their spirit of patriotism. The letter occasionally takes on a virulent tone reminiscent of the Boxer movement. In denouncing the fake charities with which the Church fooled the people, it referred to an alleged event in Fujian in 1927, in which the Christian church, under the pretense of raising orphans, cruelly killed hundreds of infants in order to use their organs for medical purposes (*Gongren* 1930, 155–56). Other accusations included the charge that missionaries spied for their countries and reported regularly to them about China's interior resources. On the whole, however, the letter did not lose sight of the main point that Christianity, both as a religion and as an agent of imperialism, kept the Chinese nation backward and ignorant.

In the part of the campaign which did not directly attack Christianity, but popular religion, Buddhism took the brunt of the attack. Here too one can detect a shadow argument that religion, especially a foreign religion, weakened the nation's ability to withstand imperialism. Certainly, a figure no less than Hu Shi had repeatedly made the point that the "Indianization of China" had produced a dark, medieval period through the spread of the defeatist religion of Buddhism (Hu Shi 1963, 84–88).[5] When the critic Fang Cao pointed out that

5. For Hu Shi, it was the foreign religion of Buddhism which constituted the dark middle period and prevented the progress of national History. The modern nation would have to break with its immediate past, dominated by Buddhism, and rejoin the primordial nation. He wrote, "[But] the native rationalistic mentality of the Chinese

Buddhism did not necessarily entail passivity, since the Mongols and the Japanese—two of China's historical aggressors—had espoused Buddhism (Fang Cao 1930b, 162), Zeng Jue replied that the real factor behind the strength of the Mongols was nomadism and that behind the Japanese was Western science. The true example of the passivity produced by Buddhism and religion was the case of India, which had remained a powerless colony (Zeng Jue 1930b, 122). Thus, we sense an effort by the radical nationalists to create a heightened awareness of the contemporary national self versus the Other. The loss of the historical foundations of the national self was compensated for by associating religion itself with imperialism, thereby heightening the rhetoric of anti-imperialism.

In 1927 and 1928, local party members in several Jiangsu counties arrested temple priests and appropriated thousands of *mu* of land (Mitani 1978, 9). In Canton, several thousand members of the "uproot superstition movement" of Guangdong province met in the great hall of the Party on September 1929 and petitioned the government "to execute a court order to place the evil shrines, temples and monasteries under legal custody and confiscate their properties. Moreover, they also raised the cry to bring down religion" (*Fenggai* 1930, 152). However, this time around the modernizers had to contend with more complex forms of resistance. Reflecting the rapidly changing political culture of the time, associational politics had become well-established and organized Buddhism had emerged in the 1920s as a political player able to intervene at the provincial and national levels (NZNJ 1936, F-134; Yang 1967, 359; Chan 1953, 56–57). The National Buddhist Association lobbied both the Jiangsu and Guangdong provincial governments. Unable to resist this pressure, the provincial administration sought to put a brake on the movement by sending down cautionary directives to local party units. However, it stopped short of reversing the party leadership's much touted program of cultural reform (*Fenggai* 1930, 116; Mitani 1978, 9).

Local party groups ignored these directives and pushed on with the campaign. The highly vocal Zeng Jue responded promptly to the efforts of the Buddhist association to preserve and restore temples and monasteries and their properties. He scoffed at the arguments of "the monks and nuns" whom he regarded, with the fewest exceptions, as criminals and morally debased. He found preposterous their

---

intelligentsia gradually reasserted itself and revolted against this humiliating domination of the whole nation by a foreign religion which was opposed to all the best traditions of the native civilization" (Hu Shi 1963, 85).

claim that KMT regulations protected their right to follow their religion. Every right had its limits, he argued, and rights could only be permitted to those who did not violate the construction of a new society built upon the Three People's Principles. This was, after all, why the Chinese Communist Party and bandits that ravaged the countryside were deprived of their rights. Since the Buddhists harmed the customs of the people, they could scarcely be permitted any rights either. The party was fully justified in depriving them of their means of livelihood (Zeng Jue 1930a, 117–18). Fang Cao noted, perhaps with some foreboding, that if the Buddhists could be deprived of their rights because they were the source of harmful customs, then, indeed, the majority of the Chinese people could be denied all rights on that count. This kind of logic amounted to increasing the suffering of the majority for the "rights" of a tiny minority (Fang Cao 1930a, 157–58).

But by late 1928 and 1929, the campaign began to encounter organized resistance led not only by Buddhist monks, but popular uprisings led by sectarians and secret societies. In particular, the radical nationalists faced a series of uprisings led by the Small Sword Society in the impoverished, hard-to-govern border regions of Northern Jiangsu (Jiangbei), Henan, Anhui, and Shandong. In a finely crafted account of the Small Sword Uprising of 1929, Mitani Takashi traces the growth of an uprising which emerged as a reaction to the campaign against popular religion but grew into a military uprising that briefly even dreamed of taking over the government in Nanking. On 3 February 1929, around the time of the old lunar New Year, the most important festival for most Chinese, thousands of armed followers of the Small Sword Society, shouting slogans such as "Down with the Three People's Principles," "Down with the Hall for Western Studies," "Support Imperialism," and "The Japanese are our Brothers," stormed the town of Suqian in Jiangbei and destroyed the Public Lecture Hall which had been erected upon the remains of the recently destroyed Eastern Peaks Temple. They also attacked the KMT party building, the telegraph office, and modern schools, including the girls' school (Mitani 1979, 141). On the 15th of February, the attack on these institutions was repeated, and this time they were joined by 50 to 60 thousand people from the rural areas around the Grand Canal. By late March, the Small Swords joined forces with the Red Spears from twenty-four counties, recruited demobilized soldiers from warlord armies, formed the Army of Great Unity (*Datong jun*), and declared the First Year of the Era of Great Unity (*Datong yuannian*). They were able to attack and seize several cities before they were defeated by the KMT forces on 11 April 1929.

Local newspaper accounts of the incident blamed the leaders of the campaign who had attacked temples, taken over their property, jailed their priests and monks and, perhaps, most of all, prohibited the festivities and ceremonials which took place during the lunar New Year celebrations, including gambling, gathering around the graves, and performing sacrifices to the ancestors and gods. They also blamed the high tax surcharges of the government. Mitani discerns two levels of the movement based on his analysis of the social landscape. One level reflected the interests of the landholding, tax-paying, antigovernment establishment in the villages, which included landholders, priests, local bullies, and the village militia. The other level reflected the lower classes of marginal peasants, vagrants, refugees, itinerant and semi-itinerant workers who were followers of the Small Sword secret society. The marginal peasants, he argues, were linked to this organization by their contacts with traveling sorcerers, fortune-tellers, medical masters, masters of secret arts, and others who possessed charismatic power. Thus secret societies led a parallel, if shadowy, existence with the village authority structure and, during chaotic periods of the Republic, joined hands with this structure to block the penetration of the new, centralizing power of the KMT regime. In 1928, this penetration came in the shape of heavy taxes, of course, but also as the campaign against superstition (Mitani 1979, 139, 143).

This line of analysis allows us to see how the reaction to the campaign embedded both the interests of specific groups like monks and rural power-holders, as well as an effort, led by secret societies and sectarians, to protect popular culture. This culture might be regarded as paternalistic and superstitious, but it comprised a world of ideas and practices concerning locality, community, family, time, work, and leisure which the party had sought to root out by attacking the calendar, festivals, and other related activities. Indeed, such was the intensity of the reaction, that we are able to identify in the movement an outline of a counternarrative in which the Army of Great Unity affiliated itself with the utopia of Great Unity, a universe which returned to the age of the sages, and which it opposed to the modern utopia (ironically also of the Great Unity) championed by the party. In the process, the party and its ideals became invested with such negative force that the Three People's Principles were denounced and the Japanese imperialism acquired a positive value (Mitani 1979, 144, 156).

The reader will appreciate the significance for a bifurcated history of two groups opposed in political discourse fighting under the singular sign of the Great Unity. It clarifies a moment in bifurcation when a new meaning has not yet succeeded in appropriating older and other dispersed meanings. The latter raise their heads at inopportune moments, whether or not self-consciously, to mock and threaten the "seamless" appropriation of the sign by the former. Thus, we should seek to develop an understanding of these oppositional narratives not only in their own utopian terms—through which we may enter the alternative worlds to which they are tied—but also in the context in which they represent a subversion of a totalizing force.

As for the radical nationalists, faced by what many of them felt to be an inexplicable hostility from the people whom they had sought to remake, they backed off, and bit by bit, the administration at the county and provincial levels were able to reassert their authority over local affairs. By 1930, the left wing of the party had been either destroyed or discredited (Wang K'e-wen 1986–87, 32). In any case, the meaning of their struggle under the lofty banner of "Down with feudalism and superstition" had changed to refer, not principally to a shining new age, but a power struggle with an encroaching state. Through none of these changes had the radicals stopped to think of how popular religion may have been meaningful in the lives of the people. Pushing the campaign forward, regardless of the popular response, had come to be of paramount importance because the anti-superstition movement had become the vehicle through which the enthusiasts could try to continue to assert local control in the face of the bureaucratization of power. In this way, the model of the free, self-conscious modern concealed a number of dispersions: once a model the radical nationalists sought to exemplify and realize, it now became a slogan under which they conducted a power struggle. Later it came to conceal a new set of reifications governed by the imperatives of the modern nation-state.

The imperatives faced by the Nationalist state at the provincial and national level were quite different from those of the party radicals. Most certainly it did not abandon its commitment to modernity. The all-important official "Standards for Preserving and Abandoning Gods and Shrines" of November 1928 spoke of religious authority as being obsolete in the age of popular sovereignty, of "superstition as an obstacle to progress," and of the superstitious nation becoming "the laughing stock of the scientific world" (ZMFH 1933, 807). But the Nationalist state was also forced to develop a strategy to reconcile its modernist ideals with the various pressures it faced from a restive populace, an organized clergy, and an assertive local party that was carrying on a runaway campaign. In other words, it had not only to politically manage the unwieldiness of the real nation, but to create a set of categories that would naturalize and normativize its conception of who and what was to belong to the sovereign people. As the state, it was able to devise systems of classification that defined and bound the arena of legitimate contestation. The Nationalist state distinguished the objects of true religious worship from superstition, thereby extending rights to Buddhists and other groups it could control.

The "Standards" sought to condemn superstition while preserving religious freedom. Accordingly, it sought to distinguish the practices, institutions, and objects of superstition that were to be abolished from the more properly religious items which were to be preserved. The "Standards" declared that historical figures who had become apotheosized but could be seen as beneficial to the community, such as Confucius and Guandi, were to be revered. Moreover, those who inspired belief with "pure faith," such as the Buddha and Laozi, were also to be respected. The worship of certain nature gods, the Daoist line of gods who encouraged the use of charms and magical texts, as well as the practices of popular religion were prohibited (ZMFH 1933, 810–14).

The radical nationalists had, of course, refused to accept this distinction between religion and superstition. For instance, Wo Fang writing in their journal, *Fengsu Gaige*, could not agree with an essay which had argued that in evolutionary terms, religion could be seen to play a motivating and leadership role, while superstitions should be seen as obstacles to progress. Indeed, the more Wo analyzed religion, the more he realized that each of its "cells" was none other than a superstition. But from the different perspective of the village, the "Standards" did not consider the argument that one person's superstition may be another's religion. Sakai Tadao, who believed that few modernizers in China were able to recognize and mobilize the anti-elite potential within popular culture, observed that the "Standards" were notably inconsistent in permitting the preservation of the worship of certain nature gods, the earth god, and the stove god while banning the worship of the city god, the dragon or rain god, and the god of wealth among others (Sakai 1951, 324; ZMFH 1933, 813). The classificatory strategy that demarcated religion from superstition revealed the play of political considerations in its effort to disenchant the world and give it to us as it is. The strategy had the ultimate effect of protecting organized religions with authoritative texts, especially organized Buddhism (NZNJ 1936, F-134). Both organizationally and doctrinally, these religions had the virtue of being historically susceptible to state control.

The KMT regime not only redefined the category of the modern, it also produced a new representation of tradition. The regime continued to consolidate its power over temple property, the rights of monks, and the religious establishment (Sakai 1951, 327). By the time of the New Life movement of the mid-1930s, it succeeded in producing an elitist "tradition" that incorporated Confucianism, organized religions and, perhaps, even the ideals of the campaign against superstition. This was the legitimate tradition that was set against the world of superstition and popular religion. It was none other than the realm of popular religion and its authority structures that came under the general ban of the "Standards" and a host of other laws, such as the "Procedure for the Abolition of Occupations of Divination, Astrology, Physiognomy and Palmistry, Sorcery and Geomancy" (1928), "Procedures for Banning and Managing Superstitious Objects and Professions" (1930), and "Prohibition of Divinatory Medicines" (1929) (ZMFH 1933, 794–96; NZNJ 1936, F-110–12). Sectarians, shamans, sorcerers, geomancers, physiognomists, and traditional healers all fell under the scope of this ban. Secret and sectarian societies—such as the Small Swords, the Boxers, the White Lotus, the Red Spears—were either historically or potentially antiestablishment or anti-state and authority within them was founded on the command of magical rituals and charms. Sorcerers, ritual specialists, and especially healers were often the leaders of these societies. By means of these laws, the nationalist state was able to proclaim its modern ideals, which included the freedom of religion, and simultaneously consolidate its political power in local society by defining legitimate believers in such a way as to exclude those whom it found difficult to bring under its political control.

CONCLUSION

I have examined the end of history syndrome in modern China in which self-consciousness and the complete break with the past signifies control over contingency and the death of self-deception. While the narrative of History had secured the role of the nation as the subject of History (see chapter 1), as a radical variant of History, the end of history discourse necessarily encountered the problem of the nation. It was extremely difficult for the radical nationalists of the 1920s to claim a cohesive national subject while denying the nation's historical past and, ultimately, its future in timeless utopias. They devised two ways to continue to claim a nationalism: First, they endowed the moment of rupture and rebirth into a new age with such charismatic power that the energies of the people reborn (read remade) could be mobilized for the new nation. Second, by associating religion and the unwanted past with imperialism, the radicals were able to heighten the contradiction between the national community and its foreign aggressors. Indeed, anti-imperialism has been the dominant form of nationalism among all nationalists who have emphasized the break with the past, especially the Chinese communists.

The effort to make the "people" in the image of the new world and the nation had extremely destructive implications for the rural community, especially when the campaign was relatively successful, as during the state-led campaigns in northern China in the early years of the twentieth century (see chapter 5) and again in the 1950s when the elimination of both temples and markets grievously eroded rural communal life (see Friedman et al. 1991). The campaign of the late 1920s is important less because it was successful than because it offers rich materials for a bifurcated history: the militant opposition generated by the campaign exposed a world of dispersed meanings that the discourse of modernity sought to erase by condemning it as feudal superstition. Launched around the lunar New Year, the Jiangbei uprising gives us a glimpse of the many communal activities and interests—from gambling to ancestral souls—affected by the destructiveness and proscriptions of the campaign. Instead of the more familiar task of having to dis-cover the dispersed meaning appropriated by a signifier, bifurcation is usefully clarified by the separate uses of *Datong* utopianism: while the nationalists appropriated this Confucian ideal to assimilate it as the telos of progressive History, the popular resistance seemed to mock the appropriation as it continued to use it to symbolize an older vision of an ideal community.

Moreover, the representation of modernity itself disguised a power struggle where the state and radical nationalists each sought to expand their power; every episode of intervention in the name of modernity often ended with a significant expansion in the power of the state. At the end of our story, a new set of reifications distinguishing religion from superstition proposed to give us the world again as pure transparency. To the extent that we ourselves assume a division between traditional and modern eras founded on a self-conscious, modern subjectivity in our historical narratives, we share a common ground with the end of history discourse (though not necessarily with its extreme views). The genealogy of "modernity" and "tradition" in the brief history of the campaigns discloses a trail of buried meanings that should alert us against accepting them as transparent categories of analysis and encourage us to locate them also as dispersed meanings in a wider historical context.

The Enlightenment narrative of the passage to modernity has repeatedly crashed against the reef of popular religion in China. The heterogenous and heterodox elements of popular culture the campaigns sought to transform into the homogenized and docile people of the nation have repeatedly resisted the incursions into their material and cultural life—sometimes with unexpected ferocity, as in the Jiangbei uprising. Nothing has been quite as unexpected as the latest return, the resurgence of organized and popular religion in post-Mao China, which is evident especially in the wealthy, southeast coastal regions and in the minority areas. How can we understand this phenomenon? I would argue that we should certainly not think of this as the persistence of some unchanging tradition, nor should we see it as the resistance of a primordial subaltern consciousness, the mirror opposite of the modern subject.

According to Ann Anagnost, the recent opening of markets has led to the reappearance of various older cultural practices which the state condemns as feudal superstition (*fengjian mixin*). One of the most important of these is the emergence or revival of local temple cults which often try to reappropriate the temples and ritual spaces that had been appropriated and marked over by the communist state as, say, "Red Flag Community Center" and the like. She gives us the examples of older women burning incense and worshipping in the midst of classroom activities in order to reappropriate the school, or the face-to-face confrontation between local party officials and a possessed spirit medium who demands the return of a temple building (Anagnost 1994, 245). Anagnost depicts this process as a contest over symbolic space that is never won or lost but continues as the recurring site of a longstanding struggle between differing symbolic orders of state and local communities (1994, 223). She insists, however, that these local traditions are retrievable in a way that *re-invents* them in the context of contemporary concerns.

Indeed, we can see how the meanings of the encounters between popular religion and the party-state are dispersed in different contexts: we can trace this dispersal back to the differences in the meanings of temple appropriation for monks and priests, itinerants and marginal peasants in the late 1920s under the banner of the Army of Great Unity. More recently, the revival of religion may reflect the restoration of family and lineages which try to step into a local power vacuum caused by the weakening of the party (Perry 1985). The proliferation of ritual display can also be seen in another context as a utilitarian and individualistic strategy of the new generation to cope with the burgeoning market economy (Siu 1989). Popular religion does not reflect an "eternal" China, but insofar as it reflects practices and beliefs that are at variance with the univocal order of History and the state, the meanings that it transmits over time and space could well come to coalesce into a rhetoric of popular dissent in modern China.

4

SECRET BROTHERHOOD AND REVOLUTIONARY
DISCOURSE IN CHINA'S REPUBLICAN REVOLUTION

IN FEBRUARY 1912, one day after he had relinquished the Provisional Presidency of the new Republic, Sun Yat-sen faced the tomb of the founder of the Ming dynasty (1368–1644) and addressed this ancestral spirit of the Han race. His address expressed a profound sense of fulfillment of a promise to avenge the Manchu (1644–1911) conquest of the holy land. "From a bad eminence of glory basely won, they (the Manchus) lorded it over this most holy soil, and our beloved China's rivers and hills were defiled by their corrupting touch, while the people fell victims to the headsman's axe or the avenging sword" (quoted in Sharman 1968, 141). After lamenting the failure of various patriotic insurrections against the Manchus, he dwelt on the present:

> Although these worthy causes were destined to ultimate defeat, the gradual trend of the national will became manifest. At last our own era dawned, the sun of freedom had risen, and a sense of the *rights* of the race animated men's minds. . . . Today it has at last restored the Government to the Chinese people, and the five races of China may dwell together in China in peace and mutual trust . . . How could we have attained this measure of victory had not your Majesty's soul in heaven bestowed upon us your protecting influence. (Sharman 1968, 142, emphasis mine)

A close reading of these passages from Sun would show that they condense several of my themes, but for the moment, let me simply note the joining of two motifs: the avenging of the ancestral spirit and the establishment of a modern republic of rights and popular sovereignty. Historiography of the nationalist revolution in China and the West (and to a lesser extent in Japan) has had difficulty

appreciating this nexus, which appears somewhat curious, if not em-
barrassing, to academia in the late twentieth century. Thus, this
historiography has tended to argue that the visceral, racist anti-
Manchuism of the Republican revolutionaries, evidenced especially
from about 1900 to 1911, represented simply a politically expedient
move to rally the popular masses and particularly the secret societies,
whom Sun and other revolutionaries sought to organize in ten uprisings between 1895 and 1907, by appealing to their (often implied)
racist hatred toward the Manchu rulers. This chapter argues that not
only was the racism of the secret societies very different from the
social Darwinian racist discourse of the revolutionaries, but that, in
some ways, a racism was imposed upon, or imputed to, these societies. This imputing was itself part of a larger narrative of a modern
nationalist romance in which the secret brotherhoods became the
silent site for resolving critical ideological problems. My task is to
reveal the appropriation of two dispersions: how the different meanings of the secret societies were appropriated by the Republican revolutionaries and, second, how the significance of social Darwinism for
the intelligentsia in its time has itself been rewritten through later
discourses, including those of contemporary academia.

SECRET SOCIETIES IN LATE NINETEENTH-CENTURY CHINA

The social history of the secret societies has been documented exten-
sively in Chinese, Japanese, and English, and I will provide only a
brief outline of it. Secret societies is the English term given to the
historical Chinese category *huitang* (associations and lodges) and was
distinguished in the literature of the imperial state from other potentially anti-state groups such as the *jiaomen* (religious sects) and *fei*
(bandits), though exactly how rigorously and with what further speci-
fication of their character, lies, as we will see, at the heart of the
matter. They are generally thought of as occupying the region of
the Yangzi River and the southern provinces, particularly those of
Guangdong and Guangxi. Different writers trace the history of these
groups back to the late Ming in the sixteenth and seventeenth centuries, while those who do not discriminate too sharply between the
sects and societies trace them back to the Mongol period in the thirteenth century and still earlier to the third century at the end of the
Han (Chesneaux 1972, 2). During the great mid-nineteenth-century
rebellions of the Taipings and others, the secret societies flourished
and established local control in various areas of south and central
China (Yokoyama 1986, 168). Although the period between these

rebellions and 1900 was one of relative quiescence, the midcentury point may still be used as the historical baseline for our discussion of the social and ideological character of secret societies until the 1911 revolution.

The names and relationships between the different secret societies are a murky area, in part because of their loose affiliations and their secretive and scattered nature. Indeed, the silences afforded by the secrecy of these groups made it especially possible for nationalists and others to interpret the societies within their own narratives, which, in turn, makes it that much harder to clarify the organizational and ideological links of these groups to each other. Broadly speaking, the umbrella name Hongmen or Triads included the Tiandihui (Heaven and Earth Society), the Sanhehui (Three Harmonies Society), the Sandianhui (Three Dots Society), the Qing Bang (Green Gang), the Hong Bang (Red Gang), and the Gelaohui (Elder Brothers Society). These groups were forced into hiding and secrecy by the Qing (Manchu) dynasty's ban on them. But only some of these groups, such as the first three named above, who operated mainly in the southern provinces, were politically anti-Manchu. The others were hunted by the state less for political activities than for engaging in criminal activities like salt smuggling (Lewis 1972, 105–6).

Common to all of these groups was a tradition not only of political secrecy, but of secret rituals. While there was perhaps not much uniformity among the rituals performed by the different groups, the life of the group was suffused with ceremonials (Lewis 1972, 103). Most elaborate were, of course, the rites of initiation, which often involved oath-taking and a blood sacrifice (of an animal), but there were also rites for opening a new lodge or branch and for conducting business. An elaborate ritual code of body signs enabled secret communication and reinforced the powerful sense of a distinct, fraternal community that the societies sought to create. This sense of fraternity was sustained by the lore of sworn brotherhood from the vernacular novels, *The Water Margin (Shuihuzhuan)*, *The Romance of the Three Kingdoms (Sanguo Yanyi)*, and the tradition of the knight-errant (*renxia*) or a kind of a Robin Hoodism. The rhetoric of fraternity and comradeship was not, however, incompatible with an extremely strict hierarchy of ranks, authoritarianism, and the exclusion of certain "unclean" groups from regular membership. (Lewis 1972, 103; Hirayama n.d., 25)

The social composition of the societies has been a subject of some debate. In the People's Republic, the debate revolves around whether the secret societies had revolutionary potential or not. Cai Shaojing

has argued that they had emerged from the peasantry and represented peasant interests (Cai Shaojing 1987, 292–95), whereas others
like Lin Zengping have argued that they were cut off from the peasants and represented rather a lumpen proletariat (Lin Zengping 1981,
353). Most authors have tended to find elements of both groups—
poor peasants and the vagrants, including boatmen, mine workers,
coolies, porters, itinerants, healers, monks, demobilized soldiers and
others. The latter half of the nineteenth century saw a definite increase in the numbers of displaced people as imperialism and rebellion uprooted them from their jobs or the land. Most noticeable was
the demobilization of the soldiers of the armies of Zeng Guofan and
others after they had put down the Taiping Rebellion. These soldiers
joined, or in many cases rejoined, the ranks of the Gelaohui along
the Yangzi River (Lin Zengping 1981, 352; Yokoyama 1986, 171–72).
But the variegated social composition of these societies should not
be ignored. Under certain circumstances, as during the Opium War
or during the Republican period in Sichuan, all classes of people,
from clerks and runners to high elites, could claim membership of
the secret societies. Certainly, the leadership of these societies was
diverse: apart from those from the above-mentioned groups, it could
include merchants, literati, military officials and even landowners
(Lust 1972, 166).

The diverse social elements within these societies supported a cor-
responding variety of goals. These included mutual aid and group
solidarity, Robin Hood type operations as well as preying on the
poor, anti-state activities and/or anti-foreign activities, religious activities, criminal activities and, occasionally, even anti-landlord activities
(Sakai 1972, 263–67; Tessan 1984, 21–22). There is a general consensus that in the late nineteenth century, the increased numbers of
displaced people joining the ranks of the societies tended to diminish
the political dimension and enhance the mutual aid goals of these
societies. Jerome Chen believes that after rebellions and consolidation
of the dynasty from the 1860s onwards, several of these societies,
such as the Qingbang and the Gelaohui in the Yangzi valley, had
reconciled themselves to the dynasty and the famous Qing era statesmen, such as Zeng Guofan and Zuo Zongtang, both of whom even
recruited large numbers of the Gelaohui into their armies (Chen 1970,
814–15).[1]

1. Chen argues that both the Gelaohui and Qingbang were politically moderate
because they worked as transporters in the imperial state's grain tribute system. After
the midcentury rebellions, the Gelaohui replaced the more subversive Heaven and
Earth Society (Tiandihui) in Hunan and worked to create mutual aid organizations in

Given the social heterogeneity of the secret societies, one can hardly expect to find ideological homogeneity among them. However, since the turn of the century, the effort to fix an originary and essentialist consciousness upon these societies has governed much of the writing about them. The core of this chapter is devoted to deconstructing this endeavor. Here I would like to show how despite, or rather, through, the *different* efforts to fix the ideology of secret societies, we can actually see the overflow of meanings and the protean nature of their ideology. It is widely believed that much of their ideology was expressed through a limited number of signifiers, taken especially from the popular novel *The Water Margin* and, to a lesser extent, from *The Romance of the Three Kingdoms*. The most important of these signifiers were *yi* (righteousness), *zhong* (loyalty), and *ren* (benevolence), all of which were drawn from orthodox Confucian vocabulary but were transformed into an "ethic for the outlaw" (Yokoyama 1986, 163). In this context, it is important to note the extent to which scholarly and popular conceptions of secret society ideology were rooted in the vernacular works of historical fiction. The several different versions—editions and rewritings—of *The Water Margin* from the fourteenth century onwards all claimed to be historical, but little of the novel is actually grounded in historical records and much more borrows from legend (Hsia 1968, 82–84). Since twentieth-century historical writings often drew on these fictional models to understand the societies, this topic affords a special view of the interpenetration of historical and fictional narratives.

In any event, no matter how closely any individual understanding of the ideology of secret societies relied on legend and fiction, the varied interpretations of historians themselves reveal that signifiers such as *yi* and *zhong* exceeded not only their usage in a Confucian ethic, but even in the popular romance of them as sworn secret brotherhoods of "the rivers and lakes" devoted to a conception of subaltern justice. For Lo Ergang, who strongly believed that the text of *The Water Margin* was a sure guide to the ideology of secret societies,[2]

---

order to return to peaceful life after the rebellions (Chen 1970, 815). The Gelaohui flourished in Hunan, Hupei, Honan, Shensi, Sichuan, Yunnan and Guizhou, whereas the Tiandihui was pushed south to Liangguang and Fujian, where they seemed not to survive in significant numbers in the twentieth century (Wang Tianjiang 1963).

2. Lo Ergang (1947) compares the text of *The Water Margin* to the rhetoric of the Tiandihui (which he believes is the parent of all secret societies) and declares the parallels and references located in the text as evidence that the text is the perfect model of the society. This can scarcely provide us with a reliable guide to secret society ideology, but it does indicate some of the idealized nodes of meaning within secret society ideology.

the ideals of *zhong* and *yi* left a varied legacy: whereas among late Ming, roving bandits and rebels, righteousness and loyalty were associated with "popular rebellion against official oppression," with the inauguration of Manchu rule, the heroes of "loyalty and righteousness" in the secret societies became engaged in recovering the fatherland from oppressive rule by a foreign race (Lo Ergang 1947, 78). Lo also reveals the ambiguity of this ideology of loyalty and righteousness: although it opposes the inequality of rich and poor, it does not propose a class ideology; although it opposes evil politics, it does not propose a populist revolution. It has a redistributive strain, but only according to the paternalistic principle of righteous charity. There is an antibureaucratic component, but also an idealization of bureaucrats (Lo Ergang 1947, 81).

Sakai Tadao believes that *zhong* and *yi* were important categories that linked secret societies and popular culture to the hegemony of elite, Confucian culture. Thus, the combination "*zhongyi*" (loyalty and righteousness), which became prominent among these sworn communities, especially in the north, during conflicts between the Han and other peoples reflects loyalty to the monarch and nation (*guo*)—categories which emerged from elite culture. At the same time, he suggests that the emphasis on "*renyi*" (benevolence and righteousness) reveals the mutual aid dimension of these groups and could become the basis of radical demands for the equalization of wealth or the reduction of taxes and rents (Sakai 1972, 113). Others, such as Wang Tianjiang, have chosen not to emphasize their racialist defense of the fatherland and focus instead on their "antifeudal" and politically rational character. They emphasize that instead of worshipping deities as did the religious sects of the north (much more on this later), the secret societies revered righteous and loyal heroes (Wang Tianjiang 1963, 89–90). Just this brief summary of some of the different ways in which the social meaning of *yi* can be understood reveals that it was a protean symbol that could be adapted in several different directions within a culture. Cut off from an authorizing institution, it possessed a moral authority in and of itself merely by reflecting its pursuit as a desirable symbol by many groups. Reminiscent of the fluidity of communities with soft, social boundaries (see

---

Incidentally, Lo's reading of the ideology from the text of *The Water Margin* is full of the subversive irony that Andrew Plaks finds in the 71-chapter abridgement of the novel by Jin Shengtan first published in 1644. Plaks distinguishes this version and interpretation of the text, which became the standard text for three centuries of Chinese readers, from earlier and other renderings of it which lack its ironic complexity (Plaks 1987, 279–359).

chapter 2), the different and changing meanings of *yi* marked the nodes of signification around any one or more of which secret society ideology circulated. In their mobilization of secret societies, the revolutionaries would try to privilege one of these nodes—anti-Manchuism—as their narrative of *discent*.

The discussion in chapter 2 identified a Confucian representation of political community in opposition to a historical racialist representation. There were moments when the two conceptions had been in fierce opposition with each other, indeed, when whether you believed in one or the other became a life and death question. And yet discursively speaking, the relation between the two conceptions of political community was in the nature of a supplement: although they were separate from each other, at different moments and in different contexts, they needed each other for their completion. Neither conception was distinct and stable. The cultural vocabulary from which the two derived were often the same, as the discussion of the language of the secret societies in the next section will show. The racialist conception of the revolutionaries, discussed in the penultimate section, however, derived more from a modern, global discourse of race tied to social Darwinism and imperialism. Thus, while the revolutionaries sought to appeal to secret society anti-Manchuism in its Confucian context in practical ways, at another level, they would have to divorce the representation of these societies from any association with Confucian culture.

COAL MINERS, CONFUCIANISM, AND THE QUESTION OF THE MANCHUS

In the late nineteenth century, Sichuan became the hotbed of anti-Christian and, more broadly, anti-Western/imperialist outbreaks led by secret societies, in particular, the Gelaohui. Tessan Hiroshi believes that these outbreaks had to do with hostilities connected with the relative preponderance of migrants and vagrants in this area. This group proved susceptible to the appeals of the secret societies, who provided them with a surrogate community, as well as to the protection and possibilities for upward mobility that the Christian churches, established in the era after 1860, offered their new converts (Tessan 1984, 20–22). Thus, their organization into rival groups exacerbated the militant tensions latent among this vagrant population. At the same time, Christianity presented a serious ideological challenge to the popular religious culture which, to a great degree, had been tacitly sanctioned by imperial orthodoxy and which appeared to have been defended by both sects and secret societies (Tessan

1984, 22; Wyman 1993, 176–77, 204–8). Thus, while the source of conflict often involved Chinese Christian converts and the popular sects or secret societies, these tensions were rapidly translated into a wider ideological conflict between Chinese culture and a foreign ideology. The situation was similar to the one in northern China, where popular anti-Christian and anti-Western outbreaks culminated in the Boxer Uprising of 1900 (Esherick 1987).

However, as in the north, perceptions of the affront to popular religious culture were inextricably linked in these movements with political and economic grievances. The animus against Chinese converts and Christian missionaries, while real enough, was also interpreted in popular culture as part of the larger question of foreign penetration in which culture, politics, and economics were all tied together. Foreign economic penetration in the upper Yangzi valley took place in the textile market, in landownership by missions and other foreigners and, later, in railway building (Tessan 1984, 20–21); but as Judy Wyman has shown, it was felt particularly acutely in mining, where fears spread about the impending mechanization of the mines by the foreigners (Wyman 1993, 212). It is no surprise that the most significant anti-Christian, anti-foreign, and pro-Qing movement of the 1880s and 1890s was led by Yu Dongchen, an uneducated coal miner and leader of the Gelaohui secret society. One of the principal reasons behind the riot of 1888, the first of three major uprisings, was that Catholic converts monopolized the main coal market, thereby pushing out the non-Catholics to a less desirable area (Wyman 1993, 209–10).

The anti-Christian riots which led to the Gelaohui uprising of Yu Dongchen began in Sichuan's Dazu county close on the heels of anti-foreign violence in Chongqing in 1886. In that year, and in 1888, 1890, and in 1898, the Roman Catholic church in the town was destroyed by a crowd each time on the day of the Lingguan religious festival, a local religious celebration. In 1890, Yu led a contingent, composed principally of coal miners, which destroyed the church, demolished the homes of converts, and killed at least twelve people. According to the French Catholic priest, the church erected in the market between two temples offended the leaders of the secret society. Again and again, converts were tortured and forced to renounce their faith in Christianity and return to the way of the Chinese gods. The movement culminated in 1898, when Yu directed it against Chinese Christian communities in southern and eastern Sichuan and kidnapped a French priest, thus provoking a serious diplomatic crisis for the Qing court. The movement subsequently spread to the neighboring provinces of Hunan, Yunnan, and Guizhou (*Dazu xianzhi* 1945, 4: 8–11; Wyman 1993, 180–203; Tessan 1984, 27–29).

Although it is not entirely clear to what extent the Qing court was sympathetic to the anti-Christian movement,[3] it did occasionally prosecute Chinese Christian converts to mollify the people. At the local level, however, magistrates, who could be sympathetic to the popular anti-Christian sentiments, often turned a blind eye or were slow to pursue the instigators of anti-Christian activities (Zhang Li 1980, 21–22). Thus did Yu Dongchen interpret these signs as tacit support for his cause and raised the slogan of "support the Qing and exterminate the foreigner." Indeed, not until the last stage of his third uprising, from October 1898 to January 1899, when the Qing court was forced to intervene to prevent a massive French attack, did the anti-foreign movement also become anti-Manchu.[4]

Yu Dongchen's locally famous "proclamation of warning" (*xiwen*), issued in mid 1898, is a very revealing text. It combines a relatively sophisticated politico-economic critique of imperialism with a defense of a nation whose representation is inspired by a Confucian populism:

> Nowadays, foreign merchants come for trade and Christian missionaries come to preach Christianity. They have stripped us of our means of livelihood on the land, destroyed the sacred relationships between the emperor and his subjects and between father and son. They used opium to poison China and fancy technology to delude the people. . . . Our national debt is heavier than a mountain (*qiushan*). They burned down our summer palace and seized our tributary states. They forced the court to open treaty ports and wished to dismember our country as if it were a melon. From antiquity to the present, there have been no barbarians like these. (*Dazu xianzhi* 1945, 5: 18)

---

3. Tessan Hiroshi (1984, 29) believes that both conservatives and the Yangwu factions in court were anti-Christian, although they may have been divided over the anti-foreign issue.

4. Tessan interprets the turn to anti-Manchuism as reflecting the transition from a gentry-supported movement to a radical movement of the popular masses. According to him, the anti-Manchu slogan basically reflected an anti-state and anti-elite orientation that lay under the surface of the movement (Tessan 1984, 27–28). However, he has to deal with the fact that the movement turned anti-Qing only when anti-imperialism reached too dangerous a level and not principally because it had become radicalized on social issues. It may well be that the process of turning against the Manchu state may have also radicalized the movement. But this does not alter that this movement led by the poor and dispossessed had a strong cultural nationalist, rather than class, orientation for most of its life.

Writing after he determined to continue the uprising against the French foreign establishment and their converts, Yu has a clear political interest in seeking to neutralize the imperial state and gentry elites. He appeals directly to the nation (*guojia*). Scholar-gentry advice will be respectfully heeded if they care to help their common cause of defending Confucianism. Bureaucrats and soldiers will not be attacked if they do not attack the righteous people. The only true targets of the uprising are the foreigners, but if the officials were to hurt their cause, "then we will regard them as foreigners and not servants of our dynasty. They will be executed by the laws of our nation (*guojia*) and will not be tolerated by the righteous people" (*Dazu xianzhi* 1945, 5: 19). There is a strategic use of language here: by identifying the nation (clearly more in its Confucian than modern sense) with the dynasty, Yu's text implicates the court with defense of the traditional Confucian concept of the nation, tries to isolate the bureaucratic faction that opposes his movement, and situates his movement (the "righteous people") as the champion of this righteous cause.

But it would be a mistake to reduce the discursive affinity with the Confucian ideological world to the merely strategic. In the face of the alien Christian doctrine, the text recognizes a common cultural vocabulary between the uprising (which it declares to be of the righteous people), the Confucian tradition, and the Manchu dynasty. It declares:

> We have been living off the produce of the land for the last 200 years. There is not one of us who is disloyal to the dynasty. The sixteen maxims (the sacred maxims of the Manchu emperor Kangxi) have been transmitted from Emperor Yao to Shun all the way down to us. We only study the Confucian classics and have never dared to receive barbarian teachings.

Somewhat later it adds, "Our emperor, (the Manchu) Xianfeng, was forced to flee to Rehe by these beastly barbarians. How can we bear such great pain?" (Yu in *Dazu xianzhi* 1945, 5: 18).

Yu Dongchen and many secret society members who invoked the language of righteousness manipulated this language only to the extent that this language defined the perimeters of meaning for them. It was possible for him to try to preempt the Qing court through the language of righteousness because the Confucian language of righteousness had, at least partially, constituted his ethos.[5] For this

---

5. The gazetteer records that Yu calls himself a "righteous person (*yimin*)" (Dazu xianzhi 1945, 4: 8) and, throughout the text as well as in his biography, one finds the message replete with references to the righteous people and his righteous cause.

reason, the Republican revolutionaries would have to acknowledge and work with this ethos, as the discussion of the Longhuahui in the following section will show. But the discursive affinity between imperial Confucianism and the popular rebels could override Han-Manchu rivalries, and Yu's rhetoric, like that of the Boxers in the north, contained the seeds of a popular counternarrative to anti-Manchuism. Thus, it was also imperative for the revolutionaries to view the secret societies not only as separate from the Qing cause, but also from Confucianism.

REVOLUTIONARY NARRATIVES OF SECRET SOCIETIES

I will examine two texts, both written by the Zhejiang revolutionary Tao Chengzhang (1878–1912), who was perhaps the most important revolutionary organizer in Zhejiang. Closely associated with Zhang Taiyan, he was one of the leading members of the Restoration Society (Guangfuhui), and from 1904 until 1907 or so, he was intermittently involved in organizing secret societies in the Yangzi valley (Rankin 1968, 322; 1971, 149). Both texts concern secret societies and revolutionaries; the second text is a particularly influential history of secret societies which was, until recently, among the most important sources of information on these societies during this period. The information therein, along with the narrative Tao devised, had wide appeal and its influence may be found in such important accounts of both politicians and academic historians as those of Hirayama Shū and Sun Yat-sen among the former and Xiao Yishan and Lo Ergang among the latter. Sun's acceptance and reworking of this narrative will be examined later.[6]

The first text is the introduction to the "Rules of the Longhuahui," an organization formed or reorganized by Tao around 1904 or 1905. This was a type of organization which Rankin believes was "part way between traditional societies and revolutionary party" (Rankin 1971, 151). Unlike some of the other such organizations developed by Tao's fellow-Zhejiang comrades, such as Xu Xilin and Qiu Jin, Tao's sought

6. The political relationship between Tao and Sun was actually very rocky. Tao was the vice-president of the Restoration Society, of which Zhang Binglin was the president. After a brief alliance between the Restoration Society and the Revolutionary Alliance of Sun Yat-sen in 1906, relations between Zhang and Sun, and consequently between the two organizations, began to decline by 1907. When Tao was sent to Southeast Asia to raise money from overseas Chinese, it is said that the rivalry with Sun almost cost him his life. According to Wong Young-tsu, Tao was finally assassinated in 1912 by Chiang Kai-shek from orders by Chen Qimei, probably with Sun Yat-sen's prior knowledge (Wong 1989, 70, 90–91).

to preserve as much as possible the traditional society organization and to emphasize ideas which were close to secret society attitudes (Rankin 1971, 151). Rankin suspects that the document may not have been drafted until 1908, when Tao and other revolutionaries were seeking to unite secret societies across several provinces in the Yangzi valley (Rankin 1971, 152). The second text, the influential history of the secret societies transcribed from a lecture given by Tao in Southeast Asia, was meant for revolutionaries and activists. Just as the first text was addressed chiefly to the secret societies, so the latter was addressed to modern revolutionary activists and their supporters.

The introduction to the Longhuahui begins by conflating two different meanings of the word *geming* (revolution). *Geming*, says the author, comes from the classic text, the *Yijing*, and means to respond to heaven and follow the people (Tao Chengzhang n.d., 122). As is well-known, in its pre-twentieth-century usage, *"geming"* was an integral part of Confucian political vocabulary: to deprive a ruler of the mandate of heaven to rule. When it returned from Japan as a neologism for modern revolution, it, of course, signified a transformation that went not merely beyond a change of dynasties, but beyond a revolution that was merely political. As the text proceeds, it becomes clear that there will be no role for an emperor, that the sense of *geming* is more modern than historical. Yet this semantic conflation reveals the first step in the strategy of the text: to mobilize secret societies around new ideas by drawing on an authoritative historical language suffused with popular Confucian ideas.

Even while it establishes this first step, the text moves in the same moment to dissociate this historical Confucian culture from the political system, in particular, from the imperial system. *Geming*, it declares, means to rebel. Rebellion (*zaofan*) is not immoral, but rather sanctioned by China's ancient culture. The charge that rebellion is immoral is made by the emperors ("who rest their buttocks on the throne") in order to discourage challengers and who have their brown-nosing officials perform Confucian rituals to sanctify this censure against rebellion (Tao Chengzhang n.d., 123). The text then repeatedly invokes Confucius and Mencius to demonstrate that they believed that the people should become emperors. Since they lived in a feudal era, the people were unable to become emperor in a practical sense; but since the unification of the state, a host of popularly known historical figures such as Liu Bang, Liu Bei, and, most of all, Zhu Yuanzhang showed that the common Chinese people could become emperors (Tao Chengzhang n.d., 125). While the narrative denounces the tyranny of the emperors, one of its goals is to celebrate a democratic potential sanctioned by the sages and inherent in the history.[7]

The separation of authentic culture from the imperial system works not simply to disclose the potential for popular rule, it works most decisively to separate culture from Manchu imperial rule. A second narrative establishing a racially exclusive Han community is almost invisibly interplotted with the first. This theme can be recognized early on, when the text registers the revulsion that Confucius must feel to have the barbarian rulers and their ancestors revere him in the great halls of the imperial palace. Surely, he never imagined he would be so harmed. The interplotting of the two narratives finds its most important (and invisibilizing) hinge in the person of the first Ming emperor—the Hongwu emperor, Zhu Yuanzhang, who was not only of the "people," but of the *Han* people—who vanquished the foreign Mongols. Other examples include Koxinga and Yue Fei ("Sir Yue" as the text identifies him) (Tao Chengzhang n.d., 126). This second narrative comes to its own with the detailing of the horrors of Manchu conquest and rule. The narrative of democratic potential fairly disappears from view during this section until the very end when they are again re-entwined with the question: Why are we so much more self-conscious about our enslavement by the Manchus now than we have been in the past? The answer reveals the inspiration of this text in a global discourse:

> It is the fortunate result of the increasing ties among nations. Originally the nations overseas did not have rulers of a foreign race rule them; rather they were oppressed by people of their own race. Then they arose and had a revolution. Now since we have gradually increased our contacts with the foreigners, the words of Confucius and Mencius have been proved to be true. Their reasoning is now clarified and in the future our revolution will be successful. All the foreigners will praise our nation. (Tao Chengzhang n.d., 127–28)

In these three or four short sentences, the different narratives are rejoined. In the single elliptical line about the foreigners being oppressed by the people of their own race making a revolution, a transition is made from race to popular revolution. Race continues to be underscored in that it is implied that revolution is that much more necessary when the oppressors are not of the same race. Secondly,

7. He notes that the ancient monarchs, such as Yao, Shun, and Yu, had abdicated their throne rather than pass it on to their sons (Tao Chengzhang n.d., 129).

legitimation is clearly sought in the foreign political experience, but it is done so only after establishing the affiliation or equivalence between modern Western civilizations and the authentic Chinese culture of antiquity, which also had a democratic potential sanctioned by Confucius and Mencius and which was now recognized by the world. Thus, the separation of a true, primordial Chinese culture from the polity plays many roles: this culture becomes the repository of democracy and revolution; it makes for national equivalence with the most powerful in the world; and, in a last area still to be explicated, the separation is necessary to bring the revolutionaries and secret societies together.

Clearly, the anti-Manchuism of the secret societies was highly ambivalent. Historically, Chinese racist constructions existed more in the relationship of a supplement to Confucian culturalist conceptions, although the two could also be opposed. The strategy (if that is what it was) of appealing to the language of Confucian culture was useful, among other reasons, in order to appeal to the shared vocabulary of righteousness and Chineseness. Yet, the revolutionaries would have to guard against the fluidity of traditional conceptions whereby the Manchus, as patrons of Confucian culture, could emerge as the champions of this culture—even among traditional champions of racial exclusivism—particularly in the face of the iconoclastic foreigners. Secret societies could reverse their slogans abruptly—from opposing to supporting the Manchus. In order to foreclose the possibility of a renewed emphasis on Confucian culture producing a pro-Manchu stance, the text not only needed to separate culture from politics, ironically, it also needed to invest Confucian culture with a racialist politics.

The second text by Tao, entitled "An Examination of the Origins and Spread of Sects and Societies," was a transcription of a speech he gave in Southeast Asia perhaps between 1907 and 1911. The most remarkable aspect of the text is its sheer silence on the question of Confucius and Confucianism, given the centrality of these subjects in the other text from which it was unlikely to have been separated by more than five or so years. To be sure, there are important references to righteousness (yi) and other traditional values, but these values will evoke a parallel or counterculture to mainstream Confucianism. Confucianism plays no role in the strategy legitimating this text addressed to nationalistic and modernizing circles of intellectuals and activists. The central irony on which this chapter seeks to focus is exemplified in this disjunction: whereas an idealized Confucianism (however invested with modern ideas and racism) provided the normative source of secret society activism and self-image in Tao's first essay, his second essay not only dispenses with this strategy, it provides the narrative framework for an anti-Confucian understanding of secret societies which others, including Sun Yat-sen, used and developed in another moment of this history. I do not mean to focus on any hypocrisy involved here; indeed, Tao himself is not explicitly anti-Confucian. Rather I want to observe the rhetorical tactics that nationalist ideology engages in to re-dress the aporia between a modern and a primordial national subject of History.

What is the legitimating strategy of this text? What is the authorizing narrative that seeks to persuade its readers of the value of its story? It is that of the development of a pure racial-national subject, unmixed with the universalism of Confucian culture, but rather embedded in the evolutionism of a modern social Darwinism. References to social Darwinian "keywords" in early twentieth-century China such as *taotai* (the elimination of the inferior) furnish the clues to grasping its role in the text (Tao Chengzhang 1957, 102). There are several other themes that weave in and out of this narrative, but I believe that they gain their legitimating power only in their conjunction with this master-narrative. The operational framework of the narrative is a comparative study of the history and relative efficacy of secret societies versus religious sects as forces historically opposed to the imperial state. To anticipate his conclusion: Tao advises his comrades that secret societies are much more rational and politically conscious than religious sects and thus suitable political allies in the republican revolution.

Tao begins by reducing the variety of sects and societies to offshoots of two main parent groups, the White Lotus sectarians located in the north and the Hongmen secret society in the south. The offshoots of the former include the Red Turbans, the Zailijiao, and the Boxers, among others. The latter includes the Triads, the Sandianhui, and the Gelaohui. This distinction is based on an environmental/cultural division of China into the Yellow River basin in the north and the region of the Yangzi basin and further south. The different modes of life and customs in these two parts have made the southerners skilled and wise; they are not superstitious and have much political consciousness. They respect the ethic of the popular vernacular novel *The Water Margin*. The northerners are simple and ignorant; they worship many gods and are superstitious (Tao Chengzhang 1957, 100). Their superstitious nature weakens their political commitment. Because the psychology (*xinli*) of the two peoples is different (Tao Chengzhang 1957, 107), the White Lotus have never been able to penetrate the south.

Sakai Tadao (1972, 264–65) and Jerome Chen have shown that this distinction between sects and societies is much overdrawn and that the two have much more in common. At any rate, such a neat difference between the two can hardly be sustained, as intermediate forms abounded, and not just in the geographical middle ground. Chen argues that the purpose of the division was to show that the Gelaohui in the Yangzi valley were politically anti-Manchu, whereas at least until 1900 and, in many areas, beyond that, they were deeply ambivalent about the role of the Manchus in their cultural universe, especially when faced with still more alien Western or Christian forces (Chen 1966, 13–16). More important, this north–south, environmental/cultural differentiation turned out to be useful for many others, including Marxist historians who were able to associate the religious sects with stagnant feudal forces and the societies with the sprouts of capitalism (Lo Ergang 1947, 78; Wang Tianjiang 1963, 89–91). Thus we need to grasp this distinction as being far more significant than its immediate goal of creating a political ally among the Gelaohui by depicting them as anti-Manchu. What was being created was a narrative framework for producing a racial-national subject, imbued with modern cultural traits—of rationality, a self-conscious, disenchanted worldview, if you will, politically conscious and committed, and, as we will see, egalitarian. Thus they would be capable, with adequate leadership, of realizing a nation that was both modern and culturally Chinese.

As in the first text, a second narrative of racial purity is established. The text links the original goals of both sects and societies to the founding moment of the culture of the Chinese people whose ancestors entered from the West and became locked in conflict with the barbarians in the area. These ancestors planted a flag to distinguish themselves from the barbarians, protect their kind and their ideas, and thus deeply bound the hearts of their people. The ancient heroes whom the Chinese people worshipped, such as the five emperors, the three kings, the Duke of Zhou and Guan Zhong were none other than their leaders, leaders who wiped out the people of other races. Between the time of the eastern Han and western Jin, the people forgot their ancestors' warning to defend themselves against the barbarians and gradually submitted to the barbarians of other races. Although, in this early period, the Chinese were subjugated by barbarian conquerors, these barbarians were of lowly origins and were quickly assimilated into Chinese culture (Tao Chengzhang 1957, 100). The Song dynasty marks a turning point in the narrative because, by ignoring the military threats from barbarians (they cared much more about internal disorder) and promoting literati culture, the Song softened the people's spirit. This is why the race and the nation declined when faced with the invasions of the Khitan, Jurchen, and Mongols, and of course, ultimately the Manchus (with the all too-brief Ming interlude of 250 years of Han Chinese rule) (Tao Chengzhang 1957, 101). Thus Tao gestures here toward the more familiar Republican revolutionary argument against literati Confucian culture (which we will see in Sun Yat-sen) without actually invoking the names of Confucius or the neo-Confucianists. The legacy of the ancestors to militarily defend the race and its culture and wipe out the barbarian enemy then fell to the sects and secret societies. The White Lotus did, of course, lead to the founding of the Ming, but because it was inspired by a foreign religion, Buddhism, they continued to feel lingering ties with the Buddhist Mongols. Only with the Manchu devastation of the central plain did the true inheritors of the race, the (secret society) Hongmen, rise to reclaim the ancestors' lands (Tao Chengzhang 1957, 101, 103).[8]

The text conducts a telling analysis of the name, Hongmen (Tao Chengzhang 1957, 101). *Men* (literally, gate) of Hongmen, Tao says, refers to the house or family of the Hongwu emperor, the Ming founder, a Han Chinese who drove out the Mongols. Members of the society thus all become equal brothers of the same family, no matter what their previous status may have been. The idea of belonging to a common family was a popular notion among the societies themselves and Tao was not adding anything new. He does add two twists, though: one, which will be discussed later, is the theme of equality; here it is enough to note that this rhetoric of equality is imposed upon a hierarchy of statuses among many of these societies. The second twist occurs when he associates this notion of a family with that of a descent group, a conception that came to reside at the heart of the idea of the nation as a family. The revolutionary Chen

---

8. The reason why the south has produced the group that will deliver the nation is explained in social Darwinian terms. As the people of the Song were pushed south by the invaders, they had to confront the fierce Mongols repeatedly and, in the process, their resolve strengthened. Having gone through the struggle for survival, the weak were eliminated and only the sharp and the capable were able to survive (Tao Chengzhang 1957, 102).

Tianhua wrote, "Common families all descend from one original family: the Han race is one big family. The Yellow Emperor is the great ancestor" (quoted in Dikötter 1992, 117). Racial loyalty came to be perceived as an extension of lineage loyalty and the myth of common ancestry and blood became a most important bond for the Republican revolutionaries' conception of the racially pure nation. (Indeed, at one point in the first essay, Tao remarks: "Are we Han Chinese not all children of the Yellow emperor?" [Tao Chengzhang n.d., 125]). In Tao's narrative, the fictive brotherhood of the secret societies plays the role of the true descendants of the original ancestors and the carriers of their prophetic warnings. Hence the various customs and practices of these societies, such as wearing the dress of the ancients. But most interesting is the way he overcomes the paradox that they, a *fictive* family or brotherhood not related by blood, should represent the true descendants. It is overcome ritually: Tao suggests that the oath-taking ceremony among secret societies of drinking or smearing the mouth with blood is a practice that links them to the ancestors because it is an ancient custom that the contemporary Manchu state does not recognize as Chinese (Tao Chengzhang 1957, 101–2). They are linked to the ancestors by the secret truth of blood.

The trope of brotherhood then serves Tao well to fuse his two concerns, which we have also seen in the earlier text: the need to construct a racial community as well as a modern society. The passages on brotherhood emphasize the equality among brothers and may be associated with other modern qualities, such as their rationality and political consciousness (Tao Chengzhang 1957, 106–8). The difference with the first text is that these qualities are not located in an abstracted Confucian culture but are embodied in the secret societies themselves as a radical and secretive culture countering the effete high culture of the literati. This sort of nationalist search for alternative traditions to Confucianism within Chinese history had become a small industry in the early twentieth century and was especially associated with the "national essence" school of nationalists such as Zhang Taiyan. Some of the greatest proponents of this search for alternative traditions—although not necessarily under the banner of "national essence"—as the foundation for a new national culture were Hu Shi and Gu Jiegang, the first in establishing the vernacular as the basis of modern Chinese, the latter, in founding an alternative history in the "penumbra of Confucianism" and folk culture. As we know, Tao was very closely associated with Zhang Taiyan in the Restoration Society and could not but have been influenced by him. Although he did not appear to be self-consciously fashioning this alternative community of the secret brotherhood, the image of it flashes here and there in the text and was clearly influential among revolutionary activists.

The clearest image of this alternative community as the repository of authentic Chinese values—the romance of the secret societies— appears in Tao's discussion of the importance of the oath that the societies vow. According to him, theirs is the oath of the Peach Garden, which bonds them in righteousness and loyalty (Tao Chengzhang 1957, 109). As is well known, the Oath of the Peach Garden is the oath of loyalty taken by the three heroes of the vernacular novel, *The Romance of the Three Kingdoms,* and is a story that has been appropriated by both popular culture and orthodoxy, each for its own purposes. Tao writes that the Hongmen unites together the hearts of the lower classes of the Chinese people with the teachings of the *Romance of the Three Kingdoms,* the *Water Margin,* and others. "By taking the oath of Liu, Guan and Zhang (the Oath of the Peach Garden) they venerate the spirit of righteousness. They energetically seek the principle of equality and therefore that of a republic" (Tao Chengzhang 1957, 109).

In this context, Tao's usage of *yi* as the means for them to establish equality and, indeed, reflect the principles of a republic is not easily assimilable within the ideological map defined by the nodes of *yi* worked out earlier. It represented an effort to fix the protean quality of *yi* and thus appropriate the romantic narrative of the secret societies that had circulated in popular culture. This appropriation involved a reworking which sought to incorporate the dual temporality that is necessary to all nationalisms: to be modern and yet retain the primordial. Thus righteousness in this narrative produced a strong, indeed, republican sense of equality and, at the same time, an undying resolve to avenge the ancestors. As it turned out, this rhetorical burden was altogether too much for the secret societies to bear, and the revolutionaries were to be much disappointed. Indeed, a few short pages after celebrating the republican form of the secret societies, Tao goes on to outline the hierarchical ranks among the societies! (Tao Chengzhang 1957, 110).

SUN YAT-SEN: THE EXPERIENCE OF THE REAL AND NARRATIVE CLOSURE

There is abundant evidence that the secret societies did not live up to the promise of the revolutionaries' narrative even when in alliance with the revolutionaries (Lust 1972, 179; Lewis 1972, 111). For instance, one of the biggest of these secret society-cum-revolutionary uprisings, the Ping-Liu-Li uprising of 1906–1907 on the Hunan-Jiangxi border, convinced the revolutionaries of their inability to control the secret societies and signaled the turn in their interest away from the societies to the New Armies. The Ping-Liu-Li uprising arose out of massive Gelaohui anger against the execution of their Hunanese leader, Ma Fuyi, by the Qing. Thus, they responded to the revolutionary call to overthrow the Manchus. But despite the efforts of the revolutionaries, the uprising became divided over its commitment to the republican cause. While one group incorporated some of the Tongmenghui political agenda and adopted the slogan of "*geming*" on its banners and badges (Lust 1972, 179),[9] the second group's anti-Manchuism came to be translated quite simply into a call for a "new Chinese empire" and forsook all ties to the Republicans (Lewis 1972, 111). Moreover, anti-foreign and anti-Christian activities among secret societies, which had been strongly discouraged by the revolutionaries in an effort to redirect their anti-foreign animus against the Manchus, did not cease in the 1900s (Rankin 1971, 131). No better evidence of their rather incomplete incorporation into the revolutionary worldview exists than, for instance, the carnivalesque celebrations by secret societies during the 1911 revolution in Sichuan. They celebrated a world that had moved backwards in time, where Gelaohui members dressed in Ming dynasty clothing and paraded as imperial officials—to the alarm of Republican revolutionaries who moved to suppress them as soon as possible (Lust 1972, 171).

The experience of the revolutionary organizer Bi Yongnian reflects well the effects of the "real" impinging on the romantic narrative of the societies. One of the early organizers of the Gelaohui in Hunan, Bi Yongnian entered Sun's Xingzhonghui after the failure of the 1898 reform movement. In 1899, he arranged a meeting of the Gelaohui leaders with the revolutionaries and Triad leaders in Hong Kong and initiated a short-lived collaboration of the forces in the south. Soon after, in 1900, several of the Gelaohui leaders abandoned the revolutionaries and switched sides, throwing their lot with Kang Youwei's "Protect the Emperor Society." They joined the Zilihui, led by Tang Caichang, which hoped to set up an independent state in south China under the Guangxu emperor. Feng Ziyou believes that they were tempted by the promise of receiving large amounts of cash from Kang's organization. Whether these actions represented avarice or simple practicality, pro-Manchuism or monarchism, these secret soci-

9. It is not at all clear, though, whether "*geming*" was being used here in its traditional or modern sense (see Lust 1972, 172).

ety leaders simply did not live up to the romantic narrative of righteousness that the revolutionaries had built. Apparently, Bi became so disgusted that he shaved his head and entered monkhood (Feng Ziyou 1943, 75).

Indeed, it was none other than Sun Yat-sen who at one point criticized the societies as hierarchical and despotic and lacking any trace of modern ideology. As one who had worked with secret societies to bring about the revolution from 1895 until 1906 and did not fully abandon them up through the revolution of 1911, Sun was most familiar with the manner in which secret societies diverged from the idealization of them underway among revolutionaries. Yet in the early years, Sun was not much troubled by their lack of republican qualities. According to Yokoyama Hiroaki, Sun's republican ideas were not very clearly developed until the formation of the Tongmenghui in Hawaii in 1905, and he did not see any great ideological incompatibility between the revolutionaries and the secret societies. Sun had participated in secret society rites and had accepted their slogans on several occasions (Yokoyama 1986, 134 for 1895–96, 143 for 1900, 154 for 1903). Indeed, even the formation in 1905 of the Tongmenghui reflected the goals of the Hawaii branch of the Hongmen. And later, when Sun organized the Gemingdang in 1913, he was accused of once again replicating the hierarchical and secretive principles of the societies (Yu 1962, 118). There is a suggestion in Yokoyama's study that Sun perhaps did not know enough about modernity in the early period to see the incompatibility between the ideas and rituals of secret societies and republicanism. I would rather look at this from another angle: Sun saw the potentialities of a modern nation less in the new and Westernized forms of associational life in the cities and more in traditional community organizations such as lineages, native place associations, and secret societies (Strand 1992, 3–5).

The few comments that Sun made about secret societies during the period between 1900 and 1911 are brief and reveal that he was mainly interested in them as militant allies in the anti-Manchu cause. Some of these comments are contained in his criticisms of the constitutional monarchists. It will be recalled that Kang's "Protect the Emperor Society" had been not unsuccessful in gaining support among some secret societies in the Yangzi valley (it is said that both Kang and Liang were made "dragon heads" by the Gelaohui), but they had recruited most widely among overseas Chinese, including the Hongmen (known as the Zhigongtang) in Hawaii and in the continental United States. At any rate, anti-Manchu sentiment among the secret society in the United States had declined considerably as they became preoccupied with American concerns. One of Sun's great political successes in the early years of the century was to eliminate the influence of the constitutional monarchists among the Overseas Chinese in America and to convert them to the Republican revolutionary cause. To be sure, Sun saw this conversion to racialist nationalism not as an imposition on the secret societies, but as a return to their founding, and thus true goals. He had identified the Hongmen as the most steadfast opponents of the Manchu regime; but he felt that the overseas Chinese had forgotten this racialist-political message as they settled into the new conditions of making a livelihood abroad. Sun saw it as his mission to remind them of their heritage and to reveal the link between this heritage and the revolutionary cause. The constitutional monarchists attacked the revolutionaries for opportunistically using the secret societies for their own ends. Sun retorted to this charge of opportunism with the comment that "revolutionaries and societies were united in will and morality, that the one responded to the voice of the other and pursued the same spirit (*qi*). They combined their strengths in their uprising" (Sun Yat-sen 1957, 808). The revolutionaries were fulfilling the original mission of the secret societies; it was the monarchists who were subverting their mission and confusing the societies by infiltrating them and seeking to recruit their support for the Qing cause (Sun Yat-sen 1957, 812).

Although the secret societies played a major role in the "Ten Great Uprisings" prior to the 1911 revolution, for many years after the establishment of the Republic, Sun did not acknowledge their role in the revolution. Indeed in 1919, when Cai Yuanpei prepared to compile a history of the national revolution and sought to incorporate the contributions of the secret societies in the history, Sun wrote back rejecting the idea and suggested instead a separate history of the secret societies. He wrote,

> The internal organization of these societies are extremely despotic, and they have sharp class differences. There is no trace of the principle of republicanism or the notion of popular sovereignty among them. Therefore their relation with the republican revolution was actually slight and it is more appropriate to write a separate history of the secret societies and not confuse the national history. (Sun Yat-sen 1954, 2)

How can we explain this attitude? At one level, it is the honest response of a revolutionary intimately involved with the societies who could not but see them in their multiple, protean aspect and from a perspective outside of the romantic narrative in which so many revolutionaries had sought to freeze their image. At this level, Sun's response was like that of Bi Yongnian who, as mentioned, took the tonsure. However, at another level one senses a discomfort in Sun's response. Was he not seeking to suppress something? After all, thousands of society members had given up their lives for the revolution and financial contributions from overseas societies had kept the organizations alive.[10] So why not give them their due? Was he uncomfortable about having been so close to the secret societies now that they were to be written about in the May 4th era when all of tradition—Confucius and popular rituals—came under an unprecedentedly devastating attack? Was he ashamed about having dealings with the underclass of society? Or was he embarrassed by the racism which he had advocated and in some cases imposed upon the societies, but for which the secret societies had since come to bear the blame?[11] We will perhaps never know the answers to this question, but five years later Sun did come to terms with the secret societies in some of his last writings. The textual strategy that he employed in dealing with them reveals how some of these concerns have been worked out in a final judgment upon the role of secret societies in the Chinese nation.

This text by Sun, which has the longest reference to the secret societies of anything he wrote, is none other than his "Third Lecture on Nationalism of the Three People's Principles," delivered on 10 February 1924. In many ways, Sun fleshes out the historical narrative outlined in Tao's second essay. Here he has much praise for the secret societies, especially in contrast to the literati elite. The secret societies had preserved the treasure of nationalist consciousness since the Kangxi period (1661–1722), while the literati as a class, intoxicated by fame and rank, had been seduced by the Manchu restoration of the examination system (Sun Yat-sen 1924, 645–46). There is a certain romanticism here as well. Not only are the secret societies seen as the carriers of the treasure of nationalism, but while the literati sold their souls to the alien dynasty, the societies were able to communi-

10. In a speech in 1923, Sun does acknowledge that "those who fought desperately to destroy the enemy were the military and the secret societies" (Sun Yat-sen 1923, 186).
11. This ambivalence can also be found in Zhuang Cheng who argues simultaneously in the same book that, on the one hand, secret societies contributed to the success of the revolution and, on the other, that the failure of the major campaigns were attributable to the weaknesses of these societies (Zhuang Cheng 1981, 15, 16–17).

cate and preserve this treasure through a natural, oral tradition. The framework of the romance is the binary between betrayal versus authenticity.

At the same time, there are some revealing differences in Sun's version of the romantic narrative of the secret societies. In the first place, the secret societies were not autonomous bodies of the "people" with an independent history of nationalist consciousness. They were organized by visionary Ming loyalists, rich in nationalist consciousness, who were forced to hide their nationalism far away from the treacherous literati circles in secret organizations among the lower classes and the vagrants of the rivers and lakes. We have seen that Sun uses the metaphor of the treasure to describe this national consciousness. The treasure needed to be put in a precious metal box and hidden away in an obscure or inconspicuous place so that a thief would not be able to find it. Similarly, the Ming loyalists sought to hide their treasure in secret organizations (precious metal box) among the lower classes (inconspicuous place), because these classes were considered lowly and no one would think of looking among them for it (Sun Yat-sen 1924, 645, 646). I am struck by the elitism of this passage, an elitism which is absent from Tao or even the earlier Sun. Not only are secret societies seen as products of a loyalist elite design, but there also seems to be a certain anxiety to explain how such a noble thing as nationalism got lodged among the lower classes.

Sun seems to want to deprive the secret societies of any meaningful agency. The elitism he reveals in the passages cited above is confirmed when he points to the limitations of these societies: ultimately they are unable to carry the national revolution through to the end because they are childlike (*youqi*) (Sun Yat-sen 1924, 647); they do not know how to use this treasure of national consciousness, so it will always be abused by others. Sun cites the story of Zuo Zongtang and the Gelaohui which had been discussed by Tao as well. Zuo's Hunan Army was filled with members of the Gelaohui. At one point Zuo discovered a wanted Gelaohui leader among his troops, but upon apprehending him, Zuo had a mutiny on his hands. The story goes that the soldiers of the Gelaohui persuasion refused to pursue the campaign unless Zuo released their leader and, in fact, unless Zuo himself entered the Gelaohui organization. Zuo allegedly did so and the Xinjiang campaign was successful. Sun then attributes the success of the campaign not to the power of the Qing, but to the secret societies fighting against barbarians. But Sun continues the narrative. Having entered the Gelaohui organization, Zuo then pro-

ceeded to destroy the organization and thereby revealed the inno-
cence and ignorance of these societies (Sun Yat-sen 1924, 647–48). By
sequencing the events of the narrative within the economy of this
one episode, Sun achieves the complete view and final judgment of
the secret societies. Although they are the repositories of an authentic national consciousness, their childlike nature requires of them a
strong external leadership in order to realize their potential.

REVOLUTIONARY IDEOLOGY AND THE GLOBAL DISCOURSE OF RACE

Earlier chapters disclosed how what came to be called social Darwinism in the late nineteenth century became a principal organizing
rhetoric for a proliferating production of imperialists, nationalists,
publicists, and the newly emergent academic disciplines across the
capitalist world, including Japan. When this global discourse of the
nation-state system took root in China at the turn of the century, it
became the most important constitutive discourse of Chinese intellectuals for the next twenty years or so, after which the rhetoric and
ethics of anti-imperialism displaced its status of preeminence. To be
sure, this discourse was cross-cut by other counterdiscourses of culture—particularly expressions of the East-West binary (see chapter
7)—but that it came to construct the reality for many Chinese intellectuals is evident from the cited examples of how evolutionist and
Darwinist assumptions continued to inform even these counterdiscourses. Here I would like to underscore the participation of Chinese
intellectuals in a discourse that was basically international in character and to show how, by reprocessing this discourse to adapt to local
needs, the revolutionary intelligentsia enabled themselves to suture
a seemingly seamless narrative of the nation's history.

Social Darwinism in China translated historical Chinese conceptions of inferior races into a conception of a new global order of a
hierarchy of races and nations. The notion of a hierarchy of civilized
races and their evolution was, of course, well developed in the West
before Darwinism made an impact in the latter half of the nineteenth
century (Stocking 1987). But in China, as elsewhere, the Darwinian
element, by emphasizing the competition among species and the
struggle for survival, not only added an element of urgency, but also
a voluntarism that made it possible and eminently desirable to rise
up in the hierarchy. Thus did nationalist intellectuals, both revolutionary and reformist, seek to mobilize the nation through this discourse. For most Chinese and, indeed, most East Asians, the unit
struggling for survival and superiority was not the individual or fam-

ily, but the race and the nation, or more precisely, the racial nation. Why race? Most scholars have suggested that racism was either a historical legacy or a political expediency to get the Manchus out, or some combination thereof. While accepting the role of both factors, I do not think we should allow these arguments to conceal the extent to which the racism of social Darwinist global discourse formed the intellectuals' view of the world in the period. Social Darwinism, too, must be understood in its "proper dispersion."

Most Western writers who wrote about or employed social Darwinism, also implied a racial or national entity (see chapter 1). Indeed, as a discourse in the service of imperialism, it was necessarily a racist doctrine abroad, whatever else it may have represented within Europe. In China, the transformation of the rhetoric into a mobilizing force to struggle ahead in evolutionary time necessarily required the construction of an agency, a specific subject of History, which in the world-order could only be the nation-state. That the nation in China was to be a racist one was a product of this constitutive discourse of the survival of the fit races, in which race was the principal source of the values that it took to be fit and civilized, as much as it was a historical inheritance or political expediency.

Thus, as was made clear in chapter 1, both the reformist Liang Qichao and the revolutionary theorist Wang Jingwei, on opposite sides of the political arena, went about building the new national subject with materials taken from the prodigious international discourse that coalesced around social Darwinism. Both drew on the nascent apparatus of ethnology, sociology, and political science in the West and Japan, as well as on their encyclopedic knowledge of the national histories of many Western countries. Whatever their transformations of this discourse, their discursive world was closer to that of the global intelligentsia than to that of the secret society. They were perhaps the most influential writers for their generation and, indeed, many of Sun Yat-sen's ideas reflected those of Wang, who, in turn, also drew on Liang and Yan Fu (even while he repudiated them). In fact, we can also find the proximate origins of several of Tao's ideas in Wang's essays. But for the purposes here, Wang's ideas in his 1905 essay, "Minzudi Guomin" (Citizens of a Nation), discussed in chapter 1, are important here because they reveal a most systematic effort to understand why it was important for the revolutionaries to constitute the nation as a race. If indeed, it was not the case that the secret societies and the "masses" forced a racism on them, but more the reverse, then it behooves us to try to understand the importance of race in their worldview.

Recall that Wang Jingwei creatively applied the lessons of social Darwinism to grasp the links between race and nation in China and, indeed, the world over. Wang believed that a state made up of a single race was infinitely superior to that made of a number of races. Wang's reasoning followed a logic we may recognize from the discussion of secret brotherhoods. Common race implied that a people are brothers and "when they are brothers, they are naturally equal" (Wang Jingwei 1905, 84). They also have freedom because the hearts of those not of our race (*zulei*) are different, so a conquered race will be kept unfree and different races will always fight. In the same spirit, he wrote that the civilized countries of the West have no race of foreign rulers, a view echoed by Tao (Wang Jingwei 1905, 97). He then outlined four different ways in which races tended to become co-extensive with nations, finding China in recent history to have occupied the third category whereby a minority conquering race assimilated a majority race (Wang Jingwei 1905, 86–87). Yet, now, since the Han had advanced in their nationalism and recognized the supreme principle of the necessity of preserving the race in the struggle for existence, the Manchus would either be absorbed or wiped out, thereby exhibiting the triumph of the fourth type (Wang Jingwei 1905, 95). Wang, like his colleagues Hu Hanmin and Zou Rong, saw the Manchus as an inferior race. The Manchus were relegated to the status of savage primitivity (in their land "they had lived in dens and wore pelts" according to Hu [Pusey 1983, 324]) and unless they assimilated they would be wiped out like "America's red savages" (Wang Jingwei 1905, 95).

In this way, the Republican revolutionaries absorbed the international discourse of racist evolutionism and deployed it to position a racially purified China, one which would then be internally egalitarian and free from disputes, to forge ahead in the evolutionary struggle of life and death. The lineaments of this logic are evident in the writings of Tao and of several generations of historians, particularly in the trope of brotherhood which combined racial vengeance with qualities of republican equality. And it clearly is a logic that is informed by a discourse from the outside, although its local reworking is of great importance. Then why did it become necessary to argue that it was politically expedient to use the racism of the secret societies only to establish a republican government (Gasster 1969, 83; Wright 1968, 23)? In American Sinology, this may have had to do with a discomfort regarding questions of race in the 1960s when the first major studies of the 1911 revolution appeared. In China, we may gain some insight into the fate of modern racial discourse and the subsequent view of secret societies when we consider the political question of what would happen to the non-Han races after the establishment of the Republic.

Before the 1911 revolution, the discussion of the fate of the non-Han communities, such as the Manchus, the Mongols, the Tibetans, the various Muslim communities, and the many smaller communities, all of whom could claim perhaps two-thirds of the territorial surface of present-day China, centered on a discussion of the ways in which they might be assimilated. Zhang Taiyan's typically maverick position that if a nation was to be racially pure, then these other races should logically be sovereign nations was not entertained seriously (Pusey 1983, 331). Wang Jingwei, although more moderate than some others, disputed Liang Qichao's notion of a great nation being made up of the small nationalities of different races within China because it denied the undeniable evolutionary superiority of the Han and the necessity and desirability of assimilation of these inferior races. In a sense, Wang had misunderstood Liang, because in the end, Liang too believed in the necessity of the assimilation of the small nationalities into the Han race in order to avoid dismemberment by the foreigners (Pusey 1983, 333; Kataoka 1984, 284).

In January of 1912, the flag of the Republic of China contained the five colors representing each of the principal racial nationalities within the Republic. It seemed to symbolize the change in rhetoric among the revolutionaries, especially as Sun Yat-sen began to speak of the doctrine of the autonomy of the five major races as the basis of the Republic. It is true that Sun's attitude to the Manchus had always been rather less virulent than most other revolutionaries, but his moderation on the question of treatment to be meted to the Manchus once the revolution was accomplished did not mean that he had always believed in the autonomy of the five races or that he or the nationalists took it seriously even after it was emblazoned on the flag. Kataoka Kazutada has done some close investigative research to show that the change in rhetoric from a racism and assimilationism to one of the autonomy of different races was in itself a politically expedient move. Not only was the fragile republic faced with secessionist movements in Mongolia and Tibet (which declared that they had been part of the empire of the Manchus, not of Zhongguo or China [Nakami 1984]), but there was the immediate fear of both invasion and retaliation on the part of the imperialist powers such as Russia and Japan if Chinese claims on these territories were actively pursued (Kataoka 1984, 292).

It is in this context that we must reconsider the political expediency argument about a necessary alliance with the secret societies. In a later commentary on an early statement of unity with the secret societies, Sun mentions that the racialist attitude of the revolutionaries was to be distinguished from that of the secret societies precisely because the revolutionaries advocated the doctrine of the constitution of the five races, which revealed their greater tolerance compared with the visceral racism of the secret societies (Sun Yat-sen 1954, 30). But Kataoka points out that Sun referred to the doctrine of the republic of the five races only after January 1912 and only when he spoke to the minorities, especially in Mongolia (part of which had declared independence in December 1911) (Kataoka 1984, 298). In a speech in September of 1912, addressed to the "brothers of the four regions," Sun spoke of the suffering of his national brothers (*tongbao*) under foreign oppressors, but who could now enjoy the Republic as masters together with their Han brothers of the inner land and jointly resist the foreign imperialists (Kataoka 1984, 300). In the meanwhile, new Tongmenghui regulations as of March 1912 revealed an ongoing commitment to a policy of assimilationism and the rapid settlement of the "border lands," all of which violated the spirit of the doctrine. In August of 1912, leaders of the new Guomindang advocated a policy of assimilation and founded an association to promote the Han settlement of the border lands. Indeed, after his tenure as provisional president, Sun hardly ever mentioned the doctrine of the five races and threw himself into the project of colonizing the border lands (Kataoka 1984, 298–300).

Thus the expediency of appealing to racism in order to mobilize the secret societies turns out to have been, to some extent at least, itself an expediency to mask a deeply, if recently, rooted discourse and continued practice of racial assimilation. But even when the discourse of race was discredited, Sun Yat-sen's continued identification of race with nation meant that the underlying link between the doctrine of the five races and the earlier anti-Manchuism was not broken. As Qi Sihe (1937) was to point out in the 1930s, this link just brought more trouble to the conception of the Chinese nation at a time when it was suffering a most cruel imperialist aggression. Since these smaller nationalities were (falsely, according to Qi) basically conceived of as independent races, this doctrine permitted Hui Muslims and Manchus and others to declare a separate nation (or, although this was not explicitly stated, could be convinced by the Japanese aggressors of the same). Qi's answer to this problem was to abandon the entire conception of race as a scientific concept. The Han and other minorities all had admixtures; the lines between the Han and the Manchus had blurred; Han and Hui had only religious differences. National-ism, he declared, emerged only from a coming together because of a common past and a will to fight the imperialists (in this case the Japanese) together (Qi Sihe 1937, 28–34). Qi's essay represented the denunciation of vestigial social Darwinism by the discourse of anti-imperialism.

Thus, the decline of social Darwinism's appeal in the 1910s, to-gether with a threatening political situation, led to the initial efforts to conceal the role of social Darwinist racism. The rise of anti-imperialism and its ideal of a morally just universe inspired by the unity of victimhood not only made racism more shameful, but led ultimately, under the Communists, to privileges (if not rights) for minority nationalities. Yet the discourse of race has not disappeared; it acquired new forms and even a certain legitimacy in areas where it was hard to recognize it in its old semblance, as for instance in the realm of eugenics (Dikötter 1992, chap. 6). And what about the secret societies? The present regimes in China and Hong Kong are commit-ted to eradicating the international network of smugglers and drug-traffickers that segments of the Triads have developed into. But in a recent interview, Tao Siju, the Minister of Public Security in the PRC, said, "As for organizations like the Triads in Hong Kong, as long as these people are patriotic, as long as they are concerned with Hong Kong's prosperity and stability, we should unite with them." He added, "When a state leader visited a foreign country, an organiza-tion that is similar to the Triads you mentioned dispatched 800 of its members to guard our state leader against any danger" (*New York Times*, 19 April 1993, A7). We may well be seeing the advent of a new stage in the political and discursive relationship between secret brotherhoods and the state.

CONCLUSION

I have argued here that anti-Manchuism represented an apparent point of contact between two different discourses. Anti-Manchuism was not simply a common area of understanding, still less a manipu-lation of something not believed (by the revolutionaries), it was a hinge which allowed the revolutionary nationalists to open a window to the world of the secret societies. They took in and tailored what could be made to "fit" and closed out the rest, which fitted rather badly with their own worldview. In this way, the revolutionaries were able to stitch together a national history of the simultaneously necessary primordiality and modernity of the nation.

The progress of national suturing began with the Republican revolutionaries convincing the secret societies that republicanism was a Confucian affair and that, therefore, they should participate in it. Meanwhile, the revolutionaries told themselves that the secret societies represented a primordial national culture that was a more authentic alternative to the literati Confucian culture or sectarian societies, both of which came to be seen as the Other of the modern nation. The core of this culture was the ethic of brotherhood representing equality (among men) and the tie of common blood. In the process, secret society racist ideas were extracted from their multifaceted ethos, which included the ambient Confucian culturalism as well as an anti-imperialism, and recast within a social Darwinian perspective that saw national survival in a competitive global arena as made possible by racial purity. To this Sun added the idea that they were childlike, incapable of independent action in a revolution—a form of politics which was, however, foreign to them. Finally, with the passing of social Darwinism, the revolutionary discourse of race was itself obscured and the racism of the revolution was attributed to the still silent secret societies.

What is the nature of the historical relationship between popular anti-Manchuism and the 1911 revolution? I believe I have sufficiently exposed the primordialist argument (made by nationalists and others) that a historical continuity was merely recovered by the Republicans, that the 1911 revolution fulfilled the goals of the secret society nationalists. But what of the strictly constructionist argument which posits that there were no historical links in the ideologies of the secret societies and the Republican revolutionaries and that the latter merely constructed a representation of the former? In this view, discourse swallows history.

Despite my emphasis on dispersion and difference concealed by historical narratives—and the next two chapters witness a dramatic rupture with history made possible by a change in the meaning and function of *fengjian* or feudalism—I wish to end this chapter by highlighting the historically enabling role of anti-Manchuism, which I have referred to above as the hinge bringing together the two parties. To be sure, in their narrative representation the revolutionaries had to devise complex strategies to recast and sustain anti-Manchu racialism as the privileged narrative of *discent*, especially since it had begun to wane in areas outside of some pockets of south China. But at a practical level, the revolutionaries were able to construct an alliance not only because of the presence of anti-Manchuism as an ideological node, but also because they relied on a host of authoritative historical words such as *geming* and *yi*, once again as hinges—Derrida calls them paleonyms—to introduce new meanings. And although the subsequent representation by the revolutionaries of the secret societies and even these hinge words might leave little trace of their transformations, it is important to note that without these historical ties the new representations themselves could probably not have assumed their present shape.

5

THE GENEALOGY OF *FENGJIAN* OR FEUDALISM: NARRATIVES OF CIVIL SOCIETY AND STATE

CHAPTERS 5 and 6 consider the ways in which alternative narratives of modernity are obscured or delegitimated in early twentieth-century China. Here I will examine the contest between the narratives of society versus that of the nation-state as alternative paths to modernity. The subject of state versus society is an old one in Chinese historiography, and in recent years Western historiography of China, following, in part, a revival of interest in civil society in the West, has witnessed a vigorous discussion on the question of whether or not China had a "civil society" and, by implication, what kind of role this civil society could play in the emergence of a modern nation. I too have found the notion of civil society a good way to capture some of the tendencies in late imperial China, but before it can be used, some conceptual ground needs to be cleared.

Illuminating as the discussion has been, the notion of civil society has been couched in extremely objectivist terms and there is hardly any discussion of the problem of narrativization. The issues of narrative, which underlie this topic, figure at several levels. The first issue raises the question, not of *if at all*, but of *how and when* it may be reasonable, in the context of China, to speak of the relevance of European historical categories such as civil society which are deeply embedded in the Enlightenment narrative of emancipation. The second problem relates to the importance not only of "civil society" or state as a factor or element in history, but its narrative representation by historical actors who then sought to propel history performatively in a particular direction; and, finally, attention to narrative raises the question of how the failure of a civil society to flourish in much of twentieth-century China may be seen not as an historical inevitability, but as the triumph in China of the discourse of the global system of nation-states.

CIVIL SOCIETY AND WESTERN HISTORIOGRAPHY OF CHINA

The reappearance of interest in European civil society has spawned a good deal of terminological confusion, and I will try to clarify my own usage of civil society from the outset. Civil society represents a domain of private and collective activity that is autonomous from the state. It includes economic activities as well as associational life and the institutions of sociability, but excludes political parties and institutionalized politics in general. The "public sphere," in particular, the bourgeois public sphere of the eighteenth century conceptualized by Jürgen Habermas, is a historically specific expression of civil society and is understood as a realm of freedom to be defended against state intrusion and domination. This realm is constituted by public opinion and debates in the coffeehouses, salons, popular literature, newspapers, and so on. Not only does this realm articulate a defense of society against state, in engaging the historically unprecedented public use of reason, it introduces a rational-critical discourse on public matters (Habermas 1989; Cohen and Arato 1992).

My use of the term civil society will incorporate this important Habermasian dimension of critique and the defense of its autonomy. However, I do not accept the rather narrow conceptualization of the "public sphere" Habermas developed in order to secure its role as the pivot of the modern transformation. Briefly, Habermas's argument for the rise of a bourgeois sphere is tied to the expansion of capitalism and the emergence of a private realm at the heart of which lay bourgeois domesticity. In this sphere, the family was idealized as the core and pure interior realm of intimate human relationships which produced private people. The public sphere was constituted by the sociability and rational-critical discourse of these private individuals, who sought to defend their privacy in the public sphere from the domination of the state. As several critics of Habermas have pointed out, and as Habermas has himself recently admitted, he had neglected the presence of several different "public spheres" and groups which the bourgeois public sphere and attention to it had excluded or obscured (see Calhoun 1992). In particular, he draws attention to the exclusion of women and a "plebeian public sphere" (after Mikhail Bakhtin) which was also "the periodically recurring violent revolt of a counterproject to the hierarchical world of domination" (Habermas 1992, 427).[1] Similarly, we too may find elements of a civil society and even of a public sphere in both rural and urban China.

Thus, drawing on the above discussion, I will use civil society to refer to an autonomous sphere of associational life that was committed to discourse of public issues and to the defense of its autonomy. Autonomy, however, has often been understood in absolute terms by scholars looking for civil society outside of Western Europe and therefore introduces an impossible, and often dangerous, touchstone for its identification. Charles Taylor has identified two streams of thought regarding the role of civil society in the emergence of modern society in the West. The one associated with John Locke emphasizes not only the autonomy of society, but its priority over the state, which has a fiduciary relation to it. Should the state violate its trust, society can recover its freedom against the government. In Locke, the autonomy of this "prepolitical" society derives from natural rights given its individuals by God. A second tradition associated most with Montesquieu does not presume a prepolitical society that is prior to the state. Society and political authority are both necessary and coeval. Society is, nonetheless, strongly anti-absolutist because its patriotic citizens seek to vigorously defend their deeply entrenched legal rights against despotism through the "mass of [its] agencies and associations." Society and state exist in a creative equilibrium in which neither can destroy the other (Taylor 1990).

The thrust of Taylor's essay sounds a cautionary note against the first position, which by potentially depoliticizing society, opens itself to appropriation by Jacobin ideologies. These ideologies have made and remade polities in the name of a prepolitical and ahistorical concept of society, whether it be expressed as the "general will," or as this chapter shows, the "people," or the "nation." It also opens itself to appropriation by theories in which the morality of the market model has sovereign status. In keeping with the Montesquieu stream, Taylor would rather see civil society as a sphere that "penetrates deeply into [political] power, fragments and decentralizes it" (Taylor 1990, 117). I would like to invoke Taylor's distinction to suggest that when China scholars in the West judge the existence and role of civil society in China in late Qing and early Republican China, they recognize not only that there is more than one model in Western

---

1. To be sure, Habermas remains committed to the idea that the "bourgeois public sphere" was the only one to hold the emancipatory potential of modernity.

society, but that it is the weaker rather than the stronger model of civil society—one in which both state and society were necessary—that may be more relevant in understanding the emergence of modern institutions in the world.

In recent years the notion of a civil society in late imperial and Republican China has been revived most explicitly by William Rowe, both in his work on Hankou and in an influential essay on the subject (1989; 1990), by Mary Rankin through her work on Zhejiang elites (1986), by David Strand on urban associational life in Beijing (1989), and others. These scholars have argued that many of the characteristics of a civil society, and even of a public sphere, had emerged in late imperial China. The presence of large-scale commercial networks, a pervasive money economy, and urban development necessitated the creation of a strong associational life to manage the economic and social infrastructure. These developments also led to the emergence of a distinctive urban culture around the Chinese tea-house, the rise of the printing press, popular literacy, and the popular novel. At the same time, a well-developed notion of a public sphere came to be expressed through the word "*gong*." As Mary Rankin has pointed out, *gong* referred to an extrabureaucratic public sphere in which elite managers and contributors displayed their responsibilities to their communities (Rankin 1990, 14–20). But the rise of the printing press and the popular novel also generated a tradition of criticism and dissent in the public realm. Writing about the eighteenth-century author of the satirical novel *Rulin Waishi* (*The Scholars*), Wu Jingzi, Paul Ropp concludes that in combining the old tradition of Confucian protest with the new trends of urban culture and popular literature, Wu established a new convention of protest and reinvigorated a minority tradition of protest in Confucian China (Ropp 1981, 246).

All of these trends—the economic and the cultural-political—intensified in the late nineteenth century to expand the role and meaning of civil society. Not only did relatively well-integrated provincial elites in the Yangzi valley expand their sphere of associational activities in the post-Taiping local society, they also began to articulate a political role for themselves through the modern commercial press as true defenders of the nation against foreign aggressors (Rankin 1986, 60, 147–69). With the *xinzheng* reforms (1902–8), many of these associations—such as chambers of commerce and professional associations—became officially recognized as *fatuan*. This may well have been a mixed development for civil society because giving them official status could compromise their autonomy by bringing them under official supervision and dependence (Strand 1989, 99).

Despite these pressures, in his inspired study of Beijing society during the Republic, David Strand traces how a vigorous civil society continued to grow throughout the late 1920s. Associational activity proliferated and even gained some ideological legitimacy. Thus, not only did elites organize into chambers of commerce and professional associations, but subaltern groups such as rickshaw pullers and water-carriers also began to organize themselves and voice their opinions and demands in the public realm. Strand notes the critical role of the civil society inherited from the late imperial period in the making of the Republican public sphere. Late imperial guilds and native place associations turn out to have been less markedly different from modern associations: like the latter, they were important organizers of collective action and had the capacity to both express and contain dissent through legitimate channels; they also shared the same weaknesses. Moreover, it was the traditional strengths of corporate self-regulation, group and territorial prerogatives that provided the Republican public sphere with some autonomous space from which to withstand the incursions of the state (Strand 1989, 175).

At the same time however, the very scholars who have inspired us to consider the presence of civil society in China have also pointed out the historical limitations of societal autonomy and initiative. Thus, Mary Rankin observes that the public as a realm of extra-bureaucratic managerial activity was not truly autonomous from elitist Confucian definitions of the common good and the depiction of the people as the passive objects of imperial concerns (Rankin 1990, 41–43). The absence of legal guarantees and individual rights were also serious limitations. In the Republic, Strand argues that even though the elite-dominated associations were able to ensure the functioning of the everyday life of the city between periods of dominance by different warlords, a tendency toward factionalism and clientelism, the scrambling for rank, and the pervasiveness of quasi-governmental functions among both modern and late imperial associations constantly weakened the autonomy of the public sphere. In the end, not only did civil society lack legal guarantees of its autonomy from the Republican state, much of this society continued to be dependent on state patronage for protection and the advancement of its individual members (Strand 1989, 157).

It would, however, be a mistake for us to conclude on the basis of the reservations mentioned above that the notion of civil society in China is irrelevant or foredoomed. If we heed Taylor's warning against idealizing the autonomy of civil society in the West, we can see that elements of a vigorous civil society, including a tradition of defense of its autonomy, had definitely emerged in China by the last decades of the Qing. At the same time, we also see the presence of counterelements, elements that severely restricted its autonomy in the same period. Precisely at the turn of our century, at this fateful juncture in Chinese history, my analysis of the objective forces allows me to say only so much: namely, that the potential for civil society to play a major role in the emergence of modern institutions certainly existed. To say any more would represent an unwarranted historical determinism.

A HYBRID NARRATIVE OF CIVIL SOCIETY

The field of Chinese historiography has tended to swing between two positions, both governed by a question derived from the Enlightenment narrative: did the history of China have an emancipatory potential, whether expressed in the "sprouts of capitalism," in a tradition of liberalism, or in a transformative civil society? The answer is made either in the affirmative or negative, but the meaningfulness of the question itself is not explored. The significance of civil society emerges from the Enlightenment narrative of History and the presence of the narrative itself has shaped, to some extent, the history of civil society. Since Chinese narratives of the imperial period did not envision the past in terms of the emancipation of the individual or the triumph of civil society over the state, the elements of civil society existed only as potential history. These very elements became retrievable as history only when two narratives, seemingly worlds apart—that of the Englightenment and the indigenous narrative of Chinese feudalism (*fengjian*)—came together for a brief period in the late nineteenth century. In the unlikely joining of these two narratives, certain literati became positioned to *actualize* this potential history of societal autonomy—to mobilize a new history from their historical mosaic. It was yet another modern discourse, that of the nation-state system, that ultimately extinguished this hybrid history.

Many historians of China believe that a civil society could not possibly have existed in China because of the long history of imperial absolutism in China and the absence of a tradition of legal and individual autonomy. While there may be some truth to this assertion, it ignores a complex of other factors that qualify its historicism, namely, the political structures and ideologies that checked the untrammeled expansion of state power. In addition to the more recent views of civil society discussed above, there is a considerable literature in Chinese, Japanese, and the Western languages suggesting the autonomy of literati culture from the state. Rather than try to summarize this literature, I shall try to show briefly how this intellectual tradition was mobilized in the late nineteenth century (see de Bary 1983; Yu Yingshi 1987).

It is widely accepted that there was a Confucian tradition of literati autonomy and dissent which developed most particularly in the Ming-Qing transition during the seventeenth century. While this did not amount to Western-style liberalism and individualism, as Jerome Grieder points out, "this was the beginning . . . of the attempt that was carried forward into the early years of the twentieth century to break the link forged in the Han dynasty that bound Confucian ideals to the service of imperial ambition" (Grieder 1981, 47). In other words, the literati tradition of autonomy and dissent, however slender and restricted, became available in the late nineteenth century as a mobilizable tradition. The space for autonomy from imperial rule sanctioned by Confucianism in the late imperial period came to be represented by the signifier *fengjian*. The work of Min Tu-ki, Mizoguchi Yūzō, and others has shown how *fengjian* discourse had served historically as a counterpoint to the tradition of the centralized imperial state. By the Qing period, *fengjian* ideas were no longer employed to displace the imperial state but as reformist programs designed to restrict the authority of the imperial state. Thus Gu Yanwu appealed to *fengjian* principles to advocate local autonomy, free from the rule of avoidance, whereby only officials from outside of the province could serve and for no more than three years in a particular county. Huang Zongxi called for the institutionalization of gentry participation in local administration to check the arbitrary exercise of power in the *junxian* system of the centralized imperial state. In the context of late imperial China, the *fengjian* tradition should be understood not in our modern representation of feudalism as a reactionary movement to bring back the past, still less to oppress peasants, but as a critique of imperial power's encroachment upon the locality and community, especially during the late Ming and early Qing when gentry power in the localities began to consolidate against the state (Mizoguchi 1991, 345–46). In other words, we have to recover its dispersed significance concealed by its semantic transformation in the twentieth century.

Reformers in the late nineteenth century, from Feng Guifen to the 1898 reformers such as Kang Youwei, Liang Qichao, and Huang Zunxian, appealed to the early Qing *fengjian* tradition to both preserve the autonomy of local society and simultaneously bring this society into the modernization project. Thinkers such as Kang Youwei also located the "public realm" (*gong*) within the *fengjian* tradition and its goal of making a public world (Min Tu-ki 1989, 119, 126; Mizoguchi 1991, 348–50). Rankin's study of Zhejiang local elite discourse reveals the persistence of appeals to *fengjian* ideas in order to curb autocratic centralism and enhance the role of local elites and public opinion in national decision making. References to the Zhou period as one favoring debate and even the "sprouts of parliamentarianism" appeared in a Shenbao editorial of 1887 (Rankin 1986, 164, 160–64). This defense of societal autonomy culminated in the reform efforts of the late 1890s—in the Hunan reform movement of Governor Chen Baozhen and Huang Zunxian and, to some extent, in the court's 100 Days Reform. For these reformers at this time, including Liang Qichao and Huang Zunxian, the *fengjian* tradition was useful not only to invoke a realm of public discussion, but also to enable the transition to their plans for constitutionally based local self-government (Liang Qichao n.d., c. 1897; Huang Zunxian n.d., c. 1897).

Huang Zunxian's opening address to the Nanxuehui or Southern Academy appealed to the virtues of the *fengjian* system in creating a modern nation. Huang argued that the *fengjian* system had a long life because it could sustain a close relationship between the rulers and the people and promote the public interest, in distinct opposition to the centralized administration or the *junxian* system in which officials chosen through the examination system oppressed the people treating them "like their fish and meat." Here, of course, Huang was invoking the historical narrative of gentry paternalism through which advocates of the *fengjian* system had stressed the superiority of local rule over rule by centralized officials. Like these earlier advocates, Gu Yanwu and Huang Zongxi, Huang pinpointed the rule of avoidance. Not only did imperial officials have little sympathy or trust with the people, they were forced to rely on a host of nonstatutory underlings—such as secretaries, clerks, and runners—who were extremely rapacious. In contrast, Huang likened rule by local notables to the nurturing attitude of a father toward his family, which was close and dear to him (Huang Zunxian n.d., c. 1897, 139–41). By infusing the present administrative system with the ancient principles of *fengjian*, not only could China attain the ideals of the ancient republic, but the principle of Great Unity could ultimately spread throughout the world.

Of course, what is of interest in this formulation is the manner in which it is used to propel China into the modern age. This was mostly left to Liang Qichao, the brains behind the radical Hunan reform movement. In an essay introducing Huang's inaugural address to the Southern Academy, Liang revealed that the goal of this society was to regenerate Hunan and the south by combining the ancient principles of *fengjian* with Western law. In this way, these areas could protect the Confucian faith and the people (even if not the nation) in the event that China was divided up by the foreign powers (Huang Zunxian n.d., c. 1897, 132–33, 138). From the Three Dynasties of antiquity until the Tang and the Song, the ancients, who were wiser than the Westerners, had employed local people to govern. Since the consolidation of imperial despotism, the bureaucracy and its underlings had oppressed the people from the outside. Now the only means of reopening the channels between those above and those below was to renew the strength of the village by returning to the intentions of the ancients and grasping the legal system of the West. The point of Western laws was to check the unpredictability and irregularities on the part of those who held power (Liang Qichao n.d., c. 1897, 133).

Thereupon, Liang went on to draw up a remarkably comprehensive vision for Hunan. The blending of *fengjian* with modern principles was extended to a detailed account of grassroots initiative: if a village decided to build a road or a bridge, then the decision would not arbitrarily be made by the bureaucrats or the village rich. The households would meet and determine who should contribute how much money or labor and, having made the decision, all would have to follow the rule in its execution. This, according to Liang, was not only the way of the Western nations, it was also the way of the villages in China, which as Huang Zunxian pointed out, had managed to retain the moral virtues of *fengjian* in their social fabric (Huang Zunxian n.d., c. 1897, 140–41). What the reformers needed to do was to extend this model to the county, the province, and finally to the nation. The means to achieve this was to establish branches of the Southern Academy from the provincial capital to the localities, which would select their most talented to participate in them. Thus the academy was a central feature of Liang's plan. Although in name it was an academy, this institution was not only a forum to learn and debate new knowledge, but also a forum to generate ways to strengthen the nation and the faith (Liang Qichao n.d., c. 1897, 134–35). The academy was to be the political expression of local society that would not only share power but jointly devise the future of China with the organs of state power.

I wish to take up the central role of the study society in two directions of inquiry. We will see below how they can be seen as elements of a civil society; here, I want to explore the gentry paternalism that Liang's vision sought to perpetrate. Liang repeatedly states that their basic goal was to extend rights or powers (*quan*) to the people. At the same time, however, it was necessary to first extend this power to the scholars because power follows knowledge: only if knowledge grows will power grow. He gives us a quick lesson in an early evolutionist understanding of the relation between power and knowledge. He cites the example of colonial India, where he believes that Indians were unable to ascend above the sixth or seventh level of occupation (*shiye*; presumably in the civil service). Since only the British were able to serve beyond this level, the learning of the Indians was blocked. However, since Indians possessed wisdom in the period before they lost their nation, this previous knowledge enabled them to ascend to the second level in the present, and they might even ascend to the first. However, not so the Africans, the American Indians, the southeast Asians, and others who are like slaves and animals (and have no knowledge). In a few decades, their kind will be extinguished (Liang Qichao n.d., c. 1897, 130). The point of this curious evolutionist example is to drive home the precedence of knowledge over power. Although the reformers wished to extend rights to the people, they first needed to extend knowledge among the scholar-gentry through the study associations. And it is through their efforts that the people and officials would be enlightened (Liang Qichao n.d., c. 1897, 131, 135).

Thus *fengjian* ideas were part of a paternalistic ideology that would empower the local gentry—in what Frederic Wakeman has called "gentry home rule"—and deferred the question of popular sovereignty. We also have to remember that the 100 Days Reform of 1898, which in many ways grew out of the Hunan experiment, evinced a plan not just for a strong society but also for a strong state. Liang and Kang's reformist ideas were based upon the Meiji reforms and that of Peter the Great and thus also served as a model for later state-building. Nonetheless, their plans for a parliament and constitutional local self-government empowering local elites reveal the importance of societal initiative as much as it was to be a program of renovation led by the central state (Mizoguchi 1991, 348–49; Grieder 1981, 81). The importance of *fengjian* ideas and their mobilization by late Qing reformers derives not only from their seeking to preserve the *autonomy* of the literati, but from the *autonomy* of society itself (of which the literati would be the guardians). Embedding societal initiative within a Confucian historical discourse represented an effort to legitimate the interdependence of state and society. As Min Tu-ki has argued so persuasively, the opening of local and provincial assemblies in the 1900s was a result of "the process of combining the spirit of traditional reforms centering around *feng-chien* (*fengjian*) ideals with modern demands for more changes" (Min Tu-ki 1989, 136).

The Southern Academy and other study societies that sprung up in the late 1890s were the first fruit of the mobilization of this counterhistory of *fengjian* to create a public sphere. These societies, which proliferated among both literati and commoners in the decade between the end of the Sino-Japanese War and the crystallization of political parties in the early 1900s, embedded critical discussion of, and autonomy from, the imperial state in the late Qing. Research in the People's Republic and elsewhere has counted about seventy-five of these societies, the most famous of which were, apart from the Southern Academy of Hunan, the Qiangxuehui (begun by Kang Youwei and Liang Qichao in 1895) and Baoguohui of Beijing (Li Wenhai 1983, 48–50). However, this number does not include the many more unnamed informal small groups that met irregularly and somewhat clandestinely because of the ban on the Qiangxuehui in 1895. These societies were committed to strengthening China by fostering public opinion and striving to attain "popular rights" (*shen minquan*). They engaged in a wide range of activities, such as the dissemination of modern knowledge through informal lending libraries and publications and the advocacy of social reform through movements against foot-binding, opium smoking, and the like (Li Wenhai 1983, 57–58, 68). The Southern Academy, for instance, provided services in such areas as public works, famine relief, the legal system, and prison reform (Sung Wook-shin 1976, 316). Such societies were quintessentially a part of the public sphere because they were not politically institutionalized. They differed from later political parties in the broadness of their goals, in the looseness of the criteria of admission, and in that they did not aim to capture political power. Yet by defying a political ban, by developing public opinion, by extending the "people's" rights, one might say that these study societies represented a practical defense of the autonomy of civil society from the imperial state.[2]

The reformers of the 1890s occupied a discursive position that was

2. By about 1904, the impetus for the defense of the public sphere moved into the burgeoning world of journalism. A recent essay by Joan Judge reveals how journalists and editors vigorously defended "public opinion" (*yulun*). The Shanghai-based newspaper *Shibao* regarded "public opinion" as the "final arbiter of moral standards and as the ultimate political tribunal before which the caprices of officialdom were tried" (Judge 1994, 65).

in-between the history of China in the Enlightenment mode and the history of China which authorized ancient forms to serve as moral guides for the present. This is a truly hybrid discourse because we are unable to determine if the discourse of modernity assimilated the historical narrative of *fengjian*, or if the promotion of associational life could be seen to further the goal of the Great Unity. Both tendencies existed. From this in-between position, the historical actors of the time seized an alternative history to create a narrative that was consonant with their understanding of the contemporary world. Later we will see how, when Liang gains a deeper commitment to the discourse of the modern nation-state system, he will come to reject what was an enabling hybridity.

Thus, if Chinese historical traditions did not only or necessarily hinder autonomous societal initiative but also prefigured the emergence of civil society at the turn of the century, we must turn our attention to the global discourse on modernity and state power in the world to understand the forces that finally sought to limit this societal initiative. We have seen how a new world order emerged toward the latter third of the nineteenth century, in which the only recognized actors on the world scene were sovereign nation-states (Bull and Watson 1976). The ideological force behind the imperative of state-building was none other than this system of nation-states. By the late nineteenth and early twentieth centuries, states all over the world were beginning to expand their role and command of society in the name of the nation.

We tend to confine our understanding of statism as a late nineteenth- and early twentieth-century phenomenon to certain European nations, Japan, and, secondarily, to countries like China. But the *discourse* of state power which authorized state expansion in the name of the nation was truly global. And this discourse was deeply entrenched in the organized intellectual centers of the nation we have come to regard as having the most powerful anti-statist tradition, the United States of America. Daniel Rodgers' remarkable work on keywords, such as the "State" in late nineteenth-century United States, shows how, like the law and the historical profession (see chapter 1 in this book), the discipline of political science, born in the post–Civil War era of intensifying class and ethnic divisions, saw its mission as an enormous "coherence-making" enterprise (Rodgers 1987, 156, 169). Rodgers views the project of these professionals (he includes Woodrow Wilson at Princeton in the 1890s among them) as an effort to replace the Revolution's language of popular rights and social contract with that of the sovereignty of the State. The State became a moral unity and a legal person; its will was the general will and it could be neither "possessed or resisted or laid claim to even by the most wild-eyed of Populists" (Rodgers 1987, 162).

Rodgers finds two sources of this extraordinary preoccupation with the omnipotence of the state which continued well into the first decades of the next century. First, the links of political science with nationalism. It is not surprising that political science, which was a "science of Union principles," sought to resolve for good the indestructibility of the nation. The second was the discipline's fascination with German theorists of the State, such as Johann Bluntschli and Rudolf von Gneist, whose theories of the science of the State were far more popular than anything they read by the English or anyone else (Rodgers 1987, 166–67). The reader familiar with modern East Asian history will be struck by this remarkable coincidence, because these German figures were the very ones who exercised such a strong influence on the course of statism in Japan and China. But, of course, it was no coincidence: as they entered the era of organized popular politics, nation-states responded by developing strong states legitimated by the rhetoric of a corporate nationalism.

In China as well, the narratives of the nation came soon enough in the early twentieth century to sanction the precedence of state over society and led to the demise of the effort to mobilize civil society toward the creation of a modern nation. Much of this discourse was transmitted by way of Japan. The example of how Yuan Shikai, president of the Chinese Republic, implemented ideas of state-building that originated with Japanese advisors and students returned from Japan will be discussed shortly. Just around the turn of the century, when Yuan was implementing his state-building goals, modern nationalism was also sweeping across China. This nationalism generated support for a strong centralized state capable of defending (and defining) the borders of the nation from the imperialist powers. As these ideas spread widely among the intelligentsia, the intellectual foundations were laid for an ideology that emphasized the sovereignty of the "national whole" and a strong state as the representative of the nation. Once again the Japanese influence was critical. Thousands of Chinese intellectuals and students in Japan between the years of 1898 and 1906 were influenced not only by the intellectual currents they encountered, but also by the reality of a strong Japanese state (Huang 1972, 36–37). The late Meiji period was one of extraordinary ferment in Japanese intellectual and political life. It was a period in which party politics was beginning to take shape around the Meiji constitution and in which radical thinkers of all stripes flourished

(Najita 1974, 102–15). But the 1890s was also a period in which the ideology of the emperor system was being developed and state-building penetrated even into the deepest recesses of community life in the villages (Pyle 1978, 96–101).[3]

While nationalist revolutionaries like Hu Hanmin and Wang Jing-wei wrote about overthrowing the monarchy, they incorporated into their long-range strategy the idea of a tutelary stage in the revolutionary process (Grieder 1981, 187). Inspired by contemporary ideas of nationalist History, they saw the national community as the community of citizens, the "constituency which creates the state, united in freedom, equality and universal affection. This is the spirit which informs the fundamental law of the state (*kuo-fa*), which is simply the general will of the citizenry" (quoted in Grieder 1981, 183). Missing in this picture of the general will is, of course, the reality of its absence: the competitiveness and messiness of civil society which is part and parcel of its dynamism. Indeed, revolutionary thinkers often spoke about the lack of privilege and classes in Chinese society (often in the same breath in which they spoke of the need for a socialistic state). A national collectivity, embodying what Wang called the "spirit of China's moral law" would naturally appear with the destruction of the Manchu state (see Gasster 1969, 141). Such a formulation of the general will, as Charles Taylor has warned us, is a disguised, but sufficient condition of statist ideology. The subsequent section examines how these two alternative narratives of the nation, the hybrid and the statist, were played out in the policies of statesmen in the twentieth century.

NARRATIVES IN ACTION: STATE BUILDING AND CIVIL SOCIETY

The first serious efforts by the Chinese state to transform itself in order to enter the system of modern nation-states took place with the *xinzheng* or New Policy reforms (c. 1902–8). The circumstances under which the Qing state was forced to undertake this project should be kept in mind. The humiliation of the Boxer defeat and the

3. Pyle notes that by means of the Town and Village Decree of 1888, for instance, 76,000 hamlets were consolidated into some 15,000 administrative towns and villages, thus enabling the central government to extend its control directly into these villages. In 1906, villages were ordered to consolidate the myriad, 190,000 Shinto shrines into a central shrine located in each administrative village. With the establishment of administrative control over local ritual life, the channels for communicating the ideology of the emperor system were completed (Pyle 1978, 100–101). Some of Yuan Shikai's efforts to establish a consolidated hierarchy of temples to the military heroes Guandi and Yue Fei may have found its inspiration in these Meiji policies.

imposition of the Boxer protocol was, of course, what convinced the imperial state that its very survival depended on a program of modernization. At the same time, it could only pay for the Boxer indemnities and the new reforms by the fiscal strengthening of the state—the enhancement of its powers to extract new revenues and contain the consequent unrest (Duara 1988a, 2–3). Thus, for the imperial state, modernization was inextricably tied to the program of state-building.

State-building is a process whereby the state seeks to increase and deepen its command over society. The concept derives from eighteenth-century Europe, when the state sought to subordinate, coopt, or destroy the relatively autonomous structures of local communities in a bid to increase its command of local resources and develop new institutions under the aegis of the state (Tilly 1975). This trend was coeval with the growth of civil society and the emergence of the public sphere and is what makes it difficult to pose a full-blown civil society historically and ontologically prior to the modern state in Europe. Modern civil society emerged in part from the survival of certain of these structures—or at least the principle underlying them, such as corporate self-regulation—and, in part, as new forms of social life spawned by capitalism (Cohen and Arato 1992, 86–87).

State-building in China involved an effort to extend the bureaucracy, rationalize its workings, increase state surveillance over communities through new administrative organs including the police, establish a new culture through modern schools and, most of all, increase its revenues (Duara 1988a, 59–64). While it was clear from the beginning of the *xinzheng* reforms that the state would inevitably play a significant role in introducing modernity and would thus need to be strengthened, it was not at all clear through what means it would expand its role and achieve its goals in rural society. Most specifically, how would it tap that vast and multitudinal realm of associational life that characterized rural society? This section focuses attention on two efforts to strengthen or "modernize" the nation by implementing two different strategies in the rural areas of north China. Each was associated, loosely to be sure, with each of the two narratives of statist nationalism and the *fengjian*-civil society hybrid encountered in the political discourse of the turn of the century.

Even in the villages and rural markets of northern China, where one rarely found powerful elite families and strong corporate organizations that were commonplace in the Yangzi valley and further south, the richness of associational life was quite astounding. The work of several scholars, including my own previous work, reveals that rural society in northern China had associations for all kinds of activities. Associations existed for self-defense and crop-watching and for economic activities such as irrigation management, the provision of credit, and co-operation in farming. Temple societies, drama associations, and pilgrimage associations flourished to satisfy religious and recreational activities, and elite-managed trusts existed for the management of education and charities.[4] To be sure, I am not arguing that this was a civil society in the European sense. On the other hand, there were certainly elements of a civil society here that modernizers could mobilize to generate their vision of a new society. How would they tap the resources, entrepreneurship, and the associational tradition itself to develop a modern society?

Two features about these associations are noteworthy. First, there was no great status distinction between degree-holders and other village leaders in the management of this sphere; many of these associations were managed by the ordinary rural people themselves. This was not a society marked by impenetrable hierarchies. Second, many, if not most of these associations took the overt form of religious associations. That is to say, even when the principal function of the association was not religious, they often performed certain rituals in common and were brought together by allegiance to a common god or temple. Take, for instance, the irrigation associations of Xingtai county in Hebei. Each irrigation association pledged allegiance to its own Dragon God temple; when it co-operated for purposes of dredging with other neighboring associations, everyone involved offered a prayer together to the larger Dragon God temple in the market town (Duara 1988a, 26–37). The role of religion in such self-defense organizations as the Red Spears are well-known (Perry 1980). Moreover, most temple associations, large and small, often possessed land and other economic resources which were used to fund their activities. Sometimes, other uses of these resources overshadowed the purely religious ones. Thus credit-rotation societies were often tied to, or grew out of, small, voluntary village religious associations such as the ones to worship the goddess of Taishan in Shandong villages. More generally, the association of public life of the village with the religious domain is clear when one sees how the village elite

4. The bibliography on this topic is extensive. I shall list just a few: Li Jinghan, *Dingxian shehui gaikuang diaocha* [*Investigation of Social Conditions in Ding County*] (1933); Hatada Takashi, *Chūgoku sonraku to kyōdōtai riron* [*Chinese Villages and the Theory of the Village Community*] (1976); Sidney Gamble, *North China Villages: Social, Political and Economic Activities Before 1933* (1963); Wang Huning, *Dangdai Zhongguo cunluo jiazu wenhua: dui Zhongguo shehui xiandaihua de yixiang tansuo* [*The Culture of the Rural Family in Contemporary China: An Investigation of the Modernization of Chinese Society*] (1991).

sought to exercise its general leadership of the village by dominating the villagewide temple societies to the tutelary deity, Tudigong or Guandi (Duara 1988a, 124–38). Thus, religious organization was associated with the realm of public affairs in the village and partially fulfilled the authoritative role that is played by the legal system in a modern civil society.

We have also encountered a different type of religious association in chapters 3 and 4—the secret societies and sectarian groups. These associations often secured the parallel, quasi-secretive community in these villages and rural markets. We have glimpsed, in the case of the Small Swords and others, how they were committed to the defense of their autonomy from the state and against those who threatened their vision of their life and world. Chapter 7 provides a better sense of the differences between the secretive and defensive versus the public and coordinating role of religious authority in rural China. For the moment, I simply wish to register the existence of fierce traditions of resistance to external authority within rural society.

In the early *xinzheng* period, two models of state-led modernizing reform were tried: that of Yuan Shikai and Zhao Erxun. Let us first consider the efforts of Zhao Erxun to strengthen the nation-state in Shanxi. As acting governor of Shanxi, Zhao, together with Wu Tingxie, acting prefect of Taiyuan, promulgated a series of reforms in 1902 that would mobilize village resources to attain state goals. Roger Thompson locates Zhao's reformist efforts within the *fengjian* tradition of reform. I am unable to trace any ties between Zhao and the reformers of the late 1890s considered above. Thompson sees him as successor to the particular lineage of this tradition linked with statecraft, to men like Gu Yanwu and Feng Guifen (Thompson 1988, 196). In matters of reform at the local level, especially at the county level and below, these thinkers had drawn from the *fengjian* tradition. Seeking to inject elements of *fengjian* into the local political system, they urged the officialization of local leaders and heritable magistracies. By the late nineteenth century, this amounted to establishing official or semi-official positions staffed by local people elected by their peers (Min Tu-ki 1989, 133). Zhao's ties with *fengjian* reformism of the 1890s was perhaps more discursive rather than direct.

Zhao sought to recruit locally prestigious and influential elites as leaders (*shezhang*) of the reconstituted administrative units known as the *xiangshe*. These units, which were to be relatively small (about ten villages) and flexible in size, were to be the principal agencies of reform. It was important to mobilize locally prestigious figures to lead and identify with these organizations not only so that they could fulfill their reform goals, but also so that they could resist the predatory yamen functionaries (Thompson 1988, 194–95). To be sure, such thinking embedded paternalistic assumptions, but in the context of an expanding state power, if such a type of local empowerment was effective, it might have been able to check the severe exactions and intrusions of state power. The ideal conditions for the success of this reform design were a moderate and accommodative form of state expansion which relied on local elites for the attainment of its goals. In this way, the vigorous associational life of the villages might have been brought into the modernization process and the narrative of *fengjian*, which would soon be regarded as anachronistic and, indeed, reactionary, might have produced a modern civil society in China.

There is every indication that Zhao sought such a solution—an accommodative, indigenous strategy to address the problems of modernity. As Thompson shows, the *xiangshe* around the turn of the century was both a community organization engaged in various local affairs—most spectacularly with the management of temple fairs and opera performances, as well as with the collection of government taxes. Thus they were important both as agents of the state and as organizations of the community. In a directive of December 1902, Zhao tried to persuade the *xiangshe* leaders to use a portion of the very substantial subscriptions collected for the operas to fund educational reform. Zhao, who saw the potential of these wealthy associations for financing the modernization program, nonetheless sought to retain these vital communal institutions as well as the prestige and reputation of their leaders (Thompson 1988, 200–202). This was a very different response to the resource potential embedded within local society than the one which became ascendant and to which I shall now turn.

The reform efforts of Yuan Shikai represent a more distinct break from late Qing reformist traditions. They reveal the influence of state-building ideas which had now become embedded in the global ideology of the nation-state system. The most immediate channel through which this influence made itself felt on the Yuan administration was the Japanese connection. Li Zongyi has effectively argued that in military and other reforms, Yuan felt that the Japanese model was most appropriate to Chinese conditions and, besides, Japanese advisors cost less as well. Even before his assumption of the presidency, Japanese advisors in Zhili under Yuan's administration grew from 13 (out of 26 in the nation as a whole) in 1901, to 85 (out of 218) in 1904, and then to 174 (out of 555) in 1908 (Li Zongyi 1980, 112–15). An entire generation of students trained in Japan, such as the renowned director of the Baoding Academy, historian of the Renaissance, and translator of Tomonaga Sanjurō's "Modern Conceptions of the Self," Jiang Fangzhen, served in key positions in his government both before and after 1911 (Boorman 1968, 314).

As Stephen McKinnon and others have shown, one of Yuan's most successful state-building reforms was the introduction of the modern police in Zhili around 1902, first into cities like Tianjin and Baoding and then into the countryside (MacKinnon 1983, 3–4). Yuan was impressed by the plans to institute a modern police force submitted by Kawashima Naniwa, the commander of the Beijing police district under Japanese control during the post–Boxer occupation of the capital (Strand 1989, 68). Trained in the new police academies, the police force emerged as professionals, engaged in surveillance and keeping order. As such, they did not resemble past surveillance forces like the Beijing gendarmerie, the neighborhood associations, or the yamen runners, and it was clear that Yuan sought to use them as a means to penetrate beyond local elites and exercise direct control over the populace. When police reform was extended to the rural areas in Zhili, an entirely new subadministrative unit, the *qu* or ward was developed for policing and tax-collecting activity. It is important to note that the *qu* did not conform to traditional centers of gentry concentration and thus represented a classic instrument of state-building which sought to bypass and erode local structures of authority. Recognizing the statist alternative to their authority, gentry elites tried to offset or block the expansion of the Beijing controlled police in their home areas (MacKinnon 1983, 4–5).

Establishing the police force was only one aspect of the modernizing agenda of the *xinzheng* reforms, although one might consider it one of the most important from the point of view of extending state control. Other reforms included the establishment of local self-government, the establishment of modern education, the rationalization of agencies involved in tax information and collection, among others (Duara 1988a, 59–73). For now, I will outline the manner in which the Yuan administration and subsequent administrations in the early twentieth century went about securing their goals in the rural areas of Zhili and Shandong. Particularly noticeable is the contrast which the attitude of the Yuan regime—especially during his governor-generalship of Zhili and Shandong in the early years of the century—presented with the efforts of Zhao Erxun.

In these villages, the administration tended to target village religion—including all of its properties and income—as the single resource which would address their various different goals, such as establishing schools, dispelling superstition and waste, increasing *tankuan* taxes (for both indemnity payments and to finance these very reforms), and formalizing village government (to implement reforms and serve as *tankuan* collector). The appropriation of temples would provide buildings for schools and village government, the desecration of divine images would eradicate the bases of superstition, the incomes of temple and religious properties would release funds for village government. Thus, the Yuan administration began the process of systematically dismantling the institutional foundations of popular religion, a process which was carried out periodically throughout the Republican period (see chapter 3).

The resistance to this appropriation is recorded in chapter 3. But just as there was resistance by sectarians, secret societies, and others, there was also a measure of success during the initial phase of this transformation, that is, in the first fifteen years or so of the twentieth century. Despite reports of peasant resistance to the appropriation from many villages in Zhili and Shandong, village governments were able to take over temple properties and buildings with considerable success (Duara 1988a, 148–55; Li Jinghan 1933, 422–23). This success was enabled by village *elite* cooperation with the goals of the state in contrast with sectarian or secret society resistance. While the state-building project of Yuan Shikai, unlike that of Zhao Erxun, did not actively incorporate a positive role for elites as representatives of their communities, nonetheless, in the early years of *xinzheng* reform, the new modernizing program attracted the village elite. The local elite saw new avenues of social mobility in the new schools and the formal positions of village government. Education had, of course, always been a route to advancement in imperial China and now it seemed to be more readily accessible to the village elite. In other words, the Yuan administration secured the cooperation of the village elite in the state-led modernization program despite itself. Through the 1910s, 1920s and 1930s, as it became increasingly evident that state revenue needs would prevail and elite roles would be displaced, this elite became more and more alienated from the state project of both state-building and modernization.

In *Culture, Power, and the State: Rural North China, 1900–1942*, I detailed the process whereby an alliance offered by the village elite to the state to participate in the mobilization of rural resources for modernization was destroyed. Though it can hardly be denied that warlordism played a most significant role in making political life intolerable for the elite, I argued that it was the manner in which the state sought to extend its power and extract rural resources that alienated not only the rural people but also the elite.[5] Right up through the 1940s, the different governments in northern China sought to extend the reach of government below the county level. I have already spoken of the establishment of the *qu*. In 1921, the *qu* was temporarily eclipsed by the *xiang* or township, and in 1928, the Nationalists, influenced by the Yan Xishan model in Shanxi, introduced the *xiangzhen* system to administer rural society directly by the state (Kuhn 1975, 284). Despite the efforts of the Nationalist government to break the elite hold over the power structure and fiscal resources of the *xiang*, they were actually unable to do so, because the *xiang*, supposedly a numerical administrative unit of between a hundred and a thousand households, was often no different from the natural village. Only with the Japanese domination of northern China did the area witness full-fledged state-building in the rural areas. By actually enforcing the *daxiang* or large administrative village, the Japanese administration forced the break-up of the local village power structure and its replacement by administrative personnel responsible only to the state.

One also needs to consider the nature of the demands that were made through these administrative channels. The Nationalists had intended the *qu* and the *xiang* to be not merely extractive agencies, but also agencies for modernization—to register the population, rationalize the land tax, develop education, participatory institutions and the economic infrastructure. As is well known, however, it was the policing and taxing functions that predominated. To a great extent, this was a result as well as a cause of the top-down statist strategy followed by the Nationalists and by some of the stable warlord powers in northern China such as Yan Xishan and Feng Yuxiang.[6] In order to effectively penetrate rural society, these regimes needed more revenues to pay their administrative personnel; yet, in order to collect these increased revenues, they had to resort to inefficient and extremely unpopular policies. Village officials had already tried to deprive the rural folk of their popular religious life; now they were expected to collect regular and irregular *tankuan* taxes from the peasants, to supervise the deed tax and commercial taxes that villagers had historically evaded, and to lead land investigations that

5. The following three paragraphs are taken from chapters 3 and 7 in my book.

6. Zhang Xin's dissertation (1991) on elite power and local administration in Henan during the Republic under Yuan Shikai, Feng Yuxiang, and the KMT regime reveals a similar political process as the one I have outline above. See, for instance, pp. 267–68.

would uncover concealed land held by elite and commoners alike. Naturally, no self-respecting village leader who wanted to maintain face in village society could afford to alienate his fellow villagers to such an extent. Ideally, the village elite could be mobilized to the cause of the state if partnership with the state could enhance their opportunities as well as their prestige in the village. In the best of times, the imperial gentry, whose affiliation with the imperial state had given them status, opportunities and responsibilities in local society, had fulfilled this goal. How much more necessary was it to solicit the partnership of prestigious local leaders when the goal was to mobilize the energies of rural society for modernization.

Instead of mobilizing rural energies or even recruiting traditional village leaders, the excessive and alienating nature of state demands tended to produce a type of political opportunist in official positions whether in the village, the township, ward, county or at higher levels. Focusing at the lower levels of rural society reveals these opportunists as the infamous *tuhao* and *lieshen*, who saw in village office an opportunity for profit and power. They made their money in the same way as did other administrative functionaries—by adding their "commission" on every tax levied on the populace. They cared not a whit about their reputation among the rural populace because the basis of their power was located in their office, or in other words, in the state. At the same time, because of the poorly integrated nature of the lower level of the bureaucracy (who were barely paid and were expected, of course, to live off the "commission"), the state was also unable to supervise or control them. The state had not only not strengthened rural associations to act as a check on the power of these opportunists, it had actually weakened them. Consequently, these figures were transformed into local tyrants.

Several reformers and observers of the time saw the connection between this type of top-down or statist approach and the growth of arbitrary power in the countryside. Liang Shuming perhaps saw it more clearly than any other. Writing in the 1930s, Liang challenged the notion that the local bully was a feudal element, a leftover of earlier society. Rather, he stressed that the appearance of this type of figure in local politics was a recent phenomenon traceable to the efforts of the state to penetrate local society from the last years of the Qing, and particularly to the recent "self-government" efforts of the Nationalists (Liang Shuming 1971a, 275–76). Liang, the modern Confucian reformer, viewed this crisis from a *fengjian* vision or, rather, nightmare of the intrusive state. He declared,

If the spirit of laissez-faire (*wuwei*), which has been the system of rule for the last several thousand years has caused
their [the peasants'] lives to be unorganized and peaceful,
then it was also the reason for the fact that no more than
a handful of local bullies and evil gentry appeared during
this period. Now wherever the fearful self-government is
being enforced, you are bound to get the creation of local
bullies even in places where there had been none before.
(Liang Shuming 1971b, 198)

While his Confucian persuasion was doubtless responsible for the
moral romanticism implied in his view of imperial history, it also
gave this practical, grassroots reformer a special insight into how the
state, governed by a different, modern narrative of expansion could
play havoc with local communities.

Liang was hardly the only one to see the depredations caused by
this form of state-building. All of the grassroots reformers, such as
Tao Xingzhi and Yan Yangchu, confronted the heavy hand of statist
intervention (see Kuhn 1959 and Hayford 1990). The scholar Fei Xiao-
tong, writing not from a Confucian but a modernizing perspective,
observed how the need to develop the Chinese economy during the
Republican period had increased the functions of the central government and how the *baojia* surveillance system had weakened the principle of self-government—or what I have been referring to as associational life—in the rural areas. Fei characterized the old system as a
double-track system where the local leadership in rural society was
informally recognized to play a role in the system by organizing
to send back unpopular orders. The carrying out of orders from
the traditionally limited imperial government was shared by three
groups: the government or yamen functionaries, the local representative or intermediary (one he calls the *shangyao*), and the leaders
among the local elite or gentry. During the Nationalist period, when
a new top-down system was adopted, all three roles were combined
in the office of the *baocun*, who was expected to implement central government orders. However, Fei noted the difficulty which the
baocun faced: on the one hand, the orders from above were onerous
and impossible to ignore, on the other the mediating role played
by the tripartite division of earlier times having disappeared, the
baocun could not get the orders implemented among the people. Thus
Fei concluded,

the local community has become a dead-end in the political
system. . . . The *pao-chia* system, thus, has not only dis-

rupted the traditional community organization but has also
hampered the developing life of the people. It has destroyed the safety valve of the traditional political system.
. . . Though it is true that through the *pao-chia* system a
more centralized system has been realized, greater effi-
ciency has resulted in form only, since when there is a
deadlock at the bottom, orders tend not to be carried out actually. (Fei Hsiao-tung 1953, 89–90)

WEAK STATES AND THE STATIST DISCOURSE

The accommodationist language of the *fengjian* narrative which appeared briefly around the turn of the century was soon eclipsed by
that of a highly interventionist state. This expanding state apparatus
excluded and destroyed autonomous societal initiatives in the modernizing process. At the same time, it also failed to reach its goals of
a modern society because it was unable to mobilize the energy and
resources of a vigorous society. But one could well say that it was
not the state-building project per se, but on the contrary, the *absence*
of a strong state capable of providing legal guarantees for civil society
that ultimately had the effect of excluding societal initiative. After all,
let us recall Charles Taylor's emphasis on the state as equally necessary to society as society to state. Indeed, the French scholar Marie
Claire Bergere has argued that civil society in China needed a strong
state to secure its borders, create the infrastructure, and guarantee
its autonomy (Bergere 1989, 8).

Thus to clarify: what we have in early twentieth-century China was
by no means a strong state, but rather a strong statist discourse which
found little use for civil society in the modernization project. This
statist discourse authorized a weak state to expand its role and command over society. However, the state-building project was inefficient and unsuccessful. Both because of the policies it undertook as
well as its failure to maintain law and order, it ended up deforming
and demobilizing civil society. Early twentieth-century China was
characterized by a weak state and a strong statist discourse.

We have seen how this statist discourse was communicated
through nationalism around the turn of the twentieth century. In this
last segment I wish to return to the figure of Liang Qichao, who was
a central player in propagating the *fengjian* vision of reform in the
years before 1898. Liang is important because he is also a central
player in propagating the statist vision of modern nationalism. The
conversion came in a matter of a few years. Liang's conversion allows
us to better understand the nexus between nationalism and statism.

By the time of his 1903 visit to the United States, Liang abandoned his earlier liberal-democratic ideas and began to advocate a tutelary autocracy as a political form most suited for a newly emergent nation-state. Liang had become keenly aware not only of the workings of the nation-state system, but also of its Darwinian and imperialist dimensions. External competition among communities now became more important to him than internal competition and he began to call for a strong state to consolidate and save China. Indeed, he noted that while liberalism and individualism had been dominant since the eighteenth century, the late nineteenth century had witnessed the expansion of state power (Chang 1971, 243–46, 254–56).

The statist turn in Liang's ideas took place during the years he spent in Japan since 1898. It bore the impact of the ideas of Katō Hiroyuki—a conservative thinker who had translated Bluntschli's work on the theory of the "organic state" and constitutional monarchy and had had a great influence on late Meiji statist developments. Katō rejected popular rights and, drawing on German social Darwinism, developed a theory of the "rights of the strong." His ideas influenced Liang's understanding of imperialism as the competition between the peoples of entire nations. Nationalism and imperialism (or colonialism) were the necessary outcome of historical evolution (Yamashita 1984, 87).

My concern here is not so much to understand the reasons for this conversion, but to see how an empowering representation such as *fengjian* becomes disempowered. What historical significance does the repression of this earlier meaning come to possess?

We saw how even in the introduction to Huang Zunxian's lecture, Liang's ideas of *fengjian* coexisted, perhaps uneasily, with certain evolutionist notions. Yet neither determined the other. The change in his thinking about *fengjian* is indicated in two essays written by him in 1898 and 1902. The first of these, "On the Principle of Succession of Monarchical and Popular Power," was written during the 1898 reforms and reflects to some extent an argument justifying the central role of the imperial state in these reforms. To be sure, Liang works within the categories of Confucian evolutionism pioneered by Kang Youwei, but the emancipatory vision of the *fengjian* ideal of no more than a year or two ago has disappeared. He interprets the three ages discussed by Confucius in the Spring and Autumn Annals as the (1) Age of Disorder or the age of many lords: the age of tribal chiefs, of the aristocracy and feudalism; (2) the Age of Ascending Peace or the age of one lord, which he equates with the centralized monarchy; and (3) the Age of Great Unity in which the people rule and all barriers among the people of the world disappear. While there is a complicated discussion of the subdivisions of each era and their value, there is, overall, a relentless progression from one to the other. *Fengjian*, or the age of many lords, takes the brunt of the attack: it is a system rife with hierarchy, warfare, and suffering. Just as America, Germany, Italy, and Japan had recently unified their separate, feuding states, so too had Confucius transformed the era of many lords into the era of a single lord which produced much goodness (Liang Qichao 1898, 26–27). This, of course, contrasts with the dominant view of the earlier reformers that Liang too once shared, a view which criticized the centralized imperial state and emphasized Confucius's ideal as the return to the pristine form of *fengjian* embodied in the Three Dynasties of antiquity.

I have tried to suggest that Liang's change of view can be, at least partially, understood in the context of state-led reforms. Certainly, Kang Youwei saw the period of Ascending Peace (*xiaokang*) dominated by the imperial state in positive terms during these years, although he was later to claim that he had long viewed it negatively (Hsiao Kung-chuan 1975, 79–80). Moreover, the progressive Confucian evolutionism to which Kang and Liang subscribed at this time, while also hybrid and generative in its own way, did not permit of a return to an ancient ideal. Indeed, Liang's strict adherence to this evolutionism causes him to suspect any trope of return, whether it is in the Chinese or Western narratives. He criticizes Yan Fu for asserting that Europe could develop democracy because of the ancient democratic traditions in Greece and Rome (which China lacked), thus implying that the embryo of democracy preceded monarchy. Liang uses the metaphor of geological evolution to see historical periods as impenetrable geological layers and in this way critique the teleology of a continuous evolution from ancient times to the present. There is one way, he writes, that he can understand this link with the severed past; and it must be one of the more striking similes in evolutionist discourse. The ideas of Greece and Rome must have erupted into the modern era as molten lava from various geological strata gushes out of the volcano's mouth (the Renaissance?) (Liang Qichao 1898, 30). But this is a chance event, not sufficiently powerful to characterize a whole era. His point is that no embryo of popular power is needed in an evolutionary scheme, whether in China or Europe. Rule by the people will necessarily emerge when the (telos of) Great Unity is attained. Unlike the democracies of the present in America and France, which still resemble the tribal chiefs of the Age of Disorder because these nations continue to fight each other, this will be the age of true democracy (Liang Qichao 1898, 31).

Liang's 1902 article, "On the Evolution of Autocratic Politics," dispenses with even this hybrid discourse of evolutionism. Liang was, by now, well on his way to adopting Katō's conservative social Darwinism and Bluntschli's conception of the organic state. The essay marks the incorporation of *fengjian* into modern evolutionism, in which it was, at best, a medieval anachronism and mostly a form of barbarism (Liang Qichao 1902b, 67–70). Tang Xiaobing (1991) has demonstrated how Liang was perhaps the first thinker to produce the History of China in the Enlightenment mode, History as linear and progressive. Moreover, chapter 1 shows that this History was the medium for the production of the nation as a part of the world system of nation-states in which it could survive only by acknowledging and participating in a competitive Darwinian world. This Historical narrative could not find a place for the hybrid narrative which looked toward ancient ideals as an empowering strategy. Despite *fengjian*'s becoming a relatively harmless political representation, its identification as Feudalism, as the Other of the master narrative of History, ensured that its critical possibilities would be lost. This loss also spelled the further loss of a narrative capable of mobilizing the dynamic associational life embedded within "traditional," popular religion.

History, which became the History of the nation-state in China and elsewhere, tends to narrate the evolving *unity* of the nation and becomes complicit in the project of the nation-state. This project privileges the unity of the nation-state and subordinates difference—unless the difference is mandated by the nation-state. Civil society in the modern world affirms the nation, but on its own terms. Strand writes about associations of rickshaw pullers and water-carriers who derived tremendous self-esteem from publicly participating in nationalist rallies, but who also used the public space to fight for their rightful demands (Strand 1989, 186–97 and chap. 11). In the eyes of the weak state, nationalist intellectuals and even warlords (who invoked the nation for their own purposes), this civil society amounted to national disunity.

We can appreciate the dilemmas of nation-builders who ultimately appealed to the unity of the nation to subordinate such fractiousness in the 1920s. But the Historical narrative of the nation-state, which celebrated its antiquity only in the vocabulary of modern discourse, had a very deep impact. By consigning such words and worlds as of *fengjian* to the dustbin of history, the narrative buried an incipient and indigenous history of civil society which a bifurcated history attentive to language has tried to recover. The old and new associations of Chinese civil society had worked heroically to manage villages and cities during warlord battles and to give night-soil collectors pride in their work. But the demands of the modern nation-state never permitted it to construct a discursive defense of its autonomy and the triumph of History buried access to a historical tradition which had once sanctioned its autonomy. We do not again see the articulation of the autonomy of civil society in the historical discourse of the twentieth century.

POSTSCRIPT: LIANG QICHAO AND THE SUPPLEMENT ON *FENGJIAN*

There is reason to believe that the genealogy of *fengjian* may not have ended quite so abruptly for Liang. The cracks and inconsistencies within a unified discourse which his hybrid vantage had once brought to view continued to nag him. The limitations of unilinear evolutionism, when applied to the Chinese experience, was one such doubt that Liang entertained, but significantly enough, he entertained it only as a supplement to his 1902 essay on the evolution of autocratic politics.

In this supplement, Liang compares the history of *fengjian* in China with that in Europe and Japan. In Europe, the destruction of feudalism was accomplished by popular power, often in alliance with the monarchy, and led ultimately to the emergence of popular sovereignty. Apparently abandoning his image of the volcanic eruption, Liang accepts the view that popular power embodied in the institutions of local self-governance had survived since the Greek republics through the feudal era. In Japan, during the three hundred years of feudalism dominated by the Tokugawa Shōgunate, the samurai held on to their autonomy in the domains. Liang compares this autonomous power to the aristocratic republics of ancient Greece. At any rate, it was this autonomy, (*zili,* comparable to, but distinguished from, popular power in the West) which also led ultimately to the emergence of popular sovereignty in Japan. By contrast, in China, feudalism was neither destroyed nor succeeded by popular power, but always by monarchical power. Neither scholars nor people participated in this overthrow, nor did they produce an ideology of opposition (Liang Qichao 1902c, 70–71).

This Chinese variance from the unilinear model is transformed into an insight that reevaluates the role of *fengjian,* albeit inexplicitly and only as a supplement. Europeans, he says, tend to regard feudalism as the worst possible form of rule. But from a Chinese perspective, feudalism possesses some value in harboring traditions of self-governance. For, as Liang says, the reason for the flourishing of the centralized state in China does not lie with the lack of popular power; nor does the reason for the lack of popular power lie with the flourishing of the centralized state. Despite their complaints about feudalism, the Europeans could have popular rule only because of the long duration of feudalism (and the tradition of self-rule) and the shortness of centralized rule, whereas China was unable to produce popular rule because feudalism declined a long time ago and centralized power (in which self-governance was impossible) ruled for so long (Liang Qichao 1902c, 71). Perhaps Liang never fully abandoned his hybrid perspective on *fengjian;* it followed him as a supplement to his evolutionism. We may wonder if it gave him the means to negotiate with the repressed.

6

PROVINCIAL NARRATIVES OF THE NATION: FEDERALISM AND CENTRALISM IN MODERN CHINA

THIS CHAPTER considers the rhetoric and politics of federalism and its enemies in China from 1900 until 1926. The signifier *fengjian* had lost much of its critical possibilities by the first decade of the twentieth century as its meaning changed to the Other of modernity. But until at least the 1927 revolution, which brought the KMT to power, the federalist forces in China continued to find relevant the politically and culturally invested space which had historically sanctioned the *fengjian* critique of centralized rule. In late imperial times, this space was the locality (*xiangtu, difang*) which covered a range of meaning from the ancestral hometown to the province. Organized around the inherited theme of empowering the locality to build the nation, the federalist alternative sought to secure the province as an autonomous, if not sovereign, power and basis upon which to construct the modern nation as a federalist polity.

I will not present an exhaustive account of the federalist movement; rather, I will try to write a bifurcated history by highlighting the relationship between two different "nation-views" in early twentieth-century China, the centralist and the federalist. No longer able to draw on the narrative of the *fengjian* tradition, advocates of federalism since the last decade of Qing rule struggled to voice their dissent from centralized rule by embedding sentiment for the locality within a series of modern discourses and theories, such as social Darwinism, constitutional theories of federalism, and an ingenious coupling of provincial autonomy with popular sovereignty. But try as they did to develop a new legitimating narrative, they were frustrated—in a bitter irony—precisely by charges that they exemplified the dark and divisive forces of *fengjian* in its modern sense. In the end, the interplay of power politics and authoritative language enabled the hegemonic, centralizing nationalist narrative to destroy and ideologically bury the federalist alternative early in the history of modern China.

THE PROVINCE AND THE LANGUAGE OF THE FEDERATED NATION

The question of the relationship between provincial and national identity in China has been argued differently by different scholars. Some have seen provincial identity as an obstacle to nationalism (Michael 1964), others as a vehicle for nationalism where provincial identity enabled the transition from a parochial to a wider identification with the nation (Fincher 1968, 224; Lary 1974). Both of these viewpoints emerge from a common modernization perspective which assumes a linear transition from tradition (parochialism or universalism) to nationalism. As Keith Schoppa points out, such views do not do justice to provincial consciousness as an integral and independent value in the Chinese outlook. He argues that provincialism and nationalism could coexist with equal degrees of intensity at any point in time, could merge into any combination of commitment, and could theoretically exist discretely (Schoppa 1977, 662). Indeed, his study of Zhejiang after 1917 demonstrates that the province became a vehicle not for national interests, but essentially for provincial interests, and "in the 1920s, it was a predominant, even positive, force for political loyalty" (Schoppa 1977, 674).

Schoppa's view of provincial identity as historically dynamic fits well with my own. I will add that it is important also to recognize the way in which this identity was shaped by different representations and discourses, not only of the province, but also of the nation. Moreover, the representation of provincial attachment in the early twentieth century was not shaped reflexively by some primordial provincial sentiment. Rather, we might say that intellectuals and leaders sought to build the province as a political community by mobilizing its traditions and hardening its cultural boundaries in response to the political forces of the late nineteenth century. These include the threat of imperialist dismemberment of China, the legacy of provincial military autonomy, the *fengjian* tradition, and the emerging rhetoric of local self-government, among others. Thus, although there was historical sentiment for the locality, the particular identification with the province had had little opportunity to grow strong roots. This weakness was both a cause and an effect of the frustrations in developing a new narrative of *discent* to replace *fengjian*.

I will describe the growth of provincial identity in China in the first quarter of the twentieth century and how it culminated in the efforts of provincial groups to construct the nation consistent with its view of the world, known as the federal self-government movement (*liansheng zizhi*) of 1920 to 1923. By and large, groups that identified with provincial ties, traditions, and interests in early twentieth-century China were also nationalistic, but their understanding of the nation was influenced by their local or provincial identifications. For them, the form and substance of the nation differed significantly from centralizers whose historical narratives of China as a centralized imperial state had no space for provincial traditions and autonomy. The most basic and representative demand of the federalist movement was that the national constitution could only be formulated on the foundations of, and subsequent to, the establishment of provincial constitutions, which in turn would be decided by a popularly elected provincial assembly. The advocates of the movement tended to see all those who would impose a national constitution upon the province—even if this constitution went under the name of federalism—as their political enemies. The contest between the federalists and centralizers was decided in two realms: in the political realm and in the realm of discourse, which determined who, and what vocabulary, could claim to define the emergent and hegemonic National imaginary—the meaning of history, national values and, indeed, Chineseness itself.

The power and impact of the centralized imperial state on Chinese historiography has been such that there have been few studies conducted of regional or provincial identity through the long history of China (Chin 1973; Peterson 1974; Grimm 1985). Thus, it is difficult to gauge the power of provincial identification before the late nineteenth century. Although I have warned against interpreting the burst of provincialist rhetoric as the resurfacing of some originary identity, provincial traditions and networks did, of course, exist historically. Literati networks and their clientele, built around provincial administrative structures, had been key in sustaining pride in provincial traditions of local history, culinary arts, style of classical theater, settlement patterns, and daily customs (Kapp 1973, 3–6; Moser 1985). Provincial associations outside of the province, such as the *bang* of workers, the *huiguan* of merchants, and *tongxianghui* or native-place associations among all sojourners were among the means whereby consciousness of the province was funneled back into the native place. But if consciousness and pride of provincial traditions were not absent, the political mobilization of provincial consciousness can only be traced to the late nineteenth century, perhaps to the counter-mobilization of local forces against the Taiping rebels (Kuhn 1970).

The intelligentsia of the turn of the century saw provincial traditions, especially in the southern provinces, as materials upon which to build an alternative political identity which would allow them to challenge the existing state and its conception of the national destiny.

By the late nineteenth century, relatively well-integrated provincial elites in the Yangzi valley began to articulate a political role for themselves as true defenders of the nation against foreign aggressors. By the 1890s, as the last chapter indicated, appeals to save the nation were accompanied by a critique of the centralized bureaucratic state and arguments for a widened role for local elites. These critiques evoked a vision of social cohesion and national reinvigoration to be achieved under the elite leadership of the provinces (Rankin 1986, 160, 147–69). In the late 1890s, provincial consciousness may have been encouraged by the increasingly autonomous actions undertaken by provincial governors and governor-generals. In 1897, Liang Qichao petitioned the governor of Hunan to declare his independence (*zili zibao*), in order to establish a base for a separate southern political unity which could challenge the center and implement local reforms (Hu Qunhui 1983, 29).

In 1899, before the delegitimation of *fengjian*, Zhang Taiyan wrote a number of essays which advocated the introduction of the historical system of military feudalism or frontier forts (*fanzhen*), in addition to the more familiar argument of the time calling for the infusion of *fengjian* principles into the polity. Curiously, Zhang reversed what would become the principal argument against the militarization of provincial authority: the weakening of the nation. Indeed, Zhang believed that history had shown that centralized rule was only suitable in the absence of a foreign threat.[1] Since the Ming dynasty when military and administrative functions in the provinces were separated (Zhang Taiyan 1899b, 104–5), neither provincial administrators nor imperial state had been capable of suppressing internal unrest or foreign threats. With the exception of the Taiping interlude, the Qing

---

1. Despite the fact that Zhang argued against the constitutional reformers and their effort to introduce local self-government some years later (Kuhn 1986, 334), the idea that centralized rule was unsuited to a period of crisis is an enduring theme in Zhang. In the preface, published more than twenty-five years later, to Chen Jiongming's essay on federalism and the unity of China (Chen Jiongming 1928), Zhang justified Chen's federalist ideals in similar terms—of the need for strong regional powers to resist foreign imperialism. In another essay, Zhang, rather idealistically, expressed the hope that these provincial leaders would, like Satsuma and Chōshū in Japan, not only resist the foreigners, but also surrender their power at the appropriate time to the imperial state (Zhang Taiyan 1899a, 102).

followed the same policy of depriving provincial authorities of military powers with the same disastrous consequences. Zhang advocated combining *fengjian* ideals with the distribution of military power in the *fanzhen* system. Governor-generals with both military and civilian powers should remain in office within a region as long as they fulfilled their duties. In this way, both local soldiers and officials would be motivated to resist foreign invasions of their native lands (Zhang Taiyan 1899b, 106–7). Zhang may well have provided a historical rationale for regional autonomy. During the Boxer movement in 1900, provincial authorities such as Yuan Shikai in Shandong, Li Hongzhang in Canton, Liu Kunyi in Nanjing, and Zhang Zhidong in Wuhan asserted their autonomy by entering into secret agreements of neutrality with the foreign powers (Li Jiannong 1956, 178).

A few years later, however, a more radical separatist rhetoric emerged with the publication of Ou Qujia's *New Guangdong* in 1903. Inspired by the example of the briefly independent Taiwan in 1895, Ou Qujia pioneered the modern rhetoric which urged autonomy and even independence of the province as a means of protesting central or outside domination. He wrote,

> The people of Guangdong are truly the masters of Guangdong. It is appropriate that with respect to Guangdong, its political, financial, military, educational, and police powers, its railroads and mines, its land, forests and oceans should all be controlled and managed by the people of Guangdong. When the people of Guangdong manage their own affairs and complete their own independence (*zili*), then it is the beginning of the independence of all China. (Ou Qujia 1903, 21)

Ou's *New Guangdong* and Yang Shouren's *New Hunan*, published a year later in 1904, sought to produce historical narratives of a cohesive provincial subject in much the same mode as nationalist narratives, although their narratives were not incompatible with the larger national project. They were also accompanied by the same tensions that attend the nationalist narrative. The Cantonese have had the makings of a glorious people and splendid traditions (maintained particularly by the secret societies [Ou Qujia 1903, 36–38]) but they have been oppressed by the Manchus, who have also caused enmities between them and the people of other provinces by, for instance, using Hunanese armies to massacre Cantonese. To be sure, Ou does not believe that the Manchus are the only cause of the incompleteness of Cantonese self-consciousness. He laments the endemic ethnic battles among the peoples of Guangdong and even among the secret societies (Ou Qujia 1903, 40–47). In Yang Shouren's text on Hunan (1904, 66–70), we confront the same anxiety regarding the incompleteness of Hunanese self-consciousness in a narrative that sounds some of the same themes that Mao would develop more than fifteen years later. In Yang's text, there is on the one hand, the greatness and independence of Hunan which developed only when Hunan and Hubei were separated and the common blood ties of the Hunanese brought them closer together. This produced the pioneering tradition of Hunanese scholarship of such great (nationalist) figures as Wang Fuzhi and Tan Sitong. On the other hand, this tradition is contrasted with the presence of ignorant mountain peoples of varied (non-Han) extraction in the more remote, inaccessible part of Hunan (Yang Shouren 1904, 68–70). There is thus an acute tension created in the text which would have to be resolved in the process of creating an independent Hunan.

This new rhetoric of provincial autonomy was embedded in social Darwinist arguments, which were just then acquiring enormous popularity and authority among Chinese intellectuals as ways of understanding the plight of China. Ou argued that the unity of China's ancient and vast land instilled a sense of complacency that prevented competition among its provinces, which in turn inhibited contact, knowledge, and ultimately a true sense of closeness between the different provinces. Since love for the nation was not as intimate as love for the province in which one was born, he urged Chinese to invest their energies in developing the competitiveness and independence of the province. Through the strivings and competition among the provinces, those which were unable to establish their own independence would be merged with (*guibing*) the successful ones, and a federated independent China could be built on the bases of these strong independent provinces (Ou Qujia 1903, 2–3).

Social Darwinist thought had provided the categories for Chinese nationalists like Yan Fu and Liang Qichao to conceive of national survival in a world dominated by imperialism. The young republican revolutionaries, many of whom, like Wang Jingwei, believed in the historical necessity of centralized rule for a future China, derived from the rhetoric of the survival of the fittest nations, the necessity for the survival of races (Pusey 1983, 327). Ou performed yet another transformation on this authoritative discourse to validate the emergent provincialism. Indeed, he turned Liang's little nationalism—a term Liang had used pejoratively to refer to the revolutionaries' racist categories—to his own purposes. What Ou called "small nationalism" (*xiao minzuzhuyi*) referred to provincial identity and immediately struck a chord among the intelligentsia. Everywhere, pamphlets, texts, such as the *New Hunan*, and magazines which featured the name of the province on their titles, such as *Zhejiang Tide, Hubei Student Circle*, and countless others began to appear. And their message was often the same: there was a need to eliminate outside, and specifically Manchu authority, coupled with the need to celebrate provincial traditions and establish provincial self-determination (Zhang Yufa 1971, 64–105; Li Dajia 1986, 15).

Ou Qujia's appeal lay in his ability to legitimate the growing provincial consciousness by affiliating it with the rhetoric of national survival. The next two decades in China witnessed the further expansion of the social and institutional foundations of provincial consciousness proceeding apace with the growth of nationalist consciousness. There was, for instance, the proliferation of native-place associations (*tongxianghui*), not only among the merchants in the form of the traditional *huiguan*, but among all sojourning or migrant communities in urban areas, especially students and workers (Goodman 1990; 1995). Provincial politicization was also aided by two other factors: the appearance in 1908 of a framework of constitutional politics in which the province, or rather provincial elites, sought to extend their rights and powers (Fincher 1968, 203); and the militarization of politics in the 1910s, during which militarists attempted to utilize the sense of provincial fellow-feeling, often, but not always, to legitimate their political aspirations.

The politicization of the province was accompanied by the provincialization of politics: the organization and structuring of politics, especially revolutionary politics and the politics of mass mobilization, along provincialist lines. Whether one looks at the anti-Manchu revolutionary nationalists in the era from 1902 until 1911 or the May 4th movement and other nationalistic movements of the 1920s, the organizing principle utilized and the divisions along which these movements broke were often provincialist (*tongxianghui*) ones (Goodman 1990, 333–58). To be sure, these were not the only ones, since other types of professional associations, both old and new, were also used, but the provincial tie was an important organizing force. For instance, among the revolutionary organizations of 1911, the Guangfuhui was made up primarily by Zhejiangese, the Xingzhonghui by Cantonese, and the Huaxinghui by Hunanese (Onogawa 1970, 214; Lee 1970, 25).

These burgeoning political and social forces continued to generate provincial consciousness, which now required a new framework to authorize it and reconcile its aspirations for provincial political community with a vision of the Chinese nation. By the second decade of the twentieth century, the rhetoric of social Darwinism, which had supplied Ou Qujia with his metaphor of competitive mini-nationalisms, had begun to outlive its appeal among intellectuals, especially since China had established its independence from the Manchus. The spokesmen for provincial autonomy now sought to validate this autonomy in Western political theories of federalism. However, when they argued for the adoption of federalism by citing the strengths of international models, federalism's want of roots in Chinese traditions was played up by its enemies. The federalists of the time seemed particularly unable to answer the charge that provincial autonomy ran counter to the historical tradition of a unified China or *dayitong*.

During the Republican Revolution of 1911, many provinces established their own constitutions as they seceded from the Qing empire. Although they did so principally to maintain local order and the constitutions were abolished after the establishment of the Republic, they did, nonetheless, reflect federalist aspirations. In particular, the demands made by the Shandong federalist association upon the Qing government dealt preponderantly with relations between the center and the province and sought a federalist system to ensure greater provincial autonomy (Li Dajia 1986, 18). In the years following the revolution, arguments for a federalist system either appealed to the superiority of Western models, especially that of the United States, or to immediate political advantages to be gained by developing a federalist system, such as weakening the Yuan Shikai regime (Tang Dezhang 1922, 4; see also Li Dajia 1986, 20, 197). For Dai Jitao in 1912, federalism was a way to incorporate minorities such as the Mongols or Tibetans into the nation-state (Lee Chiu-chin 1993, 99, 124). However, unlike social Darwinism, which had, at least, provided a compelling view of the world for many Chinese, such a language of pragmatism and comparative advantages proved to be an extraordinarily weak rhetorical strategy for legitimating federalism. But if its spokesmen during this period were unable to locate federalism within a compelling discourse, they did confront the roots of their problem when they found themselves resorting to a historical vocabulary that bore the hegemonic imprint of the centralized state.

Zhang Shizhao, who in 1912 had argued against Dai Jitao's somewhat instrumental espousal of federalism, became one of its most ardent supporters by 1914. Writing under the name of Zhang Qiutong in the journal *Jiayin*, he emphasized that the real obstacle to a federated system was the historical tradition of the centralized state or, rather, the perception of this tradition (Zhang Shizhao 1914, 1.1: 5–6). He believed that China lost the chance to become a federated nation in 1911 when the provinces had declared themselves independent from the Qing empire. They were unable to sustain their independent or autonomous stance into the Republic principally because of the persistent and powerfully negative, moral characterization of provincial autonomy as "heterodox" (*yijiao xieshuo*). Under these circumstances, some writers, while accepting the virtues of the federated system, sought to avoid the term for federalism then currently being used, *lianbang*, especially since the term *bang*, meaning state, had connotations of sovereignty in the Chinese language (Zhang Shizhao 1914, 1.1: 5)

Zhang responded to this charge at various levels. He argued first that the current Chinese understanding of *bang* in *lianbang* need not and should not connote independent nation-states that came together to form a federated nation. Rather, *bang* as a unit was comparable in principle to the historical region or province. The only difference would be that they would have greater rights and powers, not that they would be basically independent. Moreover, arguing that previously independent nations were not a necessary prerequisite for the federated nation-state, he built a case for a centralized state (such as the Chinese one) that could and should transform into a federated nation (1914, 1.1: 5–6; see also Li Jiannong 1922, 7). Thus, Zhang refused to give up the name *lianbang*. To give up the name would be to surrender to the ideology of the centralizing tradition and yield to its self-proclaimed power to name names.

The means which had been used to unify the nation had historically been top-down and militaristic. It was this centralizing, militaristic tradition that had succeeded in associating the word *lianbang* with such illegitimacy. This tradition not only charged that the federated nation was a "heterodoxy" and its proponents like "venomous snakes and fierce beasts" (*dushe mengshou*), but that in propagating regionalism and divisiveness, it went against the flow of Chinese history (Zhang Shizhao 1914, 1.1: 5). Writers like Zhang believed that it was incumbent upon the intelligentsia to expose this nexus between the centralizing, militaristic tradition and the negative associations of *lianbang*. To avoid using the word could only further obscure the relationship between politics and language. He insisted on retaining the name and advocated an educational campaign to inform public opinion (*yulun*) of the virtues of the system and to persuade it that such a system was the only way to replace a violent and militaristic unity (Zhang Shizhao 1915, 1.6: 1–7).

Zhang's call to fight the historical narrative from within, as it were, rather than appeal to an alternative tradition must have been daunting. Proponents of federalism were particularly sensitive to the charge of riding against the flow of Chinese history. Doubts were constantly raised about the authenticity of their nationalism. Was not the history of China of over two thousand years the history of the centralized state? Had not the classical cultural tradition of Confucianism been associated with, and flourished only under, the centralized state? Were not those who had historically opposed this effort necessarily warlords advocating separatism (*geju*)? There appeared to be little appreciation that Chinese historical reality was characterized as much by the absence of the centralized state as its presence and of the more significant fact that there had been a constant current of criticism of the ideology of centralization even within the Confucian tradition, expressed most recently in the Qing debates between *fengjian* and *junxian*.

It is a remarkable testimony to the swiftness of the transformation of the meaning of *fengjian* that Zhang Shizhao did not affiliate the federalist movement with the *fengjian* tradition as a counternarrative of *discent*. Not much more than ten years previously, Zhang had conducted a searing critique of imperial despotism. As a means of restraining this power, he considered a number of historical institutions, such as the election of village leaders, the tradition of *qingyi* or critical moral discussion of the polity, and most of all, the pre-imperial *fengjian* system, which he regarded as an alternative model of power-sharing (Zhang Shizhao n.d., 20–21). We may assume that his reluctance to draw on *fengjian* ideas ten years later reveals the delegitimation of these ideas in the intervening years by their appropriation into the new discourse of History. Certainly the radically modernist May 4th era would find no place for it except as its Other.

The radicalization of historical consciousness in the May 4th movement did, however, furnish an alternative discourse from which to answer the charges made by centralizers that provincial autonomy and federalism were anti-Chinese. In the pages of *Taiping Yang*, a journal devoted to the federal self-government movement of 1920 to 1923, Yang Duanliu (1922, 2–5) argued that, in fact, less than a thousand years of China's three-thousand-year history had been under centralized rule. Besides, the Confucianist conception of revering imperial authority (*zunjun pichen*) had been utilized by rulers to deceive a gullible people into an illusory sense of security. Most important, the circumstances under which the present critique of centralized rule was being made was qualitatively different from that which emerged during historical periods of disunity since it was a constructive critique made by a responsible elite schooled in modern, Western education. Thus, not only was the tradition of centralized rule morally and politically inadequate, it was also unacceptable to much of the Westernized intelligentsia. Yet, at the same time, Yang recognized that it was not practical or feasible to divide China into separate nations. Under these circumstances, the federalist option was the best available path for rebuilding the nation.

Tang Dezhang acknowledged that historical expressions of multiple sovereignties, epitomized by the Warring States period and the frontier forts (*fanzhen*) or feudatory states of the Tang, were expressions of disorder and decline and that the centralized state was associated with periods of peace. Unlike Zhang Taiyan, Tang did not dispute the association. He countered the historicism of the argument by emphasizing what became the other part of the federalist self-government program: popular sovereignty. The difference between the Zhou and Tang warlords and the present federalist movement lay in their location of sovereignty. Whereas the historical roots of disunity and warfare could be found in the autocratic aspirations of the warlords, the federalist movement emphasized popularly elected provincial governments as the means to establish a stable and responsible political system (Tang Dezhang 1922, 10). Writers such as Tang, writing in the early 1920s, no longer sought to legitimate their arguments in the construction of an alternative history, but in the new discourse of popular sovereignty. Federalists now dispensed with historical language to validate their view of the nation and turned instead to a discourse which married the language of provincial autonomy with popular rights. The opposition, however, never abandoned the historical high ground from which it attacked the movement.

The new name for the movement, "federal self-government" (*liansheng zizhi*) itself announced the marriage of provincial autonomy and the democratic ideology of self-governance. The renaming of the movement was a stroke of genius on the part of Zhang Taiyan, who, in August 1920, invented it to refer to the alliance of the provinces of Hunan and Sichuan against the military invasions by the northern warlords and the political movement that was developing within these provinces. Unlike the earlier *lianbang*, which Zhang Shizhao had valiantly sought to infuse with new meaning, the new name resonated widely. For the next three years or so, it witnessed rousing debates in prominent journals both in the provinces and the capital, massive political demonstrations in its support, and at least five provincial constitutions, including one in Hunan which functioned until 1926. How and why did these ideas suddenly burst into a political movement?

The circumstances were right. Fighting between military groups broke out in the summer of 1920. The Anfu clique in the north was overthrown by the Zhili clique and the Manchurian group. The military government in the south had also broken up as the Guangxi warlords sought to dominate Guangdong and the Yunnan militarists to dominate Sichuan. The central provinces, especially Hunan and Sichuan, caught in the unending warfare between the north and south militarists, sought to protect themselves by declaring their autonomy and establishing a federalist alliance of like-minded provinces. But the movement also witnessed a groundswell of popular support in Hunan and Guangdong and to a lesser extent in Sichuan, Hubei, and Zhejiang (Chesneaux 1969). Students, intellectuals, the new professionals, such as journalists and educators, merchants as well as provincial legislators became quickly attracted to the new slogan. Many among these groups were people whose worldviews were being shaped by the May 4th movement, which had begun in 1919 and whose intellectual influence was still very much felt. Zhang Taiyan had chosen the name for the movement wisely. It remained to be seen whether the narrative of a democratic future for the nation, rather than the uncomfortable narrative of a counterhistory—the exchange of "descent" for a new type of "dissent"—could continue to sustain the ideal of provincial autonomy.

HUNAN: AUTONOMY AND POPULAR POWER

In Hunan, the movement arose from the confluence of military and popular initiatives. A series of popular protests was launched in 1919 against the rapacious, non-Hunanese governor Zhang Jingyao who had been installed by the northern warlords. Behind the protests were students, educators, and journalists, as well as the Hunan native-place associations (tongxianghui) in other provinces, but Zhang was finally driven out by the Hunanese military leader Tan Yankai in 1920 (Li Dajia 1986, 53–54). Tan identified his military campaign with the burgeoning popular movement for a just government that was run by Hunanese. On taking power, he announced a plan for self-government:

> The meaning of our proposal for self-determination of the
> people of Hunan is neither tribalism nor separatism but
> that civilization in the Hunan region must fall on the shoul-

der of Hunanese to foster and nurture. . . . the people
of Hunan were subject to Tang Xiangming and Zhang
Jingyao's treatment of them as inferiors and as people of
other races . . . but local autonomy of each province is the
common will of our people. (Quoted in Zhang Pengyuan
1981, 538–39)

Tan's vision of self-government for Hunan run by Hunanese was
greeted with great enthusiasm by the popular movement. The leadership core of the movement was formed by the radical intelligentsia,
at the center of which was the as yet pre-Marxist Mao Zedong and
his associates. Mao and his colleagues' panegyrics to Hunanese independence were, in fact, much more enthusiastic than that of the
militarists. From the end of 1919 until October 1920, Mao wrote almost incessantly about the self-determination of Hunan. In a piece
written in September 1920, Mao constructs a history of Hunan's
thwarted "natural development" (*ziran fazhan*) (Mao Zedong 1920a,
1: 225) that is a throwback to Yang Shouren's essay of 1904. In the
period of the warring states, before the advent of the centralized
imperial state, Hunan was the state of Jing-Chu. Although the warriors and heroic princes of this state were least concerned with the
ordinary people, they were nonetheless, able to develop some of the
particular qualities of the region. This was infinitely superior to being
slaves under the dark and all-embracing rule of the later imperial
despots (Mao Zedong 1920a, 1: 225). From this point in particular,
Hunan comes under the subjugation of China and the history of
Hunan is simply a history of darkness. Only with the reform movement of 1897–1898 did the Hunanese revive their dynamism and
initiative, but they were once again suppressed by China. Now, however, because of the turmoil in China, the opportunity had arrived
for Hunanese to build a new Hunan. Redolent of Ou Qujia's rhetoric
of "little nationalisms" of the early 1900s, Mao wrote, "We must
strive first for the goal of a Republic of Hunan, to implement the new
ideals and create a new life, to build at the confluence of the Xiao
and Xiang rivers, a new heaven and earth, and to become the leader
of 27 small Chinas" (Mao Zedong 1920a, 1: 227).[2]

Stuart Schram has written that, by 1919, Mao's ideas had under-
gone a deep transformation as he became fully exposed to Enlightenment discourse. Drawn to ideas of "liberation," "revolution," and

2. All or most of Mao's documents on the Hunan self-determination movement
appear to have been translated in Schram's work (1992). I have used these and other
translations by McDonald (1976), as well as my own (Mao 1920).

"popular power," he sought, in typical May 4th fashion, to repudiate the Chinese past (Schram 1992, xxxiii). And yet, whether because of anarchist ideas or that inherited political space from which the *feng-jian* critique of the centralized state had been launched, or some combination thereof, at this moment, Mao, who would later compare himself with the ruthless centralizer, the first emperor of Chin, appears to have been genuinely opposed to great state formations. He wrote that great states such as England, France, Germany, America, and especially the Republic of China were not only not necessary for success in the "struggle for existence," but they were immensely destructive. It was not just the imperialist states which decimated and enslaved peoples, but even the Chinese Republic had succeeded in annihilating the Manchus and driving the Mongols, Hui, and Tibetans to near death and causing political chaos (Mao Zedong 1920b, 1: 217). For the past four thousand years, the Chinese state had chosen grandiose imperial schemes and, as a result, China had been outwardly strong, but inwardly weak. To be sure, Mao was not advocating tribalism or separatism. When the time arrived, China would be reunited, but it would be an effort that developed from the bottom upwards, from the initiative of militarized, autonomous provinces (Schram 1992, 527).

The popular movement in Hunan persistently conflated independence or autonomy for Hunan with radical, democratic reform. The language of provincial autonomy had become completely intertwined with the language of revolutionary transformation. The "Proposal for the 'Revolutionary Government of Hunan' to Convene a 'Hunan People's Constitutional Convention' to Enact a 'Hunan Constitution' in order to Establish a 'New Hunan,'" penned by Mao and his colleagues, argued that by defying the legal authorities, Tan had engaged in a revolutionary act welcomed by the Hunanese and had now committed himself to the path of the revolutionary transformation of Hunan. He was committed to the most radical forms of political participation, which entailed "complete," not "semi" self-rule (Mao Zedong 1920d, 1: 239–45; McDonald 1976, 771–75). According to Mao, there were two stages to self-rule: semi self-rule, in which military and bureaucratic leaders from the provinces would rule the province, and full self-rule, in which the people would rule themselves in the villages, counties, and the province. All provinces should move from the first to the second as soon as possible, but some provinces were not yet in a position to move beyond the first stage (Mao Zedong 1920c, 9: 108–9). Although they should eventually try to move to full self-rule, semi self-rule was still better than seeking the unification of China. Unity under the center which was spelled out in the two characters for the very name of China, Zhongguo (central country), was, according to Mao, the fundamental cause of the misfortune of the people (Mao Zedong 1920c, 9: 107).

Mao's text reveals a deft maneuvering of the rhetoric of self-rule (zizhi). Typically associated until this period with local self-government (difang zizhi), which had referred to enlarging the power of localities in relation to the center, Mao had skillfully smuggled the dimension of popular self-rule and democracy into the concept. While this may have seemed like a logical extension of the concept to the radicals, given their new discourse, it may not have seemed so to the others fighting for Hunanese autonomy. Militarists and the assemblymen may have acknowledged the need for democratic reforms, but to them, provincial self-government hardly meant the political revolution that the radicals called for. Indeed, as Sasagawa points out, the Hunan constitution was intended to have been an expression of enlightened self-interest on the part of those elite politicians fighting to restore the older Republican constitution (Sasagawa 1985, 177–80, 208). If the movement was built around a common identification with the province, like national identification itself, it would split along the different meanings embodied in this identification. The differences here revolved around the understanding of democratic reform.

Tan announced a plan for the old provincial assembly to draft a provincial constitution to establish an independent Hunan until such time as a new national constitution could be produced. The plan quickly ran into opposition from the popular movement. On the ninth anniversary of the Republican Revolution, 10 October 1920, twenty thousand demonstrators, including students, workers, journalists, merchants, and even peasants protested in front of the governor's yamen against the elitist and lukewarm proposals for self-government emanating from the provincial assembly. The slogans that they carried were for "universal suffrage," "direct balloting," "direct elections for county magistrates" as well as "Hunan for Hunanese," "Hunan independence," and even, "a Hunan Monroe Doctrine." Although the movement did not push its goals much further and their alternative proposal for a provincial constitution (see above) was not adopted, nonetheless, Tan and his successor Zhao Hengti, who sought to unite the different progressive forces (Sasagawa 1985, 208), did convene conferences on the provincial constitution that solicited the views of some of the most prominent intellectuals, people such as Zhang Taiyan, Cai Yuanpei, and even John Dewey (Sasagawa 1985, 188–89).[3]

The constitution that was finally drafted and implemented in November of 1921 was still, in principle, the most radical that China had seen. There was to be universal suffrage and provincial and county assemblies (Zhang Pengyuan 1981, 548–50). Education was to be free and the judiciary independent. A governor was to be selected by popular vote of citizens of the province who, in turn, were to enjoy the right of initiative, referendum, and impeachment (Li Jiannong 1956, 404–5). In actual practice, the provincial constitution did not work nearly as well as it looked. There were several reasons, but perhaps the most important was that militarists continued to dominate the government and adapt it to their own immediate interests. In 1924, Governor Zhao Hengti amended the constitution to give himself overriding power. County-level elections were not instituted and the old assemblies were reestablished without elections; the 1922 provincial elections were a sham with the open buying of votes; military expenditures could not be reduced not only because of the ambitions of the local militarists, but also because of the constant threat of invasion. As a result, the provincial government remained paralyzed for lack of funds and both radical and popular opinion began to turn away from the provincialist alternative. Opposition within the Hunanese military in 1926 forced Zhao to step down and his successor joined the National Revolutionary Army of the KMT that was leading the Northern Expedition. The provincial constitution and assembly were never again to be restored (Zhang Pengyuan 1981, 567–70; Sasagawa 1985, 197–205).

The purpose of the federal self-government movement had been twofold: "to permit each province self-government and the power to make its own constitution and to manage its domestic affairs, with which neither the central nor other provincial governments could interfere"; and "to permit a new constitution to be made by provincial representatives for the federal government" (Li Jiannong 1956, 404).

---

3. Powerful provincialist sentiments continued to unite the radical movement with wider segments of the populace and the militarists until at least 21 March 1921. On that date, Zhao permitted a movement of protest against the decision of some Hubei merchants to replace the Hunanese workers in the Changsha cotton mill (which was a Hunan provincial government mill sold by the previous government to the Hubei merchants) with workers from Hubei. It was a vast street demonstration in which students, workers, professional associations, and the Chamber of Commerce participated, declaring that the factory was the "property of 30 million Hunanese"; they succeeded in forcing the new owners to abandon their plans (Chesneaux 1969, 110).

As the Hunan constitution was being implemented, Zhao worked hard to convince the other provinces to also promulgate their own constitutions and finally work toward a federal constitution. Ten provinces responded affirmatively and, of these, Zhejiang, Sichuan, Jiangsu, Shandong, and Guangdong even drafted their constitutions (Zhang Pengyuan 1981, 570). However, these constitutions were never fully implemented and the movement was, in any event, overtaken by the centralizing nationalism of the KMT, which was committed to military unification.

It has been said of the federal self-government movement that it did not stand a chance because militarists used the movement and provincialist sentiment to further their own particular ambitions. Thus the movement is viewed as the history of separatism and divisiveness repeating itself behind the veil of democratic language of autonomy, self-government, and popular rights. The role of military men ruthlessly subordinating the movement to their own goals can scarcely be denied. However, even as we accept the critique, we should recognize that the critique emerged from confounding two dimensions of the movement, the issue of autonomy and that of democratic reform, and it may be more fruitful for us to attend to the tension between these two narratives of the movement. Certainly for the militarists and for sections of the popular movement, the issue of provincial autonomy was of greater importance than democracy. For the radicals and other intellectuals, however, provincial autonomy could only be justified by appealing to democratic values, especially in the face of the deployment of the historical narrative against them. Democracy, thus, became the standard by which the constitution of Hunan was judged and declared to have failed. It is no small irony that no other political body in China went further on the road to democracy than did Hunan.

GUANGDONG: NATIONALISM AND THE POLITICS OF BETRAYAL

The federal self-government movement in Guangdong is often characterized as expressing the most divisive aspect of the movement as a whole. At the heart of this judgment is the characterization of the so-called June 16, 1922 (6/16), rebellion of Chen Jiongming's troops against the leadership of Sun Yat-sen which destroyed Sun's hopes for an early unification of the nation. Sun recounted the event in highly charged tones of a moral and personal betrayal:

> For thirty years I have led my comrades in the fight for the republic . . . but no danger has ever been so sad as this re-

cent one. My previous failures were caused by my enemies. But this time while my enemies have been defeated, the one who rises and replaces my enemy is Chen Jiongming, who has been my protege for more than ten years. Furthermore, he is so malignant and wicked-hearted that what my real enemies dare not do he has done. It is not only a misfortune for the Republic, but also a decline in moral integrity. (Quoted in Li Jiannong 1956, 419)

It is natural to expect the official KMT historiography to denounce the "rebellion." It is slightly more unexpected to see communist leader, Chen Duxiu, once its enthusiastic supporter, suddenly turn around and denounce the federalist movement immediately after the split in Guangdong, accusing the movement of militaristic regionalism. Even more remarkable was that a person such as Li Jiannong, one-time leader of the federal self-government movement in Hunan and author of the authoritative *Political History of China*, depicted the split largely as a series of betrayals and plots by Chen Jiongming. Li viewed Chen's activities of the time essentially in terms of wider political machinations. In this scenario, Chen was allied with the Zhili faction of the Beiyang army, while Sun had formed a temporary alliance with the Fengtian clique. After the defeat of the Fengtian clique by the Zhili group, Chen no longer felt it necessary to support Sun's Northern Expedition (1956, 418). Although Li conceded that Chen may have had a better sense of the Guangdong people's desire for peace than did Sun, there is little appreciation of the idea that, in terms of his commitment and political standing, Chen represented the one force within the federal autonomist movement most capable of attaining its ideal of the nation. The so-called rebellion or coup of 6/16 actually marked the climax of a conflict between two conceptions of the nation. Its diminution as a betrayal and a coup represented a rearguard ideological operation designed to tear away the language of democracy in which the principles of the movement had come to be embedded.

The movement in Guangdong in the summer of 1919 began, much as in Hunan, as a popular protest launched by students, trade unions, and the Chamber of Commerce of the province against outside control by the Guangxi clique, specifically against the refusal of the clique to appoint Wu Tingfang, a Guangdong luminary, as civilian governor. By the winter of 1920, Chen Jiongming, commander of the Guangdong army and former governor of the province during the Republican Revolution, succeeded in driving out the Guangxi army and, under the banner of "Guangdong people rule Guangdong" (*Yueren zhi Yue*), restored Sun Yat-sen to power in the province (Chesneaux 1969, 113). Thus, Sun returned to power in the province riding on a wave of provincialist sentiment which he clearly recognized. In 1920, he remarked, "we must chase out the Guangxi clique (from Guangdong). . . . one cannot hope to improve the situation unless one puts into practice the principle that Canton must be governed by the Cantonese" (Chesneaux 1969, 120). But Sun was riding a wave for which he really did not see a future. He was anxious to reestablish the constitution of the Republic of 1912, which envisioned a centralized nation-state, and to reunify the country by military means (Lin Sheng 1922, 3).

Meanwhile, influential sectors of Guangdong society had seized on the notion of federal self-government as the ideal solution to preserve provincial autonomy while building the nation along federalist lines. Its greatest champion was none other than Chen Jiongming himself, for whose ideas of the nation we are fortunate to have a sensitive study by Winston Hsieh. Chen had been influenced by anarchism and saw the nation as an abstract category which politicians often used to hoodwink the people. This was, of course, an ironic reversal of the centralizing nationalists' charge against the advocates of provincial autonomy who, they alleged, used provincial sentiment for their own ends. Chen found the region or province to be a more meaningful unit of identification as well as one best suited for development purposes to yield practical results.

Winston Hsieh observes a contradiction between Chen's radical "antinationalist" ideas and what he finds to be his practical concern for the fate of China as a whole. Hsieh cites Chen's suspension of his campaign against Yuan Shikai during the crisis of the 21 Demands and his criticism of Sun's repeated betrayal of the national interest as a couple of examples of his practical "patriotism." It may be more useful to see these instances not as contradictions between regionalism and nationalism within Chen's personality, but rather as a representation of the nation which incorporated an important role for the province. Like many other federalists, Chen never entertained the idea of provincial independence. He embraced the federalist cause because it permitted him to build the province as the basis of the nation (Li Dajia 1986, 147). Chen had demonstrated his sincerity to both the idea of provincial autonomy and to development of the province. When he was driven out of Guangdong in 1918, he consolidated a military base and set himself up as an enlightened warlord in the twenty-six counties of the Zhangzhou region of neighboring Fujian province. The program of modernization that he undertook here in the realm of education, development of the infrastructure, and the maintenance of public order was so successful that it even drew the praise of the United States Consul (Li Dajia 1986, 148; Hsieh 1962, 211). At the same time, citing his commitment to the principle that only a Fujianese should rule Fujian, he refused to become the provincial governor of Fujian.

On returning to Guangdong, Chen, who became civil governor and commander-in-chief of the Guangdong armies, launched an ambitious program to make Guangdong a model for local self-government and a leader of the federalist movement. He extended the reform projects initiated in Zhangzhou, particularly the ideas of political reform. Surrounding himself with May 4th modernizers, Chen took several steps to implement provincial democracy. Popular elections for mayor were held at the prefectural level and the rules for voting contained an interesting requirement that voters could only obtain the right to vote if they had performed three days of manual labor (or provided the monetary equivalent)—most of which went to construct the highway system of the province. A provincial assembly was also instituted and, in 1922, Chen was replaced as governor by a civilian. The draft constitution for the province that was developed was seen as the most superior and practicable among all of the provincial constitutions, containing as it did limits on the role of the military and its budget. His fall from power soon after, however, prevented its realization (Hsieh 1962, 217–18; Li Dajia 1986, 151). Nonetheless, if there was hope for a provincial self-government movement, it was here, under the leadership of Chen Jiongming.

Chen hoped to realize his plan for the federated nation by seeking a commitment from the south-central provinces to respect the provincial autonomy of each, to unite against those who sought the path of military unification, to nurture self-government, and to work to ultimately limit the influence of the military. He also proposed that an assembly be held in Shanghai to draft the federal constitution, regarding which he had an elaborate plan (Li Dajia 1986, 153–55). Although the federal constitution never materialized, the alliance that Chen put together was effective on a few occasions in preventing invasions by rival provinces. Thus the Guangxi plan to avenge Sun's campaign against it and attack Guangdong was deterred by the federalist alliance (Li Dajia 1986, 155). Chen was aware that the militarists welcomed his plan for federalism for their own reasons, but he saw the temporary peace and unification that this would bring about as essential. It would provide a breathing space when arms could be reduced, debts could be paid, and the people's capacity for self-rule and self-defense be developed. Out of this, a real federal government might even be established (Hsieh 1962, 224). But Chen's greatest enemy was not his neighboring warlords, nor even, perhaps, the northern warlords. It was his political leader, but ideological opponent, Sun Yat-sen.

Although Sun had made some gestures in the direction of the federal self-government movement, he never seriously contemplated provincial autonomy or a federalist unity (Lin Sheng 1922, 4). When confronted with the plan for a federal constitution by the Guangdong legislators, he proposed his own plan for federalism, based on county self-government, a powerful center, and with him as the president. As Zhang Taiyan pointed out, this was a top-down plan for federation and did not really amount to federalism at all. Zhang organized a successful opposition to it and the plan was dropped. Thereafter, Sun devoted himself to the task of protecting the constitution of 1912 and sought to form a national government in Canton with himself elected as "Extraordinary President of the Chinese Republic." A little over 200 members (not enough for a quorum) of the dissolved 1917 parliament elected him on 5 May 1921. But his authority was not recognized beyond Guangdong, and even here there was opposition among the legislators and members of his own party (Li Dajia 1986, 144–45).

Despite his personal disagreement with Sun's chosen form of government and Sun's resolve to invade Guangxi in September of 1921, Chen Jiongming remained steadfast in his public support of Sun, which was as indispensable to the president as Sun's support was to Chen (Lin Sheng 1922, 3). It was only in the spring of 1922, when Sun planned to forge ahead with the Northern Expedition to dislodge the warlords from the provinces militarily and bring the nation under centralized control, did Chen express his opposition. Sun dismissed him from his posts in his national government (Lin Sheng 1922, 4). In April of 1922, Chen retired to his hometown of Huizhou. In June of that year, Sun openly challenged the military generals in Canton at a press conference and found himself the target of a military coup on 16 June which forced him to flee to Shanghai. Although Sun and his supporters have charged that it was Chen who gave the orders for the coup, there is as yet no satisfactory evidence to support the charge (Hsieh 1962, 230). Winston Hsieh believes that, more than anything else, it was the regional loyalty of the soldiers to Guangdong's autonomy which led to the coup.

Although Chen returned to power in Guangdong and restarted his program for local self-government, it was not to last. Guangdong now fell prey to incessant warfare, which doomed not only the efforts at local self-government in the province, but also the federalist movement at large since Chen had been its most credible leader. In the spring of 1922, Chen had been at the height of his career. He enjoyed popular support for his reforms and respect for his military power from the warlords. Even the "big" northern warlords like Wu Peifu and Duan Qirui, principal foes of federal self-government, sent envoys to establish peaceful relations with him (Hsieh 1962, 229). Less than a year later, in January of 1923, Sun Yat-sen's mercenary armies from Yunnan and Guangxi drove Chen out of Canton. Chen managed to hold on to east Guangdong until 1925, when he was completely routed by the Soviet-trained and backed Nationalist Army of Chiang Kai-shek.

The split of June 1922 has been depicted as a moral drama in which a warlord chose his region over the nation. It is testimony to the strength of the hegemonic nationalist narrative that Chinese commentators who have sought to set the record straight, whether at the time (Lin Sheng) or more recently (Li Dajia), have been unable to break with the terms framed by this moral drama. Their task has, of course, been made all the more difficult by the fact that Chen broke with Sun Yat-sen, Father of the Nation. It has not been enough for them to show that Chen embraced an alternative vision of the nation. They have had to show that he was an exemplary nationalist whose conduct was politically correct and morally upright. We are shown how consistently loyal Chen had been to Sun and how, even after his principled opposition and final dismissal, he never challenged the leader. His opposition to the Northern Expedition stemmed not from opposition to national unity per se, but from the need to honor his pact for mutual nonaggression among the federalist provinces (Sun was threatening to invade Hunan), from the need to continue to develop self-government in the province and, finally, because of the dire straits of provincial finances in Guangdong, which simply could not afford the northern wars (Lin Sheng 1922, 4).

It is perhaps inevitable that revisionist scholars like Li Dajia and Winston Hsieh find themselves in an uncomfortable position of having to argue that Chen was nationalist but anti-Nationalist (KMT), because the two N/nationalisms have been fused and moralized. The strength of this moralized opposition to the federal self-government movement in Guangdong, however, did not depend only on the retrospective rewriting of history on the part of the immediate victor, the KMT. The imposition of the external narrative of the state upon local historical narratives might have been easy enough to subvert, if only locally. The moralized opposition gained enormous strength when other ascendant social forces, with visions of the nation distinct from the state and even opposed to it, found common cause with the Nationalists in their opposition to the federal self-government movement.

The split between Sun and Chen marked another political break, barely noticed at the time, but with perhaps more lasting effect on the fate of federalism in China. The radical social forces of the May 4th era, led by socialists and future Marxists, had embraced both the provincialist and radical democratic agenda of the federal self-government movement.[4] The increasingly Marxist leadership of the popular movement had pinned its hopes on the radicalization of the movement, especially in Hunan. As they became disenchanted with the role of the militarist Zhao Hengti in Hunan (Sasagawa 1985, 207), communist leaders like Chen Duxiu sought to woo Chen Jiongming to join the Communist Party during his brief period of exile in Huizhou from April to June 1922. While Chen Jiongming was deeply committed to reform, he was no revolutionary, and his attitude toward the labor movement remained "austerely paternalistic" (Hsieh 1962, 234).[5] Chen Duxiu finally despaired of bringing the general to his cause and when the split with Sun occurred, he turned abruptly against Chen Jiongming and the entire federal self-government movement. Not long after, Mao too disavowed any involvement with the movement (Schram 1966, 56).

In the journal Nuli Zhoubao, Chen Duxiu offered the argument that, in principle, he favored self-government and federalism. However, under the present circumstances of feudal-style (fengjianshi) politics, it was impossible for the movement to avoid becoming a pawn in the game of the militarists, especially by small ones to protect their fief-

4. Li Dazhao's understanding of the ideals gives us a sense of how internationalist ideas could be reconciled with the province as a focus of sentimental identification. Not only did Li believe that the federal and democratic principles were inseparable, he saw the federalist idea of the confederation of self-governing units as the means of achieving his cosmopolitan ideal, his "world super-federation" (Li 1959, 130–34).

5. More recent work on Chen Jiongming's attitude toward the peasant movement reveals that his self-image as a progressive influenced by anarchist ideas and Confucian reformist ideals caused him to actually promote the peasant movement until at least 1924. Indeed, the famed revolutionary organizer, Peng Pai, was able to make great headway among Guangdong peasants in large measure because of Chen's support. By 1924, a combination of political forces whose support Chen needed, including the British in Hong Kong, Hong Kong merchants, and the local landlord lobby, ultimately prevailed upon Chen to order the disbanding of the peasant associations (Pang 1985).

doms from larger ones. Chen Duxiu derived his analysis of the present situation explicitly from history. Those advocating federalism did not understand the historical basis of disunity in China, which lay in the efforts of militaristic hegemons (*ba*) to control a particular area and its resources. Thus, the political mess in China was not, as some (including Mao and Zhang Taiyan) had argued, because centralized power had been too great and regional power too weak, but rather the other way around. So too, in the present situation, federalism was built upon the aspirations of regional militarists (*geju*) and could never achieve national unity and strength (Chen Duxiu 1922, 3–4).

Although the goal of his historical narrative differed from that of more traditional centralizing nationalists, yet by virtue of the vocabulary he used, Chen Duxiu added a powerful voice to those who hinted darkly about the moral and historically suspect nature of the movement—its antinational character. The defamation of the movement had reached a climax just after the split. Reacting to this trend, Hu Shi, a supporter of the movement, protested,

> We certainly do not seek to defend Chen Jiongming. The conduct of the soldiers of the faction supporting Chen who drove out Sun Yat-sen, can perhaps be criticized. But we definitely oppose those who employ the corpses of the old morality by using words such as "rebel leader" (*beiju*), "rebels" (*fanshang*) and "mutineers" (*panni*) to attack Chen Jiongming. (Hu Shi 1922, 2)

Chen Duxiu had insistently employed the older vocabulary including, for instance, the word *lianbang* rather than the newer, more positive *liansheng zizhi* and such terms as hegemon (*ba*) and regional militarist (*geju*). In the process, Chen Duxiu redeployed the "corpses of the old morality" as the weapons of the new morality—a morality embedded in the epochal narrative of the peoples' struggle against imperialism and feudalism. The new History had made common cause with the old imperial history and old enemies were inherited as new enemies.

Let us take stock again of the genealogy of the word *fengjian*. In imperial China, it had developed a historically critical role as a check on absolutist power. At the very end of the nineteenth century, it had flashed up again to mobilize a counternarrative of the nation. The last chapter concluded by examining how, within a few years, it had transmuted in the hands of Liang Qichao into the Other of modernity, although the Chinese variant of a principally unilinear evolutionism, in which feudalism had occurred in antiquity before the long era of the centralized imperial state, continued to feed Liang's doubts. By the time of the federalist movement, when Chen Duxiu deployed it, *fengjian* had become sheer negativity. To a great extent, the loss of the critical power of *fengjian* was predestined by the adoption of unilinear History, not simply of Europe, but of Japan. As Tetsuo Najita (1987, 208) has revealed, in early Tokugawa Japan, *fengjian* (in Japanese the compound is pronounced *hōken*, but the characters are identical) carried a positive connotation. By late Tokugawa, it took on negative connotations (Najita 1987, 260–63) as the forces working against the feudal Tokugawa regime and for the restoration of imperial power gained strength. Thus, the genealogy of *fengjian* in Japan seems to have fortuitously (?) coincided with the European narrative of linear History in which feudalism was the principal Other of modernity.

For the forces fighting against the Tokugawa regime, the signifier *hōken* or *fengjian* presented a political potency that had to be vanquished. Such was not the political reality of China, where the signifier, nonetheless, came to take on a similarly denunciatory force. To be sure, it acquired some of this force through its conversion into a socioeconomic category in Marxism as representing a mode or relations of production. But in this way it came to generate a new set of meanings around which the extremely heterogenous realities of twentieth-century China were organized; a set of meanings or an image of social reality that the late nineteenth-century conception of *fengjian* in China did not possess. Hu Shi was only partly correct in identifying Chen's words as "the corpses of the old morality," for Chen had skillfully wrapped up old words as corpses in the narrative of the new morality. This transformation of the sense of *fengjian* cost the federalists most dearly, for it effaced an entire tradition of political dissent with which they may have been able to associate themselves. It deprived them of a rhetorical strategy whereby they could claim descent as the legitimate successors to this tradition and thereby mobilize history in their cause.

The timing of Chen Duxiu's critique is significant not only for what it marked, but also for what it concealed. While there had been some criticism of the movement by the Communists as early as 1921, Chen Duxiu's renunciation and denunciation of the movement clearly marked the turning away of progressive support from it. His article appeared in September of 1922, three months after the Sun-Chen split and at the very moment during which Sun and the Soviet envoy, Joffe came close to an agreement to reorganize the KMT and militarily unify China. Some Communist leaders, for instance Li Dazhao, were already beginning to join the KMT (Li Jiannong 1956, 442). Thus, the Communist condemnation of Chen Jiongming and the movement as feudalistic and regionalistic had more to do with the new focus of their efforts—an alliance with centralizing Nationalists—than with an accurate representation of the nature of Chen Jiongming's regime.

To be sure, judging from the behavior of the warlords in Hunan and elsewhere, the substance of Chen Duxiu's general critique was undeniable at one level. And yet, Guangdong's Chen Jiongming did not fit the description of a feudalist warlord bent on keeping the nation disunited. The true causes of Chen Duxiu and the progressives' despair were not so much that militarists like Chen Jiongming would prevent the attainment of a federated nation; it was rather that they were unwilling to go along with the call for a full-scale revolution (Chesneaux [1969] echoes this view in his judgment of the movement as fundamentally conservative). But surely Chen Jiongming's regime could not be judged by such a yardstick since he never proclaimed a class revolution to be his goal. He remained true to the goals of the movement that brought him to power and sustained him till the end: the desire for provincial autonomy and the promise of democratic reform in the province and a federated nation. Nor was Chen's regime the only force to work for this ideal. Hunan's provincial constitution reflected the ideals of provincial autonomy and democracy, and, for all of its flaws in practice, it did function until it was destroyed by centralizing forces. In Zhejiang, too, the provincialist movement, led by merchants, professionals, and assemblymen under the slogan of "Zhejiang for Zhejiangese," worked hard to create an autonomous province, autonomous not only from outside warlords but, even more, from the KMT's centralized administration (Schoppa 1977, 672).

The split of June 1922 signaled the abandoning of the federalist cause by progressive forces and their turn to the call for a unified nation confronting the twin enemies of imperialism and warlordism. The radical program had become yoked to a centralizing nationalism committed to military unification. Where Mao and his radical colleagues had once seen provincial autonomy and radical democracy as inseparable, Chen Duxiu's text now depicted radical goals as unreservedly opposed to autonomy—even while Chen Jiongming continued to hold onto democratic goals. Chen Duxiu's text had effectively switched codes. No longer were the goals of federalism to be judged by the narrative of democracy; rather they were to be denounced by the narrative of History. And it was an appeal to the same History of the centralized state to which Sun and the KMT had appealed. Together the centralizers and the centralizing radicals made common cause and buried the federalist movement under allegations and insinuations of betrayed ideals which were, to begin with, not its own. When the Northern Expedition of the KMT-CCP alliance swept across the southern and central provinces, it also swept away provincial constitutions and provincial and local assemblies as so much rubble to be cleared before erecting the centralized nation-state. So successful was the undeclared cultural war that few have paused to ask why even such meager institutions of democracy and autonomy associated with the vision of a federated nation have never again been seen in China.

In one of the last pieces he wrote, Joseph Levenson argued that the Communists had converted what he considered a genuine provincialism of imperial times (that is, as a sense of provincial belonging and the fact of provincial self-sufficiency) into a museum piece, for display. It has been put on stage as "a diversified repertoire to which the nation gave attention, not as a divisive single spectacle to which the provinces gave themselves" (Levenson 1967, 278). Whether or not provincialism in the early twentieth century had older roots, the historical conjuncture outlined above was clearly a significant site of the transformation of the provinces into a "diversified repertoire" of the nation. But can it be argued from this that the federal self-government movement was the final flowering of provincialist identity, the last narrative of the nation from the locality below?

The aspirations for independence and autonomy that have emerged from Taiwan and Hong Kong in recent years suggest that nationhood continues to means different things to those who still have the means to express their difference. More recently, scholars have directed our attention to the collapse of the Maoist narrative of the "Great Han, anti-imperialist nationalism" with its glorification of an "authentic" peasant culture in the central plain that resisted foreign invasion and contamination. The new nationalisms that are emerging not only celebrate the non-Han minority nationalities like the Hui Muslims (Gladney 1991), but also what Edward Friedman identifies as an alternative southern narrative of the nation. This narrative positively reinvests precisely those alleged qualities of the south of China that are marginalized in the Maoist narrative—a dynamic entrepreneurial culture emphasizing individual freedom and a cosmopolitanism (Friedman 1993, 12). Moreover, this assertive regionalism is quickly finding its way into history textbooks as newly empowered provincial archaeological institutes make claims for the ancient origins of provincial or regional nationalities (von Falken-hausen 1993). Like the writings of the early twentieth century, these histories do not avow a separatism and, like them, they too reproduce the teleology of nationalist Histories, but they no longer extol a uni-fied national tradition. Instead, they too construct a regional or provincial narrative of the nation.

7

CRITICS OF MODERNITY IN INDIA AND CHINA

I **HAVE TRACED** the ways in which progressive History charts the evolution of the national subject through the discourses of idealistic evolutionism, social Darwinism, anti-imperialism and even Marxism. We have seen how it figures the national subject in the imagery of race, religion, class, and the state and that, while the evolution of the national subject can be complex, partial and circuitous, in most cases, the telos of the narrative remains modern self-consciousness. In this last chapter, I will consider other narratives or discourses which have challenged this History of the nation in China and India. Because these alternative narratives have been largely ignored or marginalized in both nationalist narratives and modern scholarship, it is important for a bifurcated history to explore their critical potential.

These alternative narratives center principally on the notion of "culture." The early usage of culture to oppose evolutionism can be found within Europe itself in the writings of Johann Gottfried Herder. Those figures in Asia whose alternative ideas I try to understand through the notion of culture were, perhaps, mostly unaware of Herder's usage, but the circumstances of its appearance in the two contexts have much in common. According to George Stocking, in the late eighteenth century, Herder reacted against the cultural imperialism of French and Scottish Enlightenment conceptions of universal progress and the implicit hierarchy of cultural achievement. He emphasized the variety of national character, that each national culture was an expression of its own unique *Volkgeist*, with all equally being manifestations of the divine realizing itself in the spiritual development of humanity as a whole. To be sure, while Herder may be seen as a source of pluralism and anthropological relativism, his notion of culture never closed the back door to racialist evolutionism. Each national spirit evolved from an "internal prototype": Jews would retain the spirit of their ancestors, blacks could never acquire the "finer intellects" of the Europeans, and so on (Stocking 1987, 20). Thus, if "culture" presented an oppositional stance toward the Enlightenment discourse of "civilization," which since Hegel we have identified as History, it was also capable of recalling this evolutionism as a supplement.

Within Asia, this oppositional mode has also challenged linear, evolutionary conceptions. More often than not, like Herder's critique, these challenges have targeted one or more dimensions while reproducing other assumptions of the dominant narrative of History. Thus, Zhang Taiyan and, occasionally, Lu Xun denied progress while accepting evolutionism (Ogata 1984), and Rabindranath Tagore and Liang Shuming, each in their own way, denied comparability while accepting progress. Mahatma Gandhi was one of the only significant figures to deny History in *toto*. The latter half of this chapter will seek to understand the significance of Gandhi's thought as well as the mirror in which his total and determined opposition to History was reflected. Modern scholarship has not been particularly sympathetic to these critics of the Enlightenment project. For example, history textbooks in America, India, or China either ignore most of these figures, or, where they are unable to ignore them, as in the case of Gandhi, assimilate their actions and ideas into the narrative of national liberation or into a lesson on moral courage. There is a tendency to pass over the critique of modernity.

The dominant narrative of modern Chinese history in both China and the West is the narrative of modernization. This has been seen as a painful and uncertain process, which has, nonetheless, inched toward a full modern consciousness in distinct phases. These phases are familiar enough and I will simply outline them. The narrative begins with the Opium War of 1840 and the initial refusal of the imperial state and the mandarinate to recognize the challenges posed by the West. This was followed by the self-strengthening movement, where Western learning was sought only for practical matters designed to strengthen the empire, while Chinese learning was reserved for all essential matters—the classic *ti-yong* dichotomy. With the increasing failure of the self-strengtheners to confront the military challenges of the late nineteenth century, segments of the literati and progressive bourgeoisie began to advocate institutional reform without challenging the basic principles of the Confucian imperial system. The exemplary representative of this phase is Kang Youwei and his experiments during the 100 Days of Reform. The 1911 Republican Revolution challenged, of course, the traditional political system, but it was left to the May 4th movement of 1917 to 1921 to finally and systematically attack the very cultural underpinnings of the old system.

Of course, this simple linear narrative does not do full justice to the complex responses to modern discourses that emerged in the late nineteenth and early twentieth centuries. Those who responded by questioning the project of total modernization in China have been called conservative, although Benjamin Schwartz has observed that their responses are very modern (Schwartz 1976, 4). Particularly in the Chinese political context, they have been painted in negative colors as people opposed to the epochal trends of progress and freedom. I would like to extend Charlotte Furth's very useful distinction between two forms of "conservatism" or what I call questioning narratives of modernity in China (Furth 1976, 39–41). The first form is one which tried to separate culture from politics and thus was able to find compatibilities between science, rationality, and traditional culture. In this form, culture was often subordinated to the needs of politics and technology. The second finds this distinction difficult to sustain because it sought to exalt spiritual culture over materiality. Thus, the values and ideals of this culture would necessarily shape certain essential aspects of political and material life.

Represented by the National Essence school (*guocui*) of thinkers like Zhang Binglin and Liu Shipei, the first type according to Furth, was concerned with the preservation of those cultural ideals seen as embodying the historical genius of the Chinese people (Furth 1976, 31–32; see also Chang 1987, 112, 150). As such, this school was not opposed in principle to modernity but questioned its adequacy for the life of the nation and the individual. At its edges, I find that this nationalist critique tended to merge with formulations of the East versus West binary which depicted the East as the source of spiritual culture and the West as the source of material or scientific culture, both of which, however, were necessary for humanity. Thus the critique of History through culture, while mostly used to anchor the *nation* on alternative grounds, was also linked to a redemptive *universalist* model. Most of the critiques of modernity encountered in both China and India are versions of this form. The ideas of Liang Qichao on his return from Europe after witnessing the devastation of the First World War exemplify this model of (national) culture with aspirations to redeem the universe. Liang now believed that Chinese (and Eastern) civilization had a great responsibility toward the world to counter the destructiveness of Western civilization (Hay 1970, 137–40). This model received much patronage from visiting Western philosophers like Bertrand Russell and John Dewey and from its most ardent advocate, Rabindranath Tagore, whose pan-Asianism was deeply affected by his personal friendships in China. Although Tagore's last visit to China in 1929 was not welcomed by the CCP or the KMT (Hay 1970, 323–24), even the KMT leader Dai Jitao espoused the theme of Asian spiritual unity in the magazine *New Asia* during the early 1930s where he depicted Sun Yat-sen as the father of a pan-Asianism focused on China's cultural values. In Dai, anti-imperialism and the discourse of culture coalesced into a popular Chinese image of the time which saw the entire society as a "proletariat responsible both for the Asian anti-imperialist struggle and for preserving the purity of Asian culture" (Mast and Saywell 1974, 98).

The second type of critique of modernity was embodied in what Furth calls the neo-traditional Confucianism of figures like Kang Youwei and Liang Shuming and was centrally concerned with the religious and spiritual questions. Although they were not necessarily opposed to modernity, they perceived the religious truths of Confucianism as occupying not only a separate, but a more elevated, plane than did science. In other words, this was a realm which embedded Truth that theoretically could not be judged by the standards of science or History. One may see this notion of culture in a Herderian light, but it is also continuous with the self-strengtheners' *ti-yong* formulation which regarded the moral goals of Confucianism as the ends of technological adaptation.[1] For twentieth-century Confucianists, culture could not be completely separated from politics since the religio-moral values of Confucianism could not but inform the polity and society. This was not true for the adherents of the National Essence school because the culture they advocated was in some senses subordinate, or at least, adaptable to the requirements of modernity. They could choose the substance or content of culture to suit the requirements of the age in a way in which a Confucianist could not because he sought to carry over certain substantive values and an orientation toward the world.

1. Here I am differentiating myself from the Levensonian dichotomy which sees *ti-yong* as an un-self-conscious expression of culture as telos, whereas "modern conservatives" are seen to manipulate or rationalize culture self-consciously. As I argued in chapter 3, the instrumental use of culture was alive before the modern divide, and Confucian spirituality could also function as an alternative telos in the modern era (see also Chang 1987).

Because he was inspired by the evolutionism of History, scholars have tended to regard Kang Youwei as operating essentially within its problematic. Certainly, he reveals some of the most unfeeling racial prejudices of evolutionism. In his vision of utopia in *The Great Unity*, Kang writes of the inferior races, which include all but the white and yellow races, that they will be decimated by the natural principle of the strong prevailing over the weak. For instance, the "fierce and ugly" races of India who die by many thousands in epidemics each year will hardly be able to overcome the British; since the bodies of Negroes "smell badly," it is difficult for the racial barrier against them to be leveled. Those few of the black and brown races who are not annihilated will marry with the lighter races and will ultimately become amalgamated with the white people (K'ang Yu-wei 1958, 142–43). And yet the intensity with which he subscribed to evolutionism should not blind us to another dimension of his thought which emphasized love and equality of all in the world. Hao Chang (1987) stresses the indeterminacy of Kang's ideas, which are drawn from different Confucian schools, Buddhism, as well as Western ideas. Thus Kang's evolutionism coexists (not without tension, see K'ang Yu-wei 1958, 41) with a moral quest and activism derived from a Confucian "cosmic imperative," and his utopia is informed by the moral values of *ren* (benevolence, altruism). Indeed, if one views Kang not only as a political thinker, but as a philosopher and religious leader, as did disciples like Liang Qichao, then we have to see his ultimate goal as the spread of Confucian moral and spiritual teachings in order to save the world (Chang 1987, 21–65).

However, few Confucianists of the twentieth century were practically able to realize this religio-moral vision in society, at least in a form that made it recognizably different from the modern vision of society. Were they perhaps content with Feng Youlan's suggestion that "the sage within is simply a man whose outer kingliness lies in the fact that he does what everyone does but understands it differently"? (cited in Furth 1976, 41). Liang Shuming may have been among the few who insisted that the sage's actions in the world must be realized in the form of a Confucianist moral community. Liang's rural reconstruction institutes were inspired by Mencius: The elite were to be the teachers, responsible for leading the masses and for their ethical transformation. In this sense, the teacher was to aspire to be a sage; the central institutional agent of the government was to be the school; and the cadres were to be the spiritual hierarchy of dedicated students. He loathed the self-interested, competitive spirit of Western capitalism and attacked the Westernized educational system for creating a privileged class that had lost the tradition of the morally perfect *junzi* (Alitto 1979, 200). He sought to reorganize society on the basis of the traditional ethical bonds through such hallowed institutions as the eleventh-century *xiangyue* (village compact), so that society and moral instruction "could make an indivisible whole" (Alitto 1979, 206). At the same time, like Kang, Liang Shuming never really parted with the evolutionist perspective. But it was an evolutionism that was reworked to rid it of any value hierarchy. Of the three stages of Will that he wrote about, the Western stage, the Chinese stage, and the Indian stage, each was equally and validly concerned with the problems of humanity at the appropriate stage of development. Of course, as Alitto points out, none of this critique prevented him from identifying the essence of Chinese culture as an absolute value (Alitto 1979, 84).

Many of the same processes and tendencies can also be found in the nineteenth- and twentieth-century history of India, but the narrative has not been emplotted in the same way. Here, for reasons encountered in the next section, the critique of modernity has almost as much visibility as the narrative of progress, although the sting of the former has often been removed. We may see the narrative of progress as tied together at three points by the figure of Ram Mohun Roy (1772–1833) and the Bengal Renaissance, the moderate wing of the nationalist Congress Party at the turn of the century, and by Jawaharlal Nehru, first Prime Minister of India. But the shadow of a parallel process (not quite narrativized) of the critique of History allows us to see how the orderly succession of a linear narrative, as in the progression to modernity in Chinese historiography, may be bifurcated by relating each of these developments to a reaction or countermovement in the parallel process.

The climax of the Chinese narrative, represented by the birth of full modern self-consciousness in the May 4th movement, actually begins the narrative in the Indian case. The Bengal Renaissance of the first half of the nineteenth century, championed by its initiator and central figure, Ram Mohun Roy, upheld reason and individual rights against "superstition" and the hierarchy of caste and family. True, he held onto Hinduism, but this Hinduism was transformed into a unitarianism and the repository of reason. Moreover, by virtue of the very rationalistic methods whereby he sought to establish his case, he revealed himself to be a modernist and is popularly known in India as the "Father of Modern India." Ram Mohun Roy and his followers advocated the improved status of women, as well as the adoption of English language and scientific education in Bengali (Ray

1975, 14–15). Even more radical than Roy was the Young Bengal movement of the 1820s, a smaller-scale but more thoroughly iconoclastic movement of Westernized Bengali youth led by the Anglo-Indian, Henry Vivien Derozio (1809–1831). Influenced by the philosophy of Hume and Bentham and radical thinkers like Tom Paine, they claimed to measure everything with the yardstick of reason. Their attitude toward religion, which was informed by Voltaire, led them to denounce the Hindu religion with great fervor (Ahmed 1975, 99). For the Derozians, as for the May 4th iconoclasts, the total rejection of the old was only matched by the total affirmation of the new.

As the nineteenth century drew on, however, the early form of radical iconoclasm against Hinduism and tradition in general subtly began to give way to more complex, if not always more nuanced, responses to modern ideas and practices. Bankim Chandra Chattopadhyay (1838–1894), perhaps the most acclaimed man of letters in the Calcutta of his days, and who had once described himself as a member of the Young Bengal group (Raychaudhuri 1988, 203), articulated one such response to modernity which was to find many adherents among the intelligentsia of late nineteenth- and twentieth-century India as a whole. Bankim Chandra acknowledged the significance and desirability of science and rationality. The West had achieved progress, prosperity, and freedom because it had placed reason at the heart of its culture. But the West was superior only in the culture of material life and had little to contribute to the spiritual aspect of life. Here it was the East that had the upper hand. Man was imperfect if he had developed only one side, especially the material. The perfect and complete man combined the religious truths of Hinduism with the love of reason. To be sure, figures like Chattopadhyay, just as much if not more than the Chinese, were affected by European Orientalists (Raychaudhuri 1988, 8) who, it might be said, projected a yearning for a "lost spirituality" into Oriental societies.

Bankim Chandra and other like-minded thinkers, such as Aurobindo Ghosh and Swami Vivekananda, occupy a place in the trajectory of opposition to modernism somewhere between the national culture group and the neo-traditional Confucianists. Like the former, Bankim Chandra recognized the significance and necessity of modern ideas: rationalism, progress, individualism. But his nationalism led him to claim that a purified and regenerated Hindu ideal was far superior as a rational philosophy of life than anything Western religion or philosophy had to offer. Like the National Essence school, Bankim Chandra distinguished modernism from Westernism and claimed that modernism could become part of a transcendent Hindu cultural ideal. But in practice, the tensions in his thought led him to oppose reformers who advocated reform of Hindu customs and practices by appealing to the colonial state on the basis of enlightened reason. Bankim Chandra did not oppose reform in principle; but he believed that change would and should follow from the new moral consensus that would emerge from the rejuvenated national culture, or national religion, as he preferred to call it (Chatterjee 1986, 73–79). Thus, as with Liang Shuming, politics and culture could never really remain separate: the religio-moral insight would necessarily shape the vision of the ideal society that had to be realized.

In the history of Indian nationalism, the early twentieth century is seen as marking a political break between the extremists and moderates; between those who wanted immediate independence and would use agitational politics to achieve it and those who sought more gradual, constitutional modes to attain concessions directed, ultimately, toward independence. From the perspective of culture, this political break also fits, albeit imperfectly, with the incorporation within mainstream nationalism of a discourse of the nation founded in Hindu culture as opposed to the European model of civilizational progress for the colonies. The assumptions of the latter are captured in the Moderate critique of "the un-British rule of the British in India," to which Moderates like G. K. Gokhale and Nehru's father, Motilal Nehru, subscribed. Hindu nationalism was exemplified by Gokhale's fellow Maharashtrian, the extremist B. G. Tilak, who took nationalist rhetoric out of the lawyers' chambers and into the streets to mobilize Hindus during their communal festivities. Although Gandhi drew his ideas from a variety of sources and evolved a unique blend, as depicted in chapter 2, he too drank deeply from this trope of "culture," of an irreducible (Hindu) spirituality as a foundation for his nationalism.

At this point, the Indian narrative of national modernization becomes complicated. We are at a cross-road: should we focus on Jawaharlal Nehru as the flowering of modern consciousness or on Gandhi who turns his back on History? We could, by focusing on Nehru and the segment of the intelligentsia favoring the vision of a fully modern society which dominated certain strategic points of Indian public life through most of the independence movement, develop the narrative of emancipation. To be sure, even among this group, there were few who advocated the kind of break with history seen in the May 4th movement or even among the Derozians. For Nehru the significance of traditions lay not in a transcendent spiritual or moral telos but in the historical development of the nation. All the great rulers of Indian history, such as Asoka, the Guptas, Akbar, and several other Moghul emperors attempted to develop a political framework to unite the cultural diversity of the subcontinent. This History, while giving the Indian people their unique qualities, also placed them within the progressive and emancipatory project of the Enlightenment.[2]

Like the Chinese historians discussed in chapter 1, Nehru saw the historical nation through the biological metaphor of growth and decline. The great heights of Indian thought, culture, and science had been reached as early as the eleventh century and subsequently entered a long dark period of rigidity and stagnation (Nehru 1960, 121–28). To be sure, there were short cycles of creativity thereafter, especially during the reign of Akbar and some of the other Moghul emperors, but until the modern period, which was uniquely the period of vigor and dynamism of the Europeans, there was no basic growth in India. Even within this brief outline, Nehru obviously displays an ambivalence regarding the question of a preformed national subject of ancient times. The end of creativity coincides roughly with the advent of the Islamic period, but individual Muslim monarchs are able to regenerate society periodically. Certainly there was no question of the *substance* of an ancient culture reappearing in Nehru's *Discovery of India*. That was left to Hindu nationalists of different stripes from the benign to the savagely vengeful. Even more than for the cultural nativists, culture and politics were separable for Nehru. Indeed not only were they separable, but culture occupied a distinctly subordinate position in relation to History. And as with the Chinese Marxists, a national culture may once have embodied (and will again embody) the supreme ideals of its age. Though not a Marxist, in the way in which Nehru sustained the idea of the uniqueness of national culture within a modernist vision of History, he resembled the Chinese Marxists when they were not violently antihistorical. Perhaps his ideas can be placed somewhere between the nativists and the Marxists in China.

But the narrative has to confront the figure and impact of Gandhi. He is perhaps among the most difficult political figures to understand in terms taken from modern discourses. My reading of Gandhi here owes much to works by Partha Chatterjee and Ashish Nandy. What were Gandhi's basic ideas about modern civilization? For Gandhi the religio-moral vision was so compelling that it could not brook the

2. Nehru actually develops a variation on the Hegelian progression of the universal "spirit of the age," which the modern Indian nation must once again realize.

separation of politics and culture, a distinction regarded by true believers—whether Gandhi or the variety of religious fundamentalists
found in the world today—to be a particular imposition of modernism itself. In *Hind Swaraj*, published first in 1909, Gandhi launches a
total indictment of modern civilization as it has developed in the West
and which was subsequently brought into India. Gandhi pursues a
line of argument that can also be found in the Western romantic
tradition as well as in certain Hindu and Buddhist texts. His argument, however, is not founded on a textual or scriptural tradition
but, rather, on a universalist moral philosophy. According to Gandhi,
the modern organization of society, designed to release its productive potential and produce increasing wealth and comfort for all, is
ultimately self-destructive. Modern civilization actually makes the
individual a prisoner of his or her own craving for luxury and self-
indulgence, generates a destructive competitiveness and brings about
poverty, inequality, and large-scale violence (Gandhi 1938, 24–27,
44–45).

Unlike the Marxists, who critiqued colonialism for its class character but praised it for unleashing new productive forces and technology in "stagnant, feudal societies," Gandhi criticizes precisely these
productive forces. Modern machinery can only create the desire for
more goods, it can never satisfy it. Worse, industrialism brings destruction, exploitation, and disease to a society and creates an especially exploitative relationship between the city and the village
(Gandhi 1938, 68–70). Modern industrialism cannot find a place in
Gandhi's religio-moral vision of society; neither can the modern state.
For Gandhi, whose anarchism was influenced by Tolstoy, the critique
of the modern state flows logically from his ideas about industrialism.
The modern state was only necessary because of the needs of industrialism and the coordination of large-scale organizations. Parliamen-
tary representation does not improve Gandhi's image of the state
because representative politics is based on a competitive individualism. In the new independent India, the state could never be the
appropriate machinery for the rejuvenation of village society and
economy. More important, the state as a coercive agency *could not
claim an inalienable authority*, for that authority lay in the law of
Dharma or moral duty which resided outside of the state (Iyer 1973,
253–60). Only religion possessed that transcendent authority by
means of which the existing establishment could be challenged.

Gandhi proposed a utopian society of largely autarkic village communities called Ramarajya (or the kingdom of Rama, the legendary
sage-king, see chapter 2). This was to be a patriarchy in which the

ruler, by his exemplary moral qualities, expressed the collective will. It is also a utopia in which the economic organization of production, arranged according to an idealized "varna" form of organization with a perfect system of reciprocity, would ensure that there would be no competition and differences in status. The ideal conception of Ramrajya, in fact, encapsulates the critique of all that is morally reprehensible in the economic and political organization of civil society (Chatterjee 1986, 92). The similarity of this vision to a Mencian conception of society is striking, but its similarity to a Maoist utopian vision is even more intriguing.

If we temporarily free Mao from the narrative of modernity and slice Chinese historical materials from the angle of a counternarrative, we can make much sense of both Gandhi and Mao. Both were in search of alternative forms of community, alternatives to competitive—in particular, market—models of society implicit in the emancipation ideal. Although Mao held on to the notion of economic progress, their common concern for economic and politically autarkic communes, the loathing of urban domination, the mistrust of technological expertise, and the superiority of spontaneously self-governing communities over systems of representation, whether this was the Party or Parliament, confirmed for both the necessity of subordinating politics to a communal morality.

Frederic Wakeman (1973) showed that while History itself, for Mao, remained within the progressive linearity of the Hegelian-Marxist formulation, the question of human *will* as the counterpoint to the automaticity of the unfolding of History remained unresolved, as it did in the formulation generally. The understanding of will in Mao provides an opening to influences from Chinese intellectual and moral traditions, including those from Wang Yangming to Kang Youwei. Wakeman is careful to note that this is not some timeless influence and he tracks it particularly through Kang Youwei's synthesis in the early part of the century which, although it was an incomplete synthesis, identified the telos of evolution as the morality of *ren*. This preoccupation in Mao's view is evident in that the ability to make History demanded the possession of a moral force, "a kind of revolutionary sincerity" or purity among individuals (Wakeman 1973, 324). Thus, it is the irruption of an obscured genealogy of *ren* into the dominant narrative that moved Mao, perhaps despite himself, to subvert the telos of progressive History by the quest for a moral community.

Yet, Mao was not an antimodernist, while Gandhi most definitely was. Mao's communal utopia was not transcendent; indeed, it was immanent and, frighteningly, imminent. Gandhi's utopia was based on a distinctly transcendent foundation and, as such, he was able to resist assimilation into the romantic critique of modernity. Chatterjee argues that European romantics critiqued science and rationality from within the Enlightenment discourse. They never called for the ultimate abandonment of Reason but, rather, were torn between the demands of Reason and Morality, Progress and Happiness, Historical Necessity and Human Will. These tensions did not trouble Gandhi as they did many other Indian thinkers and leaders, including Tagore (Chatterjee 1986, 99–100). The foundation of Gandhi's views of society derived fundamentally from his composite religious vision of Truth, denying History, and defying the Enlightenment problematic of his age. But the nation was not denied; at least not for the moment. Having no anchor in History, or even in history (which has no permanent anchor), the nation would have to embody the transcendent Truth.

What makes it possible for someone like Gandhi and his ideas to occupy the supremely important place that they do in Indian society and history? It is most unusual to find the general acceptability and prestige accorded such anti-modern ideas among people educated in modern society in other parts of the world. The contrast is particularly striking in the comparison with China, both with the ROC and the PRC. Although I have compared him with Mao, the comparison must break down with respect to Mao's ultimate adherence to the Enlightenment project and his violent rejection of the past. Then, of course, there is the case of Liang Shuming, who has been compared to Gandhi. Indeed, Liang liked to regard himself as a Chinese Gandhi. But the comparison with Liang Shuming is telling, because Liang's influence or prestige among China's intelligentsia is but a fraction of Gandhi's in Indian society.

To be sure, practically speaking, Gandhi accommodated, and was happily accommodated by, many modern forces, not the least of which was the emergent Indian industrial bourgeoisie, especially the house of the Birla, ranked today among the top industrial houses in the country. But regardless of whether or not his ideas are practiced in India today, the relative prestige that they occupied itself needs explanation. Moreover, although we are often reminded that Gandhi's political and economic ideas are no longer, nor were they really ever, influential in India, they have existed as a strong oppositional force criticizing the establishment. Oppositional groups inspired by Gandhian ideas seek to critique the extreme effects of modernity and search for ways of mitigating its most destructive results, whether they be the social costs of large-scale industrialism and urbanism, the untrammeled growth of state power in the name of progress, or the unforseen devastation of the environment. In particular, the environmental movement, especially in India, has led to a resurgence of interest in Gandhi's critique of modernity. The critique of modernity may have been finally domesticated by Indian nationalism, but it has not disappeared.[3]

I propose to undertake two strategies to explain the differences in the weight and influence of antimodern ideas in India and China among the intelligentsia and elites more widely. I wish to underline that my strategies refer particularly to the ways in which these politically active elites—the designers of these new nation-states—represent themselves and their visions of political community; they do not refer to some abstract entity such as Indian or Chinese political cultures. The first strategy will seek the possible institutional anchors for such antimodernist perspectives in the different political cultures of these elites. This strategy will provide the necessary but not sufficient condition to explain the difference. The second strategy considers the particular ideological conjuncture in which Gandhian ideas emerged and took root. This had much to do with the specific circumstances of imperialism and modes of resistance in the two countries: with Gandhian resistance to direct British rule and the Chinese response first to indirect imperialism and then the military and ideological resistance to Japanese imperialism. The first strategy appeals to an argument for cultural difference in the way the elite was integrated with the polity, the second to differences in ideology and cultural strategies of resistance.

Lin Yu-sheng (1979) has argued that the totalistic iconoclasm of the May 4th movement was itself made possible by the organic unity between the cultural and political order in the Chinese imperial system. In this system, universal kingship integrated the cultural-moral order with the sociopolitical order. The collapse of this pivot in the system meant the collapse of the legitimating principle of this elite's cultural-moral order, which subsequently enabled the totalistic attack

---

3. The Gandhian element is particularly developed in the "new social movements" in India, such as "eco-feminism" and the "farmers' movements." These movements tend to be anti-state, environmentally concerned, women-participatory, and oriented toward a village-centered, decentralized development (see Gail Omvedt 1992, 1994). In this context, postcolonial theory among South Asian intellectuals may be seen, in part at least, as an intellectualized and Westernized variant of a socially deeper, contemporary critique of modernity traceable to Gandhi.

on the traditional order.[4] There is a remarkably symmetrical argument made for Indian society by the Indologist Louis Dumont. Dumont (1980) argues that it is religious ideas, especially of hierarchy and pollution, and the Brahmin priesthood that held together the entire system. Kingship and politics, although protecting religion, were fundamentally dependent on religious ideas and the ritual activities of the Brahmin priesthood for their legitimation. So where, in Lin's account, the cultural and moral, as well as the more broadly social sphere, were dependent on the imperial institution for their legitimation, in Dumont's view of India, politics and society depended on religious institutions and ideas. Thus, in India, "religion encompassed the political," whereas in China, it was the political which encompassed the religious (or moral culture).

Both views may be criticized for essentializing complex cultural traditions, for reducing the enormous diversity of China and India to simple, and some would say simplistic, principles. I have found some value in their formulations as ways of understanding how elites perceived and integrated themselves with political power. Thus, in Lin's formulation, we may better think of the organic unity as a representation which informed the worldview of the literati elite and the upwardly mobile segments of society. As for Dumont, we need to qualify his assertion about religion sanctioning politics by the extent to which this relationship was relevant to the self-understanding of different, particularly lower-class, groups. By understanding these formulations as specific elite representations rather than as timeless cultural principles, we may also see how differently these elite representations have tried to shape the emergent nations in the two societies as the new sources of sovereign authority. In the comparative study that follows, I turn to a study by Arjun Appadurai of the history of a south Indian kingdom and temple community from the eighteenth until the early twentieth century. For the Chinese materials, I will use my own researches and other materials from the north China plain in the nineteenth and twentieth centuries.

Appadurai's study of the Sri Partasarati Svami temple in Madras gives us a clear picture of how authority was constructed in this society. Before the British took over the area in the late seventeenth century, a triangular relationship obtained in the community between the kings, the sectarian priests of the temple, and the temple commu-

---

4. Lin argues further that in the process of engaging in the totalistic attack, the May 4th revolutionaries reproduced the assumption of the very unity between culture and politics, seeking once again to legitimate culture by some other master narrative.

nity, the last of which also happened to be subjects of the kingdom. A set of transactions, material and symbolic, held the three together. Sovereignty lay actually with the deity of the temple. By providing royal gifts and protection (other patrons might grant more generous gifts, but could not provide protection) to the temple, the king, who demonstrated the highest form of service to the deity, came to share in the paradigmatic royalty of the deity. "By being the greatest servant of the deity, the human king sustains and displays his rule over men" (Appadurai 1981, 51). Thus, the authority of the rulers in the kingdom was, in practice, crucially dependent on their patronage of the temple.

Behind the conferral of these ritual honors and critical to the link between the temple community and the king and the royal bureaucracy, were, of course, the sectarian managers of the temple, who were also the religious leaders of the community. While the king was granted the authority to be the ultimate arbiter in temple disputes, the actual day-to-day, managerial authority of the temple community lay with these leaders; and the monarch could not encroach upon the prerogative. As Appadurai puts it,

> the ceremonial exchanges of honor between warrior-kings and sectarian leaders rendered public, stable and culturally appropriate an exchange at the level of politics and economics. These warrior-kings bartered the control of agrarian resources gained by military prowess for access to the [symbolically] re-distributive processes of temples, which were controlled by sectarian leaders. Conversely, in their own struggles with each other. . . . sectarian leaders found the support of these warrior-kings timely and profitable. (Appadurai 1981, 74)

With the expansion of the colonial British state and the growth of its control over the most intimate spheres of life, especially in the late nineteenth century, this particular interaction of religious and political structures of authority fell away and the triangular relationship was replaced by a state-civil society model of authority. At the structural level, the British dispensed with temples as the authoritative basis of rule in south India. Moreover, reversing the pattern of the past, the colonial administration sought increasingly to control the day-to-day affairs of the temple, thereby encroaching upon the authority of the temple leaders and generating enormous conflict and unending litigation. The historic process outlined was an effort at classic state-building—whereby the state attempts to appropriate the authority of local communities—albeit in the colonial context.

What was the effect of this state-making on the religious structures of authority? Needless to say, the old triangular relationship collapsed. Moreover, the authority of the sectarian leaders was being increasingly challenged. Yet, this temple, and Hindu temples all over India, continued to play a vital role in electoral politics, political mobilization, and politics in general. Control of temples continued to generate intense competition between local powerholders, their lawyers, and publicists (Washbrook 1976). Cut off from state power, sectarian and Brahmin elites sought to reinforce their religious authority within the community and temple, which continued to provide, as Appadurai argues, a last resort for working out political entitlement. Temple honors were not only valued cultural markers because they brought enhanced status to the recipient, but because they also brought control of temple resources, their followings, and their allies. Thus the continued importance of religious institutions in the power and self-perception of an important segment of the Indian elite would ensure religious ideas a role in the emergent narratives of the nation.

Consider the way in which religious and political structures of authority were articulated at the local level in China, both before and after the process of modern state-making took hold. As has been shown throughout this book, in the villages of north China during the late nineteenth and early twentieth centuries, patronage and management of the religious sphere of activity: endowing and managing temple lands, building and repairing temples, organizing temple festivities, serving on temple management committees clearly brought honor and status to those engaged in them. These activities were monopolized by the village elite, who, in terms of leisure and resources, were best able to avail of them. In many villages, these activities in the religious sphere provided the framework for managing the public affairs of the village, for instance running the crop-watching association or the self-defense corps of the village. Moreover, in some villages, temple committees also functioned as the ultimate tribunal to judge offenders in the village under the watchful eyes of the gods (Duara 1988a, chap. 5).

I have argued that the active role played by the village elite in the religious sphere was sanctioned by the cosmology of a universal bureaucracy headed by the emperor but composed of both earthly and godly bureaucrats mediating the relationship between spiritual and temporal worlds (1988a, 134–36). The activities of this universal bureaucracy provided a model for leaders to represent their authority and exercise their responsibilities. For whatever practical reasons the village elite performed their activities in the religious sphere, the bureaucrats' patronage of officially sanctioned gods and the gentry's sponsorship of both official and nonofficial gods communicated a clear message to them about the style and responsibilities of political leadership in society. It also alerts us to the way in which authority in the religious sphere at the local level was symbolically dependent on the pivotal role of universal emperorship and, more widely, on the ritual activities of the imperial bureaucracy. This is brought home most sharply when the modernizing state began to send a different message regarding the religious sphere in the villages and urged village leaders to transfer their allegiance from the religious realm to the more secular activities of the modern regime.

As I have shown in earlier chapters, at the turn of the twentieth century, the provincial administration of Zhili and Shandong under the initial leadership of Yuan Shikai sought to implement a series of modernizing reforms at the village level and target the old religious sphere as the source of "superstition" and also substantial resources. The success of this administration in appropriating temples and temple property was not inconsiderable (see chapter 5). This was due largely to cooperation by the village elites, who saw new channels of social mobility in the schools, titles, and programs which came down to the village came from a national authority. These resources functioned to certify and bolster the authority of the village elite, who monopolized official positions in this initial period (Duara 1988a, 157). In other words, the rural elite turned out to be extremely adaptive and responsive to state demands: they were able to transfer their allegiances from the religious sphere to the secular sphere relatively painlessly. They were able to do so because, for them, it had been the political within the religious that had been salient in the first place. The religious domain had ceased to be a factor in the political role of the elite any more.

What does this comparative excursus tell us about the greater prominence of critiques of modernity in India? Surely not the simplistic conclusion that religion is necessarily antimodern. Religion, in and of itself, is scarcely incompatible with modernity as the increasingly popular role of religion in the United States, Japan, or Taiwan reveals. In India, the economically most developed state is the Punjab, where Sikh religious revivalism reigns dominant. In China, the areas which have prospered most in recent years, such as the south and southeast coast, have also witnessed a massive religious revival. I believe it tells us that where elites locate their authority outside of the political power of the state, which often tends to be in organized religions, they are able not only to generate opposition, but also to articulate alternative narratives to the authoritative discourse located within this political power. Thus, a state-building program in India did not foreclose, and may even have contributed to, the expansion of a space within which certain elite groups could engage in an indigenous critique of the narrative of History associated with the colonial power. This is also how we can understand the force of Gandhi's resistance to granting moral authority to the state.

In China, since universal kingship encompassed the religious and moral order, the source of authority for local elites as well as intelligentsia resided principally in the political. We have seen how the pivotal role of the political shaped the allegiances of the elite at even the most local levels of rural society. The collapse of the political pivot which made possible the radical iconoclasm of the May 4th movement also delegitimated critiques of the emergent order originating in the nonmodern sectors of society. As discussed in chapter 3, nonmodern and nonelite popular religious movements, such as those led by the Small Sword Society, continued to flourish and challenge the hegemonic discourse, especially as it pertained to popular religion. However, lacking links with the modern intelligentsia, they were unable to articulate a counternarrative of dissent that was acceptable in the public domain.

The relative autonomy of religious authority in India enabled a man like Gandhi to be as influential as he was. But it would be a mistake to identify Gandhi entirely with the project of the nineteenth-century Hindu elite who sought to found the nation in the idea of a "spiritual culture" in opposition to History. Stephen Hay has revealed how the entire nineteenth-century Hindu renaissance was the work overwhelmingly of Brahmins in Bengal and South India. It was also largely the celebration of the high Brahmanic philosophical tradition of the Vedas and the Upanishad. While at one level, Gandhi, a non-Brahmin, drew from this tradition, Ashish Nandy (1987, 155–58) points out that, at another level, he marked a break with this tradition because Gandhi's Hinduism affirmed the noncanonical and the folk. While this may make him similar to the Chinese nativists in search of traditional roots of a modern, national culture, we should recall that for Gandhi it was often the nonmodern within these folk traditions that he valued. Gandhi's critique of modernity derived its legitimacy in substantial part from the popular, sectarian religious traditions which continued to play a vital part in the area that he came from. This corner of Gujarat was an area of eclectic and competing religious cultures, including ascetic Jainism and Christianity, and his family was strongly influenced by the devotional tradition of monotheistic Hinduism known as *bhakti*. It was from this tradition that he derived his opposition to classical, caste-bound Hinduism and projected a religious nationalism based on nonviolence and compassion. Most of all, the *bhakti* tradition gave him an orientation and style. By following in the path of *bhakti* teachers, walking about the land preaching his message, Gandhi, the latter-day saint, was able to reach out to the ordinary people (Rudolphs 1967, 158, 172).

If the continued meaningfulness of religious traditions among segments of the elite leadership of the national movement in India created a space and an audience for the critique of modernity, the substance of Gandhi's critique itself was not a necessary outcome of this space. The substance must be understood in the context of his encounter with colonial ideology. Ashis Nandy (1983) has argued that the psychological impact of colonial ideology is much more devastating and longer lasting than its political or economic effect. This impact is felt both in the colonized society as well as in the colonizing society. The justification of world colonization by Western powers required the construction of an ideology of rule that not only transformed the representation of the colonized peoples, but also recast the self-image of Western society as one that was quintessentially and definitionally the antithesis of the East. In the Indian context, the "natives" were marked variously as cowardly, effeminate, naively childlike, superstitious, ignorant and the like. In turn, the West was characterized by the images of youthfulness, aggressiveness, and mastery, exemplified so well in the British public school. In doing so, it repressed many of the antinomial Dionysian features of Western society itself, such as femininity, childlikeness, passiveness, the positive qualities of age, at great psychological cost to this society. Nandy examines the crippling effects of this ideology on those at the interface of the encounter, people such as Rudyard Kipling, E. M. Forster, and C. F. Andrews, on the one side, and Westernized Indians such as Aurobindo Ghosh on the other.

Gandhi was among the very few elite Indians to successfully resist the colonial representation of the Indian. In my opinion, upper-caste Hindu reformers tended to respond to the colonial psychological onslaught with a myopic defensiveness of a reconstructed Hindu spirituality (versus Western materiality)—itself a colonial product. Partly in consequence of this defensiveness, Hindu elites have been much more closed to the kind of self-criticism that characterized May 4th intellectuals in China. Gandhi was able to break through this defensiveness and, according to Nandy, resist the linkages at the root of colonial ideology between progressive mastery at the heart of History on the one hand, and racism, hypermasculinity, and overvalued adulthood on the other (Nandy 1983, 100). His doctrine of passive resistance and nonviolence sought to liberate activism and courage from aggressiveness and recognize them as perfectly compatible with womanhood. Keenly aware of the disfiguring effects of colonialism on the British themselves, he pointed to the abandonment of true Christian values which, he believed, could never justify colonialism.

But (and this is not part of Nandy's argument) Gandhi appears to have taken a final step of equating the irrationality and immorality of colonialism with that of modernity as a whole. So deeply implicated were the categories of modern thought with colonial ideology that to accept the Western criterion of a true antagonist—to be a player in the game of "modernization"—would be to violate one's own being, to remain imprisoned within the deforming categories of the other.

Thus the sufficient condition enabling Gandhi's critique of modernity lay in the encounter with colonial ideology and his ability to provide a psychologically valid alternative to it in his nationalism, especially for a middle class caught awkwardly between two worlds. In China, the imperialist presence was, of course, widely resented and anti-imperialism was at the core of political movements for the first half of the twentieth century. But the absence of institutionalized colonialism in most parts of China also meant that colonial ideology was not entrenched among both colonizer and colonized in the same way as it was in India and other directly colonized countries. The opposition to imperialism was chiefly political and economic and did not present the urgent need to root out imperialist ideology in the very self-perception of a people. It is interesting to speculate on the role and effects of Japanese colonial discourse in the early twentieth century.

As far as I know, few scholars have taken up this subject seriously. However, work seeking to understand the Japanese construction of History and the Orient is beginning to emerge, most notably, Stefan Tanaka's *Japan's Orient* (see also James Fujii 1993). At the center of Tanaka's concern is the Meiji production of *toyoshi* (literally, Eastern History), a historical narrative of great consequence for East Asia. From our perspective, *toyoshi* combined linear History with the oppositional discourse of "culture" in a way that Japan could resist the hierarchies of universal History and thus establish its equivalence to the West and yet create its own superiority in relation to the rest of Asia, particularly to China, which came to be designated in this discourse as Shina. As the foundation of an alternative History, the East was idealized (or Orientalized) and, for figures like Okakura Tenshin,

Japan's mission lay in reentering the Asiatic past and regaining the lost beauty of Asia. The dominant academic trend, however, tended to objectify Shina as Japan's past, as a temporal inferior, even while claiming some of the timeless qualities of Asiatic ideals as being embodied in modern Japan (Tanaka 1993, 19). While it is important to recognize the indeterminacy of *toyoshi* discourse and the fact that it inspired many Japanese to reach out to other Asians to build a positive future, nonetheless, there was, even amongst the most noble-minded of these figures, a paternalism toward Japan's Orient that seeded the violent appropriation of this discourse by Japanese imperialism (Tanaka 1993, chapter 5).

From the outset, then, it would appear that Japanese colonial ideology took a different approach to its colonial subjects that would have made a Gandhian type of response inappropriate, if not meaningless. In proclaiming the establishment of the Greater East Asian Co-prosperity Sphere as the mission of Japanese rule in the 1930s and 1940s, the Japanese imperialists were appealing to the Orientalism of *toyoshi*, which celebrated an Asiatic unity. Idyllic village communities based on the spirit of age-old cooperation were to be the building blocks of the Japanese empire, which was the only force capable of resisting the corrupting influences of Western capitalism (Hatada Takashi 1976, 10-15). Although there was a world of a difference between Gandhi and the Japanese imperialists, nonetheless, the basis of a critique founded on alternative Asian values, which Gandhi also espoused, was arguably extremely suspect in China.

CONCLUSION

I believe it is important for me to take a stand on Gandhi's thorough-going critique of modernity. In the course of writing this chapter, it occurred to me that I was faced with the irony of ending a book on China—more or less—with an extended discussion of Gandhi. Intellectually, of course, this was perfectly justified for a work that sought to deconstruct the limits imposed by national preoccupations. At another level, I had to admit that the "cunning of nationalism" had insinuated itself in my work: working through Gandhi has been a way of working with my dilemmas as a postcolonial intellectual whose self-representations have alienated me from worlds of which I had once been an intimate part. It is perhaps inevitable that, with widely varying degrees of destructiveness, all of our representations imply normative hierarchies which tend to marginalize and repress peoples and cultures. Is Gandhi relevant to understanding how and why to keep our dialogue open to the Other?

My answer is both yes and no. Gandhi's contribution was to demonstrate that it may be possible to bring vast masses of people into the political mainstream without the same violent or wrenching transformation of their self-image that nineteenth-century imperialism had produced among the intelligentsia; to locate the sources of self-empowerment (*swaraj*) not only in an external or elite discourse but within the best in their popular traditions; and to project an ideology that minimized the instrumentalization of the people with whom he worked. In these respects he also resembled grassroots reformers in China like Jimmy Yan and Liang Shuming for whom the transformative impulse was balanced by the need to preserve the local as a value, even though he was much more politically popular than were they.

In preserving the local—here religious traditions in relation to the modernizing center—as a value, Gandhi was able to transform it into a space from which the dominant ideology of the state could be critiqued—a space similar in many ways to civil society in the West. We tend not to equate religious space with civil society because the Enlightenment project was directed against the authority of the church. If, however, we may step aside from the history of modern Europe and seek our perspective from political developments for democratization in East Europe, Latin America, the Philippines and elsewhere, then we have to recognize that the critique of state and state ideologies has come from the authority provided by religious sources such as the Roman Catholic Church and Liberation Theology.

The narrative of emancipatory modernity in China has its power because it has elicited the commitment of both the Chinese state and the modern intelligentsia. Its gains for the Chinese people in many areas of life cannot go unappreciated. Moreover, despite my criticism of the Chinese intelligentsia's representation of the "people," I believe that the highly elitist Indian bureaucracy and intelligentsia (outside of the community-oriented activist groups) can learn much from Chinese egalitarianism. Yet the consuming commitment of Chinese intellectuals to the narrative of modernity has tended to produce a monologism in which gradualist reformers like Liang Shuming, Jimmy Yan, Tao Xingzhi, and others (each of whom could perhaps have played the role of a Gandhi under different circumstances) have been marginalized. In the process, this narrative has obscured the vitality of popular culture, religion, and their associational life and delegitimated the critique of modern ideologies originating outside of modern discourses. Despite the repeated persecution of the intelligentsia by the Chinese state, it is this shared narrative which has thrown so many of them repeatedly into the arms of the state and at the same time alienated both from the living cultures of the "masses" and of "tradition." While the state has made effective use of the narrative of modernity to expand its own powers, the Chinese intelligentsia has robbed itself of alternative sources of moral authority which it might have found in history and popular culture.

At the same time, Gandhi's success in politicizing the people was also limited by the fact that his politics were a meditation on the methodology of morality. We may think of his mission as the production of a self that was less epistemologically controlling, but *morally* self-aware and self-controlled. Indeed, such was his dedication to this disciplinary project that it became its own totalization and took its own toll. I find this totalization reflected in his utopianism, which was so radically oppositional that it reproduced the essentializing quality of modernity which he sought to fight. Thus, by conflating colonialism with modernity as a single, given mode of being, he objectified it and did not attend to the *historical* tensions within that could unravel it. How would Gandhi have accounted for pacificist traditions in modern society, for the power of the environmental movement, for the increased visibility of androgyny, for the "age revolution"? Gandhi did not recognize that any deconstruction of a system of ideas must also fall prey to this system. To put it more affirmatively, "It is a question of explicitly and systematically posing the problem of the status of a discourse which borrows from a heritage the resources necessary for the de-construction of that heritage itself" (Derrida 1978, 282).

In not posing the problem of his affiliation with that which he critiqued, Gandhi could not see that the transcendent Truth which his conception of the nation sought to embody was exactly parallel to the nation as the transcendent subject of History, an essence which remained even as all tangible histories were rewritten, dispersed, or had died out. In seeking to displace History as the foundation of the nation, Gandhi banished historicity itself and ended up with a transcendental ideal, the more impossible to realize. Our task is to banish History, but at the same time, to rescue history. We do so with the knowledge that the nation cannot be essentialized as a transcendent reality, beyond self-serving regimes and bickering interest groups. Nations live simultaneously as relations of power, as representations of community, and as yearnings for transcendence. As the complex and ever-changing relationship between these three terms, the nation can only be grasped by marshaling all of the resources that history has to offer.

CONCLUSION

IN THIS BOOK I have sought to understand the nation as a *meaningful* entity, as different visions and narratives of community. The prevalent characterization of the nation, however, has tended to emphasize its formal dimension as a territorial, sovereign nation-state. This model, which has been generated by the global system of nation-states, has an intimate kinship with national Histories that depict the nation as a self-same ancient entity evolving into the collective subject of the modern nation-state. Armed with this narrative of History, and with a battery of discourses from social Darwinism to Marxism which often reproduced the assumptions of History, modernizing nationalists and the nation-state in China have sought to either obliterate or appropriate the otherness of those who do not belong to its ideal of self-consciousness—such as popular religious groups or secret societies—into the narrative of History. Even when the idea of a national History has not been challenged, proponents of a centralizing, statist narrative have destroyed and buried alternative paths to a modern nation. We saw how nationalistic organizations such as the KMT and the CCP, claiming a collective national subject within the state, caused the political and ideological demise of the federalist movement and the *fengjian*/civil society endeavor.

And yet when I turned to the very discourses and narratives which at one level buttressed the assumptions of national History, I found that each also produced acute tensions with the formal conception of the nation as the collective, territorial sovereign. Consider not only the cross-cutting representations of class, religion, and race or the transnational aspirations of anti-imperialism and of historical representations, but even social Darwinism. Thus, social Darwinism, which had just about locked together race and nation in China, could be found, in a local reading of it, to sanction autonomous provinces that deferred their union with the nation in the rhetoric of early twentieth-century federalists. Note also the language of the "end of history": nationalist radicals, advocating the Hegelian telos of self-consciousness in the campaign against popular religion, struggled hard to justify the nation as the moral community when they had to deny both its past and its future. These discourses and competing narratives of community produce the nation as the object not only of identity and loyalty, but of contestation, indeed bloody contestation, such as in the American or Chinese civil wars or the partition of India at independence.[1]

In order to grasp how these discourses have been able to generate such oppositional functions, I have found it necessary to read these discourses and national History as changing and partial means of producing identities and not as coherent and cohesive totalities. In particular, I showed, in chapters 2 and 3, the importance of distancing ourselves from viewing a modern value such as self-consciousness as the essence of an era or society. Thus we have seen totalizing representations of community in the past supplement universalist ideologies, just as we have seen modern nations riven by alternative and historical visions of community. I have made an effort to break down these totalities by what means I have found at hand, whether by attending to suppressed or incipient narratives in history or through the deconstructive concept of the "supplement."[2]

The nation as the site of contested meanings not only shapes the lives of people, it may also occasionally threaten its very form as the sovereign, territorial nation-state of History. Alternative conceptions of community or universalist yearnings which inhabit the representation of the nation, such as Marxist internationalism in Russia or China or Shiite fundamentalism in Iran, have presented this threat historically. Today, the threat to this form seems more palpable than

1. See Ellis and Wildavsky (1990) for a reading of the American Civil War, at least partially, as a contest between alternative narratives of society. According to them, the civil war was triggered by the growth of the radical abolitionist rhetoric and its refusal to "temporize with evil." In turn, this escalation prompted a counternarrative of community in the South justifying the master-slave relation as the foundation of a good society. The polarization of these visions of community made it impossible to sustain both within the framework of a single nation.

2. Despite my efforts, I acknowledge that, occasionally, my own usage of "modernity" or "tradition" may be more essentialist than I had realized. But I would rather admit to a blurred line between a category and its critique than pretend to be able to fully dismantle concepts that have so informed my own view of the world.

ever in the emergence of the European community and the probable reaction to it in the form of regional trading blocs. The needs of transnational capitalism may well become linked with trans- or cross-national representations of community to endanger the nation-state.

Contemporary capitalism appears to endanger the nation-state form not only from outside, but also from within. My comments below regarding capitalism's effect on the nation-state are admittedly speculative, but these effects may be one reason why History as the evolving unity of the nation seems to be giving way to "multicultur-alist" trends in many parts of the world. To some, the collapse of multi-ethnic states such as Yugoslavia or the Soviet Union may spell the resurgence of a trend toward the "ethnically cleansed" cohesive national subject and so reveal the former as an aberration. In my view, however, it is almost impossible to return to or create the mono-ethnic nation-state. I refer not only to the extraordinary hetero-geneity of populations as a result of migration and movement of people and cultures in both capitalist and ex-socialist states, but par-ticularly the increasing presence in contemporary capitalism of an "ethnic division of labor." This topic is a burgeoning, if relatively recent, area of inquiry and it is hardly appropriate to introduce it in a conclusion. But let me present a personal conversation that brought home to me with particular clarity the idea that if, in some ways, capitalism required a homogenized work-force (Gellner 1983), today it also finds the ethnic division of labor very useful.

An Indian software engineer in California's Silicon Valley once told me: most hardware engineers are Chinese; they have strong science abilities and no language (English) or social (American) skills. Most software engineers are Indian; they have math and language abilities, but no social skills. Most management is American; they have the social skills. This collocation of culture (imputed abilities) and eth-nicity with the division of labor is complex enough, but it becomes still more complicated when we realize that large numbers of Asian women are employed in computer manufacturing sweatshops be-cause of the "docile" nature of Asian women. Here the division of labor also reproduces the patriarchy of the "Asian family" through more and more intricate patterns in which culture, ethnicity, and capital are entwined. New books reviewed in business magazines and the popular press about the special talents of certain ethnicities of the world to make it in the capitalist world reinforces the tendency to link the tensions of capitalism with "peoples" and cultures rather than classes, states, or capital itself (Duara 1993).

There is something frighteningly similar between this conception of special ethnic skills and abilities and the social Darwinian conception of races with special civilizational endowments. This time, however, contemporary capitalism's spawning and use of a diversity and mobility of people(s) will make it increasingly difficult for nation-states to claim to be made up exclusively of one ethnicity/race. While economic imperatives in modern nations necessitate this mobility and diversity, the political apparatus of the nation-state is often unable to contain the disruptions that it generates (Appadurai 1993). Different ethnicities have fit into, or are perceived to have fit into, different occupational and cultural niches, such as Asian grocers in inner-city America, South Asian female domestics in West Asia, Thai workers in Taiwan, and Turks in Europe. Given the conflict potential within these niches, ethnic tensions, and identitarian movements, new narratives of *discent* and multiculturalism will spread across a great range of societies and will make it still more difficult for nation-states to celebrate their evolution as the self-same subject of History. Thus the form of the nation-state and, in particular, its relationship to History is likely to change.

What about China? Will there be a decoupling of History and the nation-state here? Will the form of the territorial sovereign nation-state be affected here? In many ways, it is more difficult to imagine this decoupling in China than in most other places. Ethnic minority activities and mass migrations, though greater than before, are still more closely controlled than elsewhere. An intensification of economic ties with Overseas Han Chinese from other nation-states in East and Southeast Asia has led to a renewed confidence in Han ethnicity. Finally, the dissolution of both Confucian and communist universalism as meaningful alternatives to nationalism has tended to revive a raw social Darwinistic nationalism. Yet even here there are countervailing trends that threaten the centralized nation-state. Provincial autarky has encouraged the emergence of new identities—in particular an emergent southern identity coalescing around Hong Kong-based capital and culture and defined against both migrant labor and the "closed mentality" of northerners (see Friedman 1993 and chapter 6). Moreover, as in Europe, the nation-state form may turn out to be an unsuited or inadequate means to manage the burgeoning economic ties between foreign and Chinese economic interests, particularly as these ties develop in Chinese coastal provinces independently of the center.

But no matter how much longer the nation-state form remains or whether History continues to sanction the nation, the powerful repressive and appropriative functions of national History need to be continually challenged. Much of the political, intellectual, and moral challenge to History in Asia centered on the idea that I have expediently designated as "culture." The moral authority of the discourse of culture derived often from universalist and redemptive yearnings such as can be found in the telos of *Datong* or Gandhi's *Ramrajya*. This universalism ironically authorized a particular space of irreducible difference (the nation) from which one could resist assimilation into History. Culture as the space of difference enabled thinkers like Liang Shuming and Gandhi to give us critical insights into the repressive functions of Enlightenment History. But the simultaneous commitment to the nation among these advocates of transcendent values and spiritual culture enabled the nation-state to appropriate this space, drain its redemptive universalism, and subvert its critical function. As the space of irreducible difference, culture has been invoked to authorize the subordination of women and political and economic rights within a nation.

More recently, the critique of linear History has generated some important creative and alternative historical writing, including that of the Annales school, Michel de Certeau, Michel Foucault, and still more recent poststructuralist and postcolonial writers (see Attridge et al. 1987; Spivak 1988). My own critique of it as national History represented by the notion of bifurcation has been influenced by some of this literature. My critique differs from most earlier critiques of nationalist historiography in that I focus less on the falsehoods of nationalist historical writing than on the narrative structure of this History as the evolving national subject. Since much contemporary historiography shares several assumptions of a linear history with modern historical actors pursuing Enlightenment goals—such as an evolving subject or a causal model—much of this professional history also falls prey to this critique. I have tried to show in various chapters how these shared assumptions render invisible several thorny issues. These include the notion of self-consciousness as the essence of modernity (chapters 2 and 3), the rewriting of social Darwinist racism (chapter 4), and, most of all, the invisibility of the changed function of signifiers such as *fengjian* (chapters 5 and 6) and others rendered by the common problematic of History.

Bifurcated history not only substitutes multiplicity for the evolution of the same, it denies that the movement of history is causally linear, that only antecedent causes produce effects within a cause-effect chain. It views history as transactional, where the present, by appropriating, repressing, and reconstituting dispersed meanings of the past, also reproduces the past. At the same time, in investigating the process of appropriation, bifurcated history seeks not only to evoke the dispersed meaning but to disclose the ways in which this past may have provided the cause, the conditions, or the affinities which enabled the transformation.

An appropriation of the past often reveals traces or influences of this past for a while, but occasionally, a trace may be entirely erased or rewritten within an astonishingly short period of time for reasons that still need to be fully explored. The most dramatic instance of this erasure—akin to Foucault's "systematic reversal" of meaning—is the transformation of the meaning and role of *fengjian* between the last few years of nineteenth century and the first few years of the twentieth century. We can see here the immense power of the narrative of History to overcome and assimilate the past for its own purposes. Similarly, the post-May 4th representation of the "people" (*renmin, minzhong*) embedded within a teleology of national History broke with earlier representations, not to speak of the cultures of real people past or present. But while we must acknowledge and excavate these breaks with the past, I do not believe that they suggest a great systemic or epistemic rupture between two different orders. These "orders" are the deterministic conceptual totalities underlying much modern scholarship of nationalism as well as of China about which I have gone on at some length.

Let me review how a bifurcated history attentive to the appropriating process has revealed some of the different ways in which the past is or was relevant to the present. I have explored the role of several signifiers which, at the turn of the twentieth century, have functioned to obscure their older meanings; yet radical transformations were less frequent than the working off of old meanings and grafting on of related meanings. Often the new meaning indexed a change of emphasis or came to be metaphorically or metonymically linked to earlier meanings. Thus, for instance, the ambivalence of *geming* as revolution and as loss of heavenly mandate among Republican revolutionaries, the common root of *zu* for both lineage and race, the maneuvering of *zizhi* (self-governance) between local autonomy and popular rule, and even the use of *Datong* (Great Unity) as the telos of progressive History reveal a process of gradual change before a new meaning is transposed on the old one. New meanings are not simply exchanged for old meanings; they are also justified or understood in terms of old meanings.

These signifiers are like the colonial functionaries of powerful historical narratives. The latter confer upon the former the new historical meaning or mission but are also themselves indigenized or historicized by them. Furthermore, dominant narratives also appropriate the meanings of indigenous or historical narratives by similarly gradualistic means, by rearranging and inflecting the meanings of older narratives or their sequences. My best example here is the manner in which the Republican revolutionaries adapted the romantic narrative of secret societies in popular fiction and managed to invest these societies with the qualities of both republican equality and racial vengeance in the new nationalist History. This was a subtle transformation that needed not only the romantic structure of the narrative but also the historical context of secret society periodic anti-Manchuism to sustain its believability. Similarly, the construction of a hybrid narrative of *discent* to mobilize societal initiative and construct a modern society at the end of the nineteenth century sought to fit new Western ideas with the earlier *fengjian* critique of autocracy. Through these complex transactions between language and history, narratives acquire the power of rhetorical persuasion even though they conceal, repress, and abstract from dispersed histories.

Historical groups able to so mobilize a narrative to transform the meanings of a culture and community have the power to produce history not only as the past but also for the future. The narrative positions them to propel future history in the immanent direction or telos of the narrative. The Chinese adoption of Enlightenment History and its narrative structures is perhaps as important in the shaping of twentieth-century Chinese history as any objective factor. The meanings of these objective factors, which are as much cause as effect, would have been considerably different with another narrative. The May 4th movement, itself immensely productive of subsequent history, is unthinkable without grasping how Chinese history came to be narrativized in the Enlightenment mode at the turn of this century. Thus we see how certain powerful narratives, such as History, can themselves play a role in shaping the present. Conversely, the federalist movement was unable to endow the province with sufficient meaning to sustain its mobilization because of both political and rhetorical weaknesses. The latter derived from the growing monopolization of language by the History of the nation-state. Language as an arena of historical contest is where we may witness the historicity of History.

There is a final realm in which a bifurcated view reveals history outside of the categories of History: in the return of the repressed. The Army of Great Unity (*Datongjun*) (chapter 3) challenged the nationalist suppression of religion in the name of the Great Unity. They defied (un-self-consciously, as it were) the nationalists' appropriation of the Great Unity as the telos of progressive History to sanction this suppression. The Gelaohui celebration of the Republican Revolution in Ming dynasty regalia mocked the appropriation of them as embodying the spirit of republicanism. Most of all, the return of popular religion and its pervasive presence throughout modern Chinese history belies its absence or marginalization in the dominant narratives of Chinese History.

There are three moments in a bifurcated history that together grant us some distance to see history beyond, or perhaps, between the discourses and narratives of the scholarly world and historical actors. In a first moment, we seek to grasp the appropriating efforts of a narrative through a critical reading of its language, attending not only to its strategies of constructing representations, but to its tactics of working with historical meanings. In a second moment, we attend to the gaps and failures of this narrative attempt to contain the "real" and most especially to signs of the dispersed "real" when they reappear elsewhere, as with the Gelaohui carnival. In a final moment, we gain a distance from the differences between our own disciplinary goals and those of the object discourses (social Darwinism, sectarian utopianism, modernization theory). It is important, however, not to see this distance as yielding absolute truth but as an enabling advantage that comes from being at a different place and a different time.

The hermeneutics of these three moments allows us to locate a history within the fissures in, at the limits of, and in the spaces between discourses. From this vantage-ground, critical historiography has the ability to historicize and de-totalize power. In revealing the historicity of an identity presumed to be originary, exclusive and cohesive, bifurcated histories belie the claims of those who would harden the boundaries of society in the name of cultural authenticity. This is an authenticity that lacks the capacity for tolerance and interdependence because it will not admit of the Other within itself.

REFERENCES

Agnew, John A. 1987. *Place and Politics: The Geographical Mediation of State and Society*. London: Allen & Unwin.

Ahmed, A. F. Salahuddin. 1975. "Rammohun Roy and his Contemporaries." In V. C. Joshi, ed., *Rammohun Roy and the Process of Modernization in India*, pp 89–103. Delhi: Vikas Publishing House.

Alitto, Guy S. 1979. *The Last Confucian: Liang Shu-ming and the Chinese Dilemma of Modernity*. Berkeley: University of California Press.

Anagnost, Ann S. 1994. "The Politics of Ritual Displacement." In Charles F. Keyes, Laurel Kendall, and Helen Hardacre, eds., *Asian Visions of Authority: Religion and the Modern States of East and Southeast Asia*. Honolulu: University of Hawaii Press.

Anderson, Benedict. 1991. *Imagined Communities: Reflections on the Origins and Spread of Nationalism*. London: Verso. (Revised and expanded version of 1983 text.)

Anderson, Marston 1985. "The Morality of Form: Lu Xun and the Modern Chinese Short Story." In Leo Ou-fan Lee, ed., *Lu Xun and His Legacy*. Berkeley: University of California Press.

Appadurai, Arjun. 1981. *Conflict and Worship under Colonial Rule: A South Indian Case*. Cambridge: Cambridge University Press.

———. 1993. "Patriotism and Its Futures." *Public Culture* 5, no. 2 (Spring): 411–29.

Armstrong, John A. 1982. *Nations before Nationalism*. Chapel Hill: University of North Carolina Press.

Attridge, David, G. Bennington, and R. Young, eds. 1987. *Post-structuralism and the Question of History*. Cambridge: Cambridge University Press.

Balibar, Etienne. 1991. "The Nation Form: History and Ideology." In Etienne Balibar and Immanuel Wallerstein, eds., *Race, Nation, Class: Ambiguous Identities*, pp. 86–106. London: Verso Press.

Banton, Michael. 1980. "The Idiom of Race: A Critique of Presentism." *Research in Race and Ethnic Relations* 2: 21–42.

———. 1983. *Racial and Ethnic Competition.* New York: Cambridge University Press.

Barlow, Tani. 1989. "Introduction." In Tani Barlow, with Gary J. Bjorge, eds., *I Myself Am Woman: Selected Writings of Ding Ling.* Boston: Beacon Press.

Bayly, Chris. 1983. *Rulers, Townsmen and Bazaars: North Indian Society in the Age of British Expansion.* Cambridge, UK: Cambridge University Press.

———. 1985. "The Pre-history of 'Communalism': Religious Conflict in India, 1700–1850." *Modern Asian Studies* 19, no. 2: 177–204.

Benard, Cheryl, and Zalmay Khalilzad. 1984. *"The Government of God": Iran's Islamic Republic.* New York: Columbia University Press.

Benjamin, Walter. 1969. "Theses on the Philosophy of History." In *Illuminations*, pp. 253–64. New York: Schocken Books.

Bergere, Marie-Claire. 1989. *The Golden Age of the Chinese Bourgeoisie, 1911–1937,* translated by Janet Lloyd. Cambridge: Cambridge University Press.

Bernstein, Richard J. 1983. *Beyond Objectivism and Relativism: Science, Hermeneutics and Praxis.* Philadelphia: University of Pennsylvania Press.

Bhabha, Homi K., ed. 1990. *Nation and Narration.* London: Routledge.

Boli-Bennet, John, and John W. Meyer. 1978. "The Ideology of Childhood and the State: Rules Distinguishing Children in National Constitutions, 1870–1970." *American Sociological Review* 43: 797–812.

Boorman, Howard L. 1968. *Biographical Dictionary of Republican China.* New York: Columbia University Press.

Breuilly, John. 1982. *Nationalism and the State.* Chicago: University of Chicago Press.

Bull, Hedley, and Adam Watson, eds., 1976. *The Expansion of International Society.* Oxford: Clarendon Press.

Cai Shaojing. 1987. *Zhongguo jindai huitangshi yanjiu [Studies in the Modern History of Chinese Secret Societies].* Beijing: Zhonghua Shuju.

Calhoun, Craig, ed. 1992. *Habermas and the Public Sphere.* Cambridge, MA: MIT Press.

Chan, Wing-tsit. 1953. *Religious Trends in Modern China.* New York: Columbia University Press.

Chang, Hao. 1971. *Liang Ch'i-ch'ao and Intellectual Transition in China, 1890–1907.* Cambridge: Harvard University Press.

———. 1987. *Chinese Intellectuals in Crisis: Search for Order and Meaning (1890–1911).* Berkeley: University of California Press.

Chatterjee, Partha. 1986. *Nationalist Thought and the Colonial World: A Derivative Discourse.* London: Zed Books.

Chen, Jerome. 1966. "Secret Societies." *Ch'ing-shih Wen-ti* 1, no. 3: 13–16.

———. 1970. "Rebels Between Rebellions—Secret Societies in the Novel, P'eng Kung Au." *Journal of Asian Studies* 29, no. 4 (August): 807–22.

Chen, Leslie H. 1988. "A Collection of Historical Materials for a Biography of Chen Chiung-ming [1878–1933]." Unpublished essay. Alexandria, VA.

Chen Duxiu. 1915 (1984). "Aiguoxin yu Zijuexin" [Patriotism and Self-consciousness]. *Jiayin* 1, no. 4. Reprinted in *Chen Duxiu wenzhang xuanbian* (1984), 67–72. Bejing: Shenghuo dushu xinzhi sanlian shudian.

———. 1922. "Duiyu xianzai Zhongguo zhengzhi wenti de wojian" [Regarding my Views on the Contemporary Political Situation in China]. *Nuli Zhoubao*, 3 September.

Chen Jiongming. 1928. *Zhongguo tongyi zhuyi* [*My Humble Opinion on Chinese Unity*]. With a preface by Zhang Taiyan. Unpublished. From the collection of Leslie H. Chen, Alexandria, VA.

Chesneaux, Jean. 1969. "The Federalist Movement in China, 1920–23." In Jack Gray, ed., *Modern China's Search for a Political Form*, pp. 96–137. Oxford: Oxford University Press.

———. 1972. "Secret Societies in China's Historical Evolution." In Jean Chesneaux, ed., *Popular Movements and Secret Societies in China, 1840–1950*, pp. 1–22. Stanford: Stanford University Press.

Chin, Frank F. K. 1973. "The Element of Regionalism in Medieval China: Observations on the Founding of the Eastern Chin." In *Twenty-ninth International Congress of Orientalists*, vol. 7, pp. 67–71. Paris: L'Asiathèque.

Chow, Rey. 1991. *Woman and Chinese Modernity: The Politics of Reading between East and West*. Minneapolis: University of Minnesota Press.

Cohen, Jean L., and Andrew Arato, 1992. *Civil Society and Political Theory*. Cambridge, MA: MIT Press.

Cohen, Paul A. 1984. *Discovering History in China: American Historical Writing on the Recent Chinese Past*. New York: Columbia University Press.

———. 1992. "The Contested Past: The Boxers as History and Myth." *Journal of Asian Studies* 51, no. 1: 82–113.

Cohn, Bernard S. 1983. "Representing Authority in Victorian India." In Eric Hobsbawm and Terence Ranger, eds., *The Invention of Tradition*, pp. 165–209. Cambridge, UK: Cambridge University Press.

Connor, Walker. 1972. "Nation-Building or Nation-Destroying?" *World Politics* 24: 319–55.

Crossley, Pamela. 1987. "*Manzhou yuanliu kao* and the Formalization of the Manchu Heritage." *Journal of Asian Studies* 46, no. 4: 761–90.

———. 1990a. "Thinking about Ethnicity in Early Modern China." *Late Imperial China* 11, no. 1: 1–35.

———. 1990b. *Orphan Warriors: Three Manchu Generations and the End of the Qing*. Princeton: Princeton University Press.

Dazu xianzhi. (See *Minguo chongxiu Dazu xianzhi*.)

de Bary, William Theodore. 1983. *The Liberal Tradition in China*. New York: Columbia University Press.

de Certeau, Michel. 1988. *The Writing of History*, translated by Tom Conley. New York: Columbia University Press.

Derrida, Jacques. 1981. *Positions*, translated and annotated by Alan Bass. Chicago: University of Chicago Press.

———. 1978. *Writing and Difference*, translated by Alan Bass. Chicago: University of Chicago Press.

Deutsch, Karl W. 1961. "Social Mobilization and Political Development." *American Political Science Review* 55, no. 3: 493–514.

Dewoskin, Kenneth J. 1977. "The Six Dynasties *Chih-kuai* and the Birth of Fiction." In Andrew H. Plaks, ed., *Chinese Narrative: Critical and Theoretical Essays*, pp. 21–52. Princeton, NJ: Princeton University Press.

Dikötter, Frank. 1992. *The Discourse of Race in Modern China*. Stanford: Stanford University Press.

Dimock, Peter. 1992. "The American Revolution as Legitimating Social Narrative." Paper presented at the Organization of American Historians, Chicago, 5 April.

———. 5 April 1992. Personal communication with the author.

Dow, Tsung-I. 1982. "The Confucian Concept of a Nation and Its Historical Practice." *Asian Profile* 10, no. 4: 347–62.

Duara, Prasenjit. 1988a. *Culture, Power and the State: Rural North China, 1900–1942*. Stanford: Stanford University Press.

———. 1988b. "Superscribing Symbols: The Myth of Guandi, Chinese God of War." *Journal of Asian Studies* 47, no. 4: 778–95.

———. 1991. "Knowledge and Power in the Discourse of Modernity: The Campaigns against Popular Religion in Early Twentieth Century China." *The Journal of Asian Studies* 50, no. 1: 67–83.

———. 1993. "The Displacement of Tension to the Tension of Displacement." *Radical History Review* 57 (Fall): 60–64.

Dumont, Louis. 1980. *Homo Hierarchicus: The Caste System and Its Implications*. Chicago: University of Chicago Press.

Eley, Geoff. 1981. "Nationalism and Social History." *Social History* 6, no. 1: 83–107.

Elliot, Mark. 1990. "Bannermen and Townsmen: Ethnic Tension in Nineteenth Century Jiangnan." *Late Imperial China* 11, no. 1: 36–74.

Ellis, Richard, and Aaron Wildavsky. 1990. "A Cultural Analysis of the Role of Abolitionists in the Coming of the Civil War." *Comparative Studies in Society and History* 32, no. 1: 89–116.

Embree, Ainslee T. 1985. "Indian Civilization and Regional Cultures: The Two Realities." In Paul Wallace, ed., *Region and Nation in India*, pp. 19–39. New Delhi: Oxford University Press.

Esherick, Joseph W. 1987. *The Origins of the Boxer Uprising*. Berkeley: University of California Press.

Fang Cao. 1930a. "Zeng Jue xiansheng weiduguo 'sanminzhuyi' ba" [I Suppose Mr. Zeng Jue Has Not Yet Read His "Three People's Principles"]. In *Fenggai*, pp. 157–59. Guangzhou: Guangzhou Tebie Shidangbu Xuanchuanbu.

———. 1930b. "Sanminzhuyi yu zongjiao wenti" [The Three People's Principles and the Problem of Religion]. In *Fenggai*, pp. 160–69. Guangzhou: Guangzhou Tebie Shidangbu Xuanchuanbu.

Fei Hsiao-tung. 1953. *China's Gentry: Essays on Rural-Urban Relations*. Chicago: University of Chicago Press.

Fenggai. Abbreviation for Fengsu Gaige Weiyuanhui [Committee to Reform

Customs], ed. 1930. *Fengsu Gaige Congkan* [*Essays Reprinted from the Reform Customs Weekly*]. Guangzhou: Guangzhou Tebie Shidangbu Xuanchuanbu.

Feng Ziyou. 1943. *Geming Yishi* [*Reminiscences of the Revolution*], vol. 1. Chongqing: Shangwu Yinshuguan.

Fincher, John. 1968. "Political Provincialism and National Revolution." In Mary C. Wright, ed., *China in Revolution*, pp. 185–227. New Haven: Yale University Press.

———. 1972. "China as Race, Culture, and Nation: Notes on Fang Hsiao-ju's Discussion of Dynastic Legitimacy." In David C. Buxbaum and Frederick W. Mote, eds., *Transition and Permanence: Chinese History and Culture: A Festschrift in Honor of Dr. Hsiao Kung-ch'uan*, pp 59–69. Seattle: University of Washington Press.

Fischer, Michael M. J., and Mehdi Abedi. 1990. *Debating Muslims: Cultural Dialogues in Postmodernity and Tradition*. Madison: University of Wisconsin Press.

Fitzgerald, John. 1988. "Nation and Class in Chinese Nationalist Thought." Unpublished ms. Department of History, University of Melbourne.

———. 1990. "The Misconceived Revolution: State and Society in China's Nationalist Revolution, 1923–1926." *Journal of Asian Studies* 49, no. 2: 323–43.

Fletcher, Joseph. 1978a. "Ch'ing Inner Asia c. 1800." In John K. Fairbank, ed., *The Cambridge History of China*, vol. 10, part 1, pp. 35–106. Cambridge, UK: Cambridge University Press.

———. 1978b. "The Heyday of Ch'ing Order in Mongolia, Sinkiang and Tibet." In John K. Fairbank, ed., *The Cambridge History of China*, vol. 10, part 1, pp. 351–408. Cambridge, UK: Cambridge University Press.

Fogel, Joshua A. 1977. "Race and Class in Chinese Historiography: Divergent Interpretations of Zhang Bing-lin and Anti-Manchuism in the 1911 Revolution." *Modern China* 3, no. 3: 346–75.

———. 1984. *Politics and Sinology: The Case of Naito Konan (1866–1934)*. Cambridge, MA: Council on East Asian Studies, Harvard University.

Foucault, Michel. 1977. "Nietzsche, Genealogy, History." In Donald F. Bouchard, ed., *Language, Counter-Memory, Practice*, translated by Donald F. Bouchard and Sherry Simon, pp. 139–64. Ithaca, NY: Cornell University Press.

———. 1972. *The Archaeology of Knowledge*, translated from the French by A. M. Sheridan Smith. London: Tavistock Publishers.

Friedman, Edward. 1993. "A Failed Chinese Modernity." *Daedalus* (Spring): 1–18.

Friedman, Edward, Paul G. Pickowicz, and Mark Selden, with Kay Ann Johnson. 1991. *Chinese Village, Socialist State*. New Haven: Yale University Press.

Fujii, James A. 1993. "Writing Out Asia: Modernity, Canon, and Natsume Soseki's *Kokoro*." *Positions: East Asia Cultures Critiques* 1, no. 1 (Spring): 194–223.

Furth, Charlotte. 1976. "Culture and Politics in Modern Chinese Conservatism." In Charlotte Furth, ed., *The Limits of Change: Essays on Conservative Alternatives in Republican China*, pp. 22–53. Cambridge, MA: Harvard University Press.

Fu Sinian. 1928. "Zhongguo lishi fenqizhi yanjiu" [Researches in the Periodization of Chinese History]. In *Beijing Daxue Rikan*, 17–23 April. (Reprinted in *Fu Sinian Quanji*, vol. 4: 176–85.)

Gamble, Sidney D. 1963. *North China Villages: Social Political and Economic Activities before 1933*. Berkeley: University of California Press.

Gandhi, Mohandas Karamchand. 1938 edition. *Hind Swaraj or Indian Home Rule*. Ahmedabad: Navajivan Press.

Gasster, Michael. 1969. *Chinese Intellectuals and the Revolution of 1911: The Birth of Modern Chinese Radicalism*. Seattle: University of Washington Press.

Gellner, Ernest. 1983. *Nations and Nationalism*. Ithaca, NY: Cornell University Press.

———. 1982. "Relativism and Universals." In Martin Hollis and Steve Lukes, eds., *Rationality and Relativism*, pp. 181–201. Cambridge, MA: MIT Press.

Gernet, Jacques. 1972. *A History of Chinese Civilization*, translated by J. R. Foster. Cambridge, UK: Cambridge University Press.

Gladney, Dru C. 1991. *Muslim Chinese: Ethnic Nationalism in the People's Republic*. Cambridge, MA: Council on East Asian Studies, Harvard University.

Gluck, Carol. 1985. *Japan's Modern Myths: Ideology in the Late Meiji Period*. Princeton: Princeton University Press.

Gongren. Abbreviation for *Fengsu Gaige Weiyuanhui Gongren* [Workers of the Committee to Reform Customs], 1930. "Wei fandui Jidujiao gao tongbao shu" [Letter Informing Our Brothers to Oppose Christianity]. In *Fenggai*, pp. 155–56. Guangzhou: Guangzhou Tebie Shidangbu Xuanchuanbu.

Goodman, Bryna. 1995. *Native Place, City and Nation: Regional Networks and Identities*. Berkeley: University of California Press.

———. 1990. "The Native Place and the City: Immigrant Consciousness and Organizations in Shanghai, 1853–1927." Ph. D. diss., History Department, Stanford University.

Grieder, Jerome B. 1981. *Intellectuals and the State in Modern China*. New York: Free Press.

Grillo, R. D. 1980. "Introduction." In R. D. Grillo, ed., *"Nation" and "State" in Europe: Anthropological Perspectives*, pp. 1–30. London: Academic Press.

Grimm, Tilemann. 1985. "Intellectual Groups in 15th and 16th century Kiangsi: A Study of Regionalism in Forming Elites." In Gert Naundorf, Karl-Heinz Pohl, and Hans-Hermann Schmidt, eds., *Religion und Philosophie in Ostasien: Festscrift fur Hans Steininger zum 65. Geburtstag*, pp. 425–43. Wurzburg: Konigshausen + Neumann.

Gu Jiegang. 1938. *Zhongguo Jiangyu Yangeshi* [A History of the Evolution of China's Border Regions]. Changsha: Shangwu Yinshuguan.

———. 1966 reprint. *An Autobiography of a Chinese Historian*, translated Arthur W. Hummel. Taipei: Ch'eng-wen Publishing Co.

Habermas, Jürgen. 1992. "Further Reflections on the Public Sphere." In Craig

Calhoun, ed., *Habermas and the Public Sphere*, pp. 421–60. Cambridge, MA: MIT Press.

——. 1989. *The Structural Transformation of the Public Sphere*. Cambridge: MIT Press.

Habib, Irfan. 1963. *The Agrarian System of Moghul India, 1556–1701*. New York: Asia Publishing House.

Handelman, Don, and Lea Shamgar-Handelman. 1990. "Shaping Time: The Choice of the National Emblem in Israel." In Emiko Ohnuki-Tierney, ed., *Culture Through Time: Anthropological Approaches*, pp. 193–226. Stanford: Stanford University Press.

Hatada Takashi. 1976. *Chūgoku Sonraku to Kyōdōtai Riron*. Tokyo: Iwanami Shoten.

Hay, Stephen N. 1970. *Asian Ideas of East and West: Tagore and His Critics in Japan, China and India*. Cambridge, MA: Harvard University Press.

Hayford, Charles W. 1990. *To the People: James Yen and Village China*. New York: Columbia University Press.

Hegel, Georg W. F. 1956. *The Philosophy of History*, translated by J. Sibree. New York: Dover Publications.

Hevia, James. 1990. "Making China 'Perfectly Equal.'" *Journal of Historical Sociology* 3, no. 4: 379–400.

Hinton, William. 1966. *Fanshen: A Documentary of Revolution in a Chinese Village*. New York: Vintage Books.

Hirayama, Shū. n.d. *Zhongguo mimi shehuishi* [*A History of Chinese Secret Societies*]. (Reprint of 1912 Shanghai edition) Taibei: Guting shuwu.

Hobsbawm, Eric J. 1990. *Nations and Nationalisms since 1780*. Cambridge, UK: Cambridge University Press.

Hobson, Marian. 1987. "History Traces." In Derek Attridge, et al., eds., *Post-structuralism and the Question of History*, pp. 101–15. Cambridge, UK: Cambridge University Press.

Hofstadter, Richard. 1955. *Social Darwinism in American Thought*. Boston: Beacon Press.

Honig, Emily. 1989. "Subei People in Republican-Era Shanghai." *Modern China* 15, no. 3: 243–74.

Hsia, C. T. 1968. *The Classic Chinese Novel: A Critical Introduction*. New York: Columbia University Press.

Hsiao Kung-chuan. 1975. *A Modern China and a New World: K'ang Yu-wei, Reformer and Utopian, 1858–1927*. Seattle: University of Washington Press.

Hsieh, Winston. 1962. "The Ideas and Ideals of a Warlord: Ch'en Chiung-ming." *Papers on China*, no. 16: 198–251. Harvard University, East Asia Research Center.

Huang, Martin Weizong. 1990. "The Inescapable Predicament: The Narrator and His Discourse in the True Story of Ah Q." *Modern China* 16, no. 4: 430–49.

Huang, Philip C. 1972. *Liang Ch'i-ch'ao and Modern Chinese Liberalism*. Seattle: University of Washington Press.

Huang Zunxian. n.d. c. 1897. Quoted in Liang Qichao, n.d. c. 1897. "Hunan Guangdong qingxing" [Conditions in Hunan and Guangdong]. In *Wuxu zhengbianji, Yinbingshi Zhuanji*, vol. 1, pp. 139–41. Taibei: Zhonghua Shuju.

Huang Shaodan. 1930. "Cong renlei jinhuade qushizhong taolun zongjiao wenti" [Discussion of the Religious Problem from the Trend of Human Evolution]. In *Fenggai*, pp. 85–93. Guangzhou: Guangzhou Tebie Shidangbu Xuanchuanbu.

Hu Qunhui. 1983. *Minzhude difang zhuyi yu liansheng zizhi* [*Localism and the Federal Self-government Movement in the Early Republic*]. Taibei: Zhengzhong Shuju.

Hu Shi. 1922. Editorial in *Nuli Zhoubao*, 23 July.

———. 1963 reprint. *The Chinese Renaissance: The Haskell Lectures, 1933*. New York: Paragon Book Reprint Company.

Huters, Theodore. 1984. "Blossoms in the Snow: Lu Xun and the Dilemma of Modern Chinese Literature." *Modern China* 10, no. 1: 49–77.

Iyer, Raghavan N. 1973. *The Moral and Political Thought of Mahatma Gandhi*. New York: Oxford University Press.

Jansen, Marius. B. 1967. *The Japanese and Sun Yat-sen*. Cambridge: Harvard University Press.

Joshi, V. C., ed. 1975. *Rammohun Roy and the Process of Modernization in India*. Delhi: Vikas Publishing House.

Judge, Joan. 1994. "Public Opinion and the New Politics of Contestation in the Late Qing, 1904–1911." *Modern China* 20, no. 1: 64–91.

K'ang Yu-wei. 1958. *Ta T'ung Shu: The One World Philosophy of K'ang Yu-wei*, translated from the Chinese with Introduction and Notes by Laurence G. Thompson. London: George Allen and Unwin, Ltd.

Kapp, Robert A. 1973. *Szechwan and the Chinese Republic: Provincial Militarism and Central Power, 1911–1938*. New Haven: Yale University Press.

Kataoka, Kazutada. 1984. "Shingai kakumei jiki no gozoku kyōwaron o megutte" [Regarding the Theory of Five Races in the 1911 Revolutionary Period]. In Tanaka Masayoshi sensei taikan kinen ronji, ed., *Chūgoku Kindaishi no shomondai* [*Several Problems of Modern Chinese History*], pp. 279–306. Tokyo: Kokusho Kankoku.

Keylor, William R. 1975. *Academy and Community in France: The Foundation of the French Historical Profession*. Cambridge, MA: Harvard University Press.

Kolb, David. 1986. *The Critique of Pure Modernity: Hegel, Heidegger, and After*. Chicago: University of Chicago Press.

Kuhn, Philip A. 1959. "T'ao Hsing-chih, 1891–1946, An Educational Reformer." *Harvard Papers on China*, vol. 13: 163–94.

———. 1970. *Rebellion and Its Enemies in Late Imperial China: Militarization and Social Structure, 1796–1864*. Cambridge MA: Harvard University Press.

———. 1975. "Local Self-government under the Republic: Problems of Control, Autonomy and Mobilization." In Frederic Wakeman, Jr., and Carolyn Grant, eds., *Conflict and Control in Late Imperial China*, pp. 257–98. Berkeley: University of California Press.

_____. 1977. "The Origins of the Taiping Vision: Cross Cultural Dimensions of Chinese Rebellions." *Comparative Studies in Society and History* 19, no. 3: 350–66.

_____. 1986. "The Development of Local Government." In John K. Fairbank and A. Feuerwerker, eds., *The Cambridge History of China*, vol. 13, part 2, pp. 329–60. Cambridge: Cambridge University Press.

_____. 1990. *Soulstealers: The Chinese Sorcery Scare of 1768.* Cambridge, MA: Harvard University Press.

Kwok, Danny W. Y. 1965. *Scientism in Chinese Thought, 1900–1950.* New Haven: Yale University Press.

Laclau, Ernesto, and Chantal Mouffe. 1985. *Hegemony and Socialist Strategy: Towards a Radical Democratic Politics.* London: Verso Press.

Langlois, John D., Jr. 1980. "Chinese Culturalism and the Yuan Analogy: Seventeenth-Century Perspectives." *Harvard Journal of Asiatic Studies* 40, no. 2: 355–98.

Laroui, Abdallah. 1976. *The Crisis of the Arab Intellectual: Traditionalism or Historicism?*, translated from the French by Diarmid Cammell. Berkeley: University of California Press.

Larson, Wendy. 1991. "Definition and Suppression: Women's Literature in Post-May 4th China." Paper presented at the Association of Asian Studies Annual Meeting, 11–14 April, New Orleans.

Lary, Diana. 1974. *Region and Nation.* Cambridge: Cambridge University Press.

Lee, Leo Ou-fan. 1987. *Voices from the Iron House: A Study of Lu Xun.* Bloomington: Indiana University Press.

Lee, Ta-ling. 1970. *The Foundations of the Chinese Revolution, 1905–1912.* New York: St. John's University Press.

Lee Chiu-chin. 1993. "From Liberal to Nationalist: Tai Chi-tao's Pursuit of a New World Order." Ph. D. diss. submitted to the University of Chicago.

Lei Haizong. 1936. "Duandai wenti yu Zhongguo lishi di fenqi" [The Problem of Periodization and the Division of Chinese History]. *Shehui Kexue* 2, no. 1 (October). (Reprinted in *Zhongguo Jindaishi Luncong*, pp. 271–305. Taipei: Zhengzhong shuju.)

Levenson, Joseph R. 1965. *Confucian China and Its Modern Fate: A Trilogy.* Berkeley: University of California Press.

_____. 1967. "The Province, the Nation and the World: The Problem of Chinese Identity." In Albert Feuerwerker, et al., eds., *Approaches to Modern Chinese History*, pp. 268–88. Berkeley: University of California Press.

Lévi-Strauss, Claude. 1962. "History and Dialectic." In the *Savage Mind*, pp. 245–69. Chicago: University of Chicago Press.

Levinas, Emmanuel. 1969 *Totality and Infinity*, translated by Alphonso Lingis. Pittsburgh: Dequesne University Press.

Lewis, Charlton M. 1972. "Some Notes on the Ko-lao Hui in Late Ch'ing China." In Jean Chesneaux, ed., *Popular Movements and Secret Societies in China, 1840–1950*, pp. 97–112. Stanford: Stanford University Press.

Liang Qichao. n.d. c. 1897. "Hunan Guangdong qingxing" [Conditions in

Hunan and Guangdong]. In *Wuxu zhengbianji* [*Record of the Coup of 1898*], *Yinbingshi Zhuanji* [*Collected Works from an Ice-Drinker's Studio*], vol. 1, pp. 129–46. Taibei: Zhonghua Shuju.

———. 1898. "Lun junzheng minzheng xiangshanzhi li" [On the Principle of Succession of Monarchy and Popular Power]. In *Wuxu Bianfa* [*The Reforms of 1898*], 2: 26–31. Shanghai: Shenzhou Guoguangshe, 1953.

———. 1901. "Zhongguoshi xulun" [A Systematic Discussion of Chinese History]. In Lin Zhijun, ed., *Yinbingshiwenji* [*Collected Essays from an Ice-Drinker's Studio*], no. 3. 1970 reprint of 1932 edition. Taibei: Taiwan Zhonghua shuju. 1–12.

———. 1902a. "Xinshixue" [New History]. In Lin Zhijun, ed., *Yinbingshiwenji* [*Collected Essays from an Ice-Drinker's Studio*], no. 4, pp. 1–33. 1970 reprint of 1932 edition. Taibei: Taiwan Zhonghua shuju.

———. 1902b. "Zhongguo zhuanzhi zhengzhi jinhua shilun" [A Historical Essay on the Evolution of Autocratic Politics in China]. In *Yinbingshiwenji* [*Collected Essays from an Ice-Drinker's Studio*], no. 4, pp. 59–90. Taibei: Zhonghua Shuju.

———. 1902c. "Fulun Zhongguo fengjianzhi zhi yu Ouzhou Riben bijiao" [Appendix: Comparing Chinese Feudalism with that of Europe and Japan]. In *Yinbingshiwenji* [*Collected Essays from an Ice-Drinker's Studio*], no. 4, pp. 70–71. Taibei: Zhonghua Shuju.

Liang Shuming. 1971a. "Beiyou suojian jilue" [Records of Observations during my Northern Travels]. In *Zhongguo Minzu Zijiu Yundongzhi Zuihou Juewu* [*The Final Awakening of the Chinese People's Movement for Self-Salvation*], pp. 257–88. Taibei: Shulin.

———. 1971b. "Gangao jinzhiyan difang zizhizhe" [Warning to People Who Talk of Self-government Today]. In *Zhongguo Minzu Zijiu Yundongzhi Zuihou Juewu* [*The Final Awakening of the Chinese People's Movement for Self-Salvation*], pp. 193–206. Taibei: Shulin.

Li Dajia. 1986. *Minguo zhuniande liansheng zizhi yundong* [*The Federal Self-government Movement in the Early Republic*]. Taibei: Hongwenguan.

Li Dazhao. 1959. "Lianzhi zhuyi yu shijie zuzhi" [Federalism and World Organization]. In *Li Dazhao Xuanji* [*Selected Works of Li Dazhao*], pp. 130–34. Beijing: Renmin chubanshe.

Li Guoqi. 1970. "Zhongguo jindai minzu sixiang" [Modern Chinese Nationalist Thought]. In Li Guoqi, ed., *Minzuzhuyi* [*Nationalism*], pp. 19–43. Taibei: Shibao Chuban Gongsi.

Li Jiannong. 1956. *The Political History of China, 1840–1928*, translated and edited by Ssu-yu Teng and Jeremy Ingalls. Princeton, NJ: Van Nostrand Co.

———. 1922. "Minguo Tongyi Wenti" [The Problem of Chinese Unity]. *Taipingyang* 3, no. 7: 1–10.

Li Jinghan. 1933. *Dingxian shehui gaikuang diaocha* [*The Investigation of Social Conditions in Ding County*]. Beijing: Zhonghua Pingmin Jiaoyu Zujinhui.

Lin Sheng. 1922. "Zaishu Sun-Chen zhi zheng" [Rewriting the Conflict between Sun Yat-sen and Chen Jiongming]. In *Nuli Zhoubao* (27 August): 3–4.

Lin Yu-sheng. 1979. *The Crisis of Chinese Consciousness: Radical Anti-traditionalism in the May Fourth Era*. Madison: University of Wisconsin Press.

Lin Zengping. 1981. "Xinhai geming shiqi Tiandihuidi xingzhi wenti" [The Question of the Nature of the Tiandihui during the Period of the 1911 Revolution]. In *Xinhai geming shilun wenxuan* [*Anthology of Historical Studies of the 1911 Revolution*], pp. 352–65. Beijing: Sanlian shudian.

Liu, Lydia. 1995. *Trans-lingual Practice: Literature, National Culture and Translated Modernity—China 1900-1937*. Stanford: Stanford University Press.

———. 1994. "The Female Body and Nationalist Discourse: *The Field of Life and Death* Revisited." In Inderpal Grewal and Caren Kaplan, eds., *Scattered Hegemonies: Postmodernity and Transnational Feminist Practices*, pp. 37–62. Minneapolis: University of Minnesota Press.

Li Wenhai. 1983. "Wuxu weixin yundong shiqidi xuehui zuzhi" [The Organizations of Study Societies during the Period of the 1898 Restoration Period]. In Hu Shengwu, ed., *Wuxu Weixin Yundongshi Lunji* [*Collection of Essays on the History of the 1898 Restoration Movement*], pp. 48–78. Changsha: Hunan renmin chubanshe.

Li Zongyi. 1980. *Yuan Shikai zhuan* [*Biography of Yuan Shikai*]. Beijing: Zhonghua shudian.

Lo Ergang. 1947. *Tiandihui wenxianlu* [*Documents of the Heaven and Earth Society*]. Shanghai: Zhengzhong Shuju.

Lu Fangshang. 1989. *Gemingzhi Zaiqi: Zhongguo guomindang gaizuqian dui xinsizhaode huiying* [*Rekindle the Revolution: The Kuomintang's Response to New Thought before the Revolution*]. Taibei: Zhongyang yanjiuyuan jindaishi yanjiusuo (57).

Lust, John. 1972. "Secret Societies, Popular Movements, and the 1911 Revolution." In Jean Chesneaux, ed., *Popular Movements and Secret Societies in China, 1840-1950*, pp. 165–200. Stanford: Stanford University Press.

Lutz, Jessie G. 1988. *Chinese Politics and Christian Missions: The Anti-Christian Movements of 1920-1928*. Notre Dame, IN: Cross Cultural Publications, Inc.

Lu Xun. 1927. "Wei-Jin fengdu ji wenzhang yu yao ji jiu zhi guanxi" [Letters and Life-style in the Wei-Jin Period and Their Connection to Drugs and Alcohol]. In *Lu Xun Quanji* [*Collected Works of Lu Xun*], vol. 3: 486–507.

Mao Zedong, 1920a. "Hunan shou Zhongguozhi lei yi lishi ji xianzhuang zhengmingzhi" [Hunan Is Burdened by China: Historical and Contemporary Evidence]. In Mao Zedong wenxian ziliao yanjiuhui, eds., *Mao Zedongji bujuan* [*Supplementary Volumes to Mao Zedong's Collected Writings*], vol. 1., pp. 225–27. Tokyo: Zōzōsha.

———. 1920b. "Hunan jianshe wentidi genben wenti—Hunan gongheguo" [The Basic Issue in Hunan's Reconstruction—The Republic of Hunan]. In Mao Zedong wenxian ziliao yanjiuhui, eds., *Mao Zedongji bujuan* [*Supplementary Volumes to Mao Zedong's Collected Writings*], vol. 1., pp. 217–19. Tokyo: Zōzōsha.

————. 1920c. "Fandui Tongyi" [Oppose Unification]. In Mao Zedong wen-xian ziliao yanjiuhui, eds., *Mao Zedongji bujuan* [*Supplementary Volumes to Mao Zedong's Collected Writings*], vol. 9, pp. 107–9. Tokyo: Zōzōsha.

————. 1920d. "You 'Hunan geming zhengfu' zhaoji 'Hunan renmin xianfa huiyi' zhiding 'Hunan xianfa' yi jianshe 'Xin Hunan' zhi jianyi" [Proposal for the 'Revolutionary Government of Hunan' to Convene a 'Hunan People's Constitutional Convention' to Enact a 'Hunan Constitution' in order to Establish a 'New Hunan"]. In Mao Zedong wenxian ziliao yanjiuhui, eds., *Mao Zedongji bujuan* [*Supplementary Volumes to Mao Zedong's Collected Writings*], vol. 1., pp. 239–45. Tokyo: Zōzōsha.

McDonald, Angus W., Jr. 1976. "Mao Tse-tung and the Hunan Self-government Movement, 1920: An Introduction and Five Translations." *China Quarterly* 68: 751–77.

Mackinnon, Stephen R. 1980. *Power and Politics in Late Imperial China.* Berkeley: University of California Press.

————. 1983. "A Late Qing-GMD-PRC Connection: Police as an Arm of the Modern Chinese State." *Selected Papers in Asian Studies*, new series, 14. Published by Western Conference of the Association of Asian Studies.

McNeill, William. 1982. *The Pursuit of Power.* Chicago: University of Chicago Press.

Martin, Dorothea A. L. 1990. *The Making of a Sino-Marxist World View: Perceptions and Interpretations of World History in the People's Republic of China.* London and New York: M. E. Sharpe, Inc.

Marx, Karl. 1853. "Revolution in China and in Europe." In Henry Christman, ed., *The American Journals of Marx and Engles*, 14 June. New York: New American Library.

————. 1853. "The British Rule in India." In Henry Christman, ed., *The American Journals of Marx and Engles*, 25 June. New York: New American Library.

Mast III, Herman, and William G. Saywell. 1974. "Revolution Out of Tradition: The Political Ideology of Tai Chi-t'ao." *Journal of Asian Studies* 34, no. 1 (November): 73–98.

Meisner, Maurice. 1967. *Li Ta-chao and the Origins of Chinese Marxism.* Cambridge, MA: Harvard University Press.

Metzgar, H. Michael. 1976. "The Crisis of 1900 in Yunnan: Late Ch'ing Militancy in Transition." *Journal of Asian Studies* 35, no. 2 (February): 185–201.

Metzger, Thomas A. 1977. *Escape from Predicament: Neo-Confucianism and China's Evolving Political Culture.* New York: Columbia University Press.

Meyer, John W. 1980. "The World Polity and the Authority of the Nation State." In Albert Bergesen, ed., *Studies of the Modern World System*, pp. 109–137. New York: Academic Press.

Michael, Franz. 1964. "Introduction" to Stanley Spector, *Li Hung-chang and the Huai Army.* Seattle: University of Washington Press.

Minguo chongxiu Dazu xianzhi [*Revised Gazetteer of Dazu County in the Republic*]. 1945. Volumes 4 and 5. Dazu county: Zhongguo xuedian beiquan fenguan.

Min Tu-ki. 1989. *National Polity and Local Power: The Transformation of Late Imperial China*. Edited by Philip A. Kuhn and Timothy Brook. Cambridge, MA: Council of East Asian Studies, Harvard University.

Mitani, Takashi. 1978. "Nankin seiken to 'meishin daha undō'" [The Nanjing Regime and the "Antisuperstition Movement"]. *Rekishigaku kenkyū* 455, no. 4: 1–14.

———. 1979. "Kōhoku minshu bōdō (senkyūhaku nijūkyū nen) ni tsuite" [Concerning the Popular Riot of 1929 in Jiangbei]. *Hitotsubashi Ronsō* 83, no. 3: 137–57.

Mizoguchi, Yūzō. 1991. "Zhongguo minquan sixiangde tese" [The Special Character of the Concept of Popular Rights in China]. In Zhongyang yanjiuyuan jinshi yanjiusuo, ed., *Zhongguo xiandaihua lunwenji*, pp. 343–62. Taibei: Zhongyang yanjiuyuan jinshi yanjiusuo.

Moser, Leo J. 1985. *The Chinese Mosaic: The Peoples and Provinces of China*. Boulder, CO: Westview Press.

NZNJ. Abbreviation for *Neizheng Nianjian* [Yearbook of the Ministry of the Interior], chapter 9: "Zongjiao Tuanti" [Religious Organizations]. 1936. Shanghai: Shangwu Yinshuguan.

Nagai, Michio. 1954. "Herbert Spencer in Early Meiji Japan." *Far Eastern Quarterly* 14, no. 1 (November): 55–64.

Najita, Tetsuo. 1974. *Japan: The Intellectual Foundations of Modern Japanese Politics*. Chicago: University of Chicago Press.

———. 1987. *Visions of Virtue in Tokugawa Japan: The Kaitokudō Merchant Academy of Osaka*. Chicago: University of Chicago Press.

Nakami, Tatsuo. 1984. "A Protest against the Concept of the "Middle Kingdom": The Mongols and the 1911 Revolution." In Eto Shinkichi, et al., eds., *The 1911 Revolution in China*, pp. 129–49. Tokyo: Tokyo University Press.

Nandy, Ashis. 1983. *The Intimate Enemy: Loss and Recovery of Self under Colonialism*. Delhi: Oxford University Press.

———. 1987. *Traditions, Tyranny and Utopias: Essays in the Politics of Awareness*. Delhi: Oxford University Press.

Naquin, Susan, and Evelyn S. Rawski. 1987. *Chinese Society in the Eighteenth Century*. New Haven: Yale University Press.

Nehru, Jawaharlal. 1960. *The Discovery of India*. New York: Anchor Books.

Niranjana, Tejaswini. 1992. *Citing Translation: History, Post-structuralism and the Colonial Context*. Berkeley: University of California Press.

Novick, Peter. 1988. *That Noble Profession: The "Objectivity Question" and the American Historical Profession*. Cambridge, UK: Cambridge University Press.

Ogata, Yasushi. 1984. "Shinmatsu shinkaron no shisōteki issō to sono kaishū" [The Intellectual Status of Evolutionary Thought in the Late Qing and Its Consequences]. *Tōdai Chūtetsubun Gakkai Hō*, no. 9 (June 1984): 37–57.

Omvedt, Gail. 1992. "'Green Earth, Women's Power, Human Liberation': Women in Peasant Movements in India." *Development Dialogue*, nos. 1–2: 116–30.

————. 1994. *Reinventing Revolution: India's New Social Movements.* London and New York: M. E. Sharpe.

Onogawa, Hidemi. 1970. "Zhang Binglinde paiman sixiang" [The Anti-Manchu Thought of Zhang Binglin]. In Li Guoqi, ed., *Minzuzhuyi,* pp. 207–60. Taibei: Shibao Chuban Gongsi.

Ou Qujia. 1903. (Reprinted 1971.) "Xin Guangdong" [New Guangdong]. In Zhang Yufa, ed., *Wan Qing geming wenxue* [*Writings from the Late Qing Revolution*], pp. 1–49. Taibei: Xinzhi zazhishe.

Pang Yong-pil. 1985. "Warlord's Chen Jiongming's Policy on the Peasant Movement of the 1920s." *The Journal of Asiatic Studies* 28, no. 1: 129–54.

Perry, Elizabeth J. 1980. *Rebels and Revolutionaries in North China, 1845–1945.* Stanford: Stanford University Press.

————. 1985. "Rural Violence in Socialist China." *China Quarterly* 103 (September): 414–40.

Peterson, Charles A. 1974. "Regional Defense against the Central Power: The Huai-Hsi Campaign, 815–817." In Frank A. Kiernan, Jr., and John K. Fairbank, eds., *Chinese Ways in Warfare,* pp. 123–50. Cambridge: Harvard University Press.

Plaks, Andrew H. 1987. *The Four Masterworks of the Ming Novel.* Princeton: Princeton University Press.

Pollock, Sheldon. 1989. "Mimamsa and the Problem of History in Traditional India." *Journal of American Oriental Society* 109, no. 4: 603–10.

————. 1993. "Ramayana and Political Imagination in India." *Journal of Asian Studies* 52, no. 2: 261–97.

Pong, David. 1973. "Confucian Patriotism and the Destruction of the Woosung Railway, 1877." *Modern Asian Studies* 7, no. 4: 647–76.

Potter, David Morris. 1968. "The Historian's Use of Nationalism and Vice Versa." In David Morris Potter, ed., *The South and the Sectional Conflict,* pp. 34–83. Baton Rouge: Louisiana State University Press.

Price, Don C. 1992. "Early Chinese Revolutionaries: Autonomy, Family and Nationalism." In Academica Sinica, Modern History Institute, ed., *Family Process and Political Process in Modern Chinese History,* part 2. Taipei: Academica Sinica, Modern History Institute.

Pusey, James Reeve. 1983. *China and Charles Darwin.* Cambridge, MA: Council on East Asian Studies, Harvard University.

Pyle, Kenneth B. 1978. *The Making of Modern Japan.* Lexington, MA: D. C. Heath and Co.

Qi Sihe. 1937. "Minzu yu Zhongzu" [Race and Nation]. *Yugong* 8, nos. 1–2–3: 1–33.

Ranger, Terence. 1983. "The Invention of Tradition in Colonial Africa." In Eric Hobsbawm and Terence Ranger, eds., *The Invention of Tradition,* pp. 211–62. Cambridge, UK: Cambridge University Press.

Rankin, Mary B. 1968. "The Revolutionary Movement in Chekiang: A Study in the Tenacity of Tradition." In Mary C. Wright, ed., *China in Revolution: The First Phase, 1900–1913,* pp. 319–64. New Haven: Yale University Press.

———. 1971. *Early Chinese Revolutionaries: Radical Chinese Intellectuals in Shanghai and Chekiang, 1902–1911*. Cambridge, MA: Council on East Asian Studies, Harvard University.

———. 1986. *Elite Activism and Political Transformation in China: Zhejiang Province, 1865–1911*. Stanford: Stanford University Press.

———. 1990. "The Origins of a Chinese Public Sphere: Local Elites and Community Affairs in the Late Imperial Period." *Études chinoises* 10, no. 2: 13–60.

Ray, Rajat K. 1975. "Introduction." In V. C. Joshi, ed., *Rammohun Roy and the Process of Modernization in India*, pp 1–20. Delhi: Vikas Publishing House.

Raychaudhuri, Tapan. 1988. *Europe Reconsidered: Perceptions of the West in Nineteenth Century Bengal*. Delhi: Oxford University Press.

Ricoeur, Paul. 1984. *Time and Narrative*, vol. 1. Chicago: University of Chicago Press.

———. 1988. *Time and Narrative*, vol. 3. Chicago: University of Chicago Press.

———. 1991. "The Human Experience of Time and Narrative." In Mario J. Valdes, ed., *Reflection and Imagination: A Paul Ricoeur Reader*, pp. 99–117. Toronto: University of Toronto Press.

Rodgers, Daniel T. 1987. *Contested Truths: Keywords in American Politics since Independence*. New York: Basic Books.

Ropp, Paul S. 1981. *Dissent in Early Modern China: Ju-lin Wai-shih and Ch'ing Social Criticism*. Ann Arbor: University of Michigan Press.

Rosen, Philip. 1993. "Traces of the Past: From Historicity to Film." In David E. Klemm and William Schweiker, eds., *Meanings in Texts and Action: Questioning Paul Ricoeur*, pp. 67–89. Charlottesville: University of Virginia Press.

Roth, Guenther, and Wolfgang Schluchter. 1979. *Max Weber's Vision of History*. Berkeley: University of California Press.

Rowe, William T. 1989. *Hankow: Conflict and Community in a Chinese City, 1796–1895*. Stanford: Stanford University Press.

———. 1990. "The Public Sphere in Modern China." *Modern China* 16, no. 3 (July): 309–29.

Rudolph, Lloyd I., and Susanne H. Rudolph. 1967. *The Modernity of Tradition: Political Development in India*. Chicago: University of Chicago Press.

———. 1985. "The Subcontinental Empire and Regional Kingdom in Indian State Formation." In Paul Wallace, ed., *Region and Nation in India*, pp. 40–59. New Delhi: Oxford University Press.

Sakai, Tadao. 1951. "Gendai Chūgoku bunka to kyūshūkyō" [Contemporary Chinese Culture and the Old Religion]. In Niida Noboru, ed., *Kindai Chūgoku no Shakai to Keizai*, pp. 313–41. Tokyo: Tōko Shoin.

———. 1972. "'Bang' no minshū no isshiki" [Consciousness of the People in Secret Societies]. *Tōyōshi kenkyū* 31, no. 2: 90–115.

Sasagawa, Yūji. 1985. "Senkyūhaku nijū nendai zenhanno Konan shosei minshūka undō" [The Movement to Democratize Provincial Politics in Hunan in the First Half of the 1920s]. In Yokoyama Sugiru, ed., *Chugokū no Kindaika to Chihō Seiji*, pp. 171–216. Tokyo: Keisō Shoho.

Schneider, Laurence A. 1971. *Ku Chieh-kang and China's New History: Nationalism and the Quest for Alternative Traditions.* Berkeley: University of California Press.

Schoppa, Keith R. 1977. "Province and Nation: The Chekiang Provincial Autonomy Movement, 1917–1927." *Journal of Asian Studies* 36, no. 4: 661–74.

———. 1989. *Xiang Lake: Nine Centuries of Chinese Life.* New Haven: Yale University Press.

Schram, Stuart R. 1966. *Mao Tse-tung.* New York: Simon and Schuster.

———, ed. 1992. *Mao's Road to Power: Revolutionary Writings, 1912–1949. Volume I: The Pre-Marxist Period, 1912–1920.* Armonk, NY: M. E. Sharpe.

Schwarcz, Vera. 1984. *The Chinese Enlightenment: Intellectuals and the Legacy of the May Fourth Movement of 1919.* Berkeley: University of California Press.

Schwartz, Benjamin. 1976. "Notes on Conservatism in General and China in Particular." In Charlotte Furth, ed., *The Limits of Change: Essays on Conservative Alternatives in Republican China,* pp 3–22. Cambridge, MA: Harvard University Press.

Scott, Joan W. 1988. *Gender and the Politics of History.* New York: Columbia University Press.

Sharman, Lyon. 1968 reprint. *Sun Yat-sen: His Life and Its Meaning.* Stanford: Stanford University Press.

Shimada Kenji. 1990. *Pioneer of the Chinese Revolution: Zhang Binglin and Confucianism,* translated by Joshua A. Fogel. Stanford: Stanford University Press.

Siu, Helen. 1989. "Re-cycling Rituals: Politics and Popular Culture in Contemporary Rural China." In Perry Link, et al., eds., *Unofficial China: Popular Culture and Thought in the People's Republic,* pp. 121–37. Boulder, CO: Westview Press.

Skinner, G. William. 1964–65. "Marketing and Social Structure in Rural China." *Journal of Asian Studies* 24, nos. 1: 3–43, and 2: 195–228.

———, ed. 1977. *The City in Late Imperial China.* Stanford: Stanford University Press.

Smith, Anthony D. 1986. *The Ethnic Origins of Nations.* Oxford: Blackwell.

Smith, Arthur H. 1899 (1970 reprint). *Village Life in China.* Boston: Little, Brown and Co.

Snyder, Louis L. 1983. "Nationalism and the Flawed Concept of Ethnicity." *Canadian Review of Studies in Nationalism* 10, no. 2: 253–65.

Soja, Edward W. 1989. *Post-modern Geographies: The Re-assertion of Space in Critical Social Theory.* London: Verso Press.

South China Morning Post. 22 December 1993. "Move to Ban Birth of 'Inferior People.'" Hong Kong. 1, 18.

Spivak, Gayatri Chakravorty. 1988. "Subaltern Studies: Deconstructing Historiography." In Ranajit Guha and Gayatri C. Spivak, eds., *Selected Subaltern Studies,* pp. 3–32. Oxford: Oxford University Press.

Stein, Burton. 1980. *Peasant, State and Society in Medieval South India.* Delhi, New York: Oxford University Press.

Stocking, George. W. 1987. *Victorian Anthropology.* New York: The Free Press.

Strand, David. 1989. *Rickshaw Beijing: City People and Politics in 1920s China.* Berkeley: University of California Press.

———. 1993. "Images of Society and the Rhetoric of Development in the *Sanmin zhuyi.*" Unpublished ms. Dickinson College, PA.

Sung Wook-shin. 1976. "Reform Through Study Societies in the Late Ch'ing Period, 1895–1900: The Nan Hsueh-hui." In Paul A. Cohen and John E. Schrecker, eds., *Reform in Nineteenth Century China,* pp. 310–16. Cambridge: East Asian Research Center, Harvard University.

Sun Yat-sen. 1923. "Zhongguo gemingshi" [A History of the Chinese Revolution]. In *Guofu quanji* [*The Complete Works of the Father of the Nation*], vol. 2, pp. 181–92. Taibei: Zhongguo guomin zhongyang weiyuanhui.

———. 1924. "Sanminzhuyi" [The Three People's Principles: Third Lecture]. In *Sun Zhongshan xuanji* [*The Selected Works of Sun Yat-sen*], pp. 615–89. Beijing: Renmin Chubanshe. Reprinted 1981.

———. 1954. *Guofu geming yuanqi xiangzhu* [*A Detailed Commentary on the Father of the Nation's "The Beginning and Rise of the Revolution"*], edited by Xu Shishen. Taibei: Zhengzhong shuju.

———. 1957. "Po 'Baohuang bao'" [Refuting "The Monarchists' Journal"]. In *Zhongguo jindai sixiangshi cankao ziliao jianpian* [*A Brief Reference to Materials on the Intellectual History of Modern China*], pp. 804–10. Beijing: Shanglian shudian.

———. 1986 (reprint). *Sanminzhuyi* [*The Three People's Principles*]. Taipei: Zhongyang Wenwu Gongyingshe.

Tambiah, Stanley Jeyaraja. 1985. *Culture, Thought and Social Action.* Cambridge, MA: Harvard University Press.

Tanaka, Stefan. 1993. *Japan's Orient: Rendering Pasts into History.* Berkeley: University of California Press.

Tang Dezhang. 1922. "Liansheng zizhi yu xianzaizhi Zhongguo" [Federal Self-government and Contemporary China]. *Taipingyang* 3, no. 7: 1–11.

Tang Xiaobing. 1991. "Writing a History of Modernity: A Study of the Historical Consciousness of Liang Ch'i-ch'ao." Ph. D. diss. submitted to Duke University.

Tao Chengzhang. n.d. "Longhuahui zhangcheng" [Regulations of the Dragon Flower Society]. In Shū Hirayama, n.d., *Zhongguo mimi shehuishi* [*A History of Chinese Secret Societies*], pp. 122–47. Taibei: Guting shuwu.

———. 1957. "Jiaohui yuanliukao." In Chai Degeng et al., compilers, *Xinhai geming* [*The 1911 Revolution*], vol 3, pp. 99–111. Shanghai: Shanghai renmin chubanshe.

Taylor, Charles. 1990. "Modes of Civil Society." *Public Culture* (Fall) 3, no. 1: 95–118.

Tessan, Hiroshi. 1984. "Shinmatsu Shisen ni okeru hanshokuminchika to kyūkyō undō" [The Semi-colonialization of Sichuan in the Late Qing and the Anti-Catholic Movement]. *Rekishigaku Kenkyū* 6, no. 529: 17–33.

Thompson, Roger. 1988. "Statecraft and Self-government: Competing Visions of Community and State in Late Imperial China." *Modern China* 14, no. 2: 188–221.

Tilly, Charles. 1975. "Introduction." In Charles Tilly, ed., *The Formation of National States in Western Europe*. Princeton: Princeton University Press.

Trauzettel, Rolf. 1975. "Sung Patriotism as a First Step toward Chinese Nationalism." In John W. Haeger, ed., *Crisis and Prosperity in Sung China*, pp. 199–214. Tucson: University of Arizona Press.

Treichler, Paula A. 1992. "Beyond Cosmo: AIDS, Identity, and Inscriptions of Gender." *Camera Obscura* 28: 23–76.

von Falkenhausen, Lothar. 1993. "The Regionalist Paradigm in Chinese Archaeology." Unpublished mss. University of California, Los Angeles.

Wagle, Narendra K. 1989. "Hindu Muslim Interactions in Medieval Maharashtra." In G. D. Sontheimer and H. Kulke, eds., *Hinduism Reconsidered*, pp. 51–66. New Delhi: Manohar.

Wakeman, Frederic, Jr. 1966. *Strangers at the Gate: Social Disorder in South China, 1839–1861*. Berkeley: University of California Press.

———. 1973. *History and Will: Philosophical Perspectives of Mao Tse-tung's Thought*. Berkeley: University of California Press.

Wallerstein, Immanuel. 1974. *The Modern World-System*. New York: Academic Press.

———. 1991. "The Construction of Peoplehood: Racism, Nationalism, Ethnicity." In Etienne Balibar and Immanuel Wallerstein, eds., *Race, Nation, Class: Ambiguous Identities*, pp. 71–85. London: Verso Press.

Wang Gungwu. 1968. "Early Ming Relations with Southeast Asia: A Background Essay." In John K. Fairbank, ed., *The Chinese World Order: Traditional China's Foreign Relations*, pp. 34–62. Cambridge, MA: Harvard University Press.

Wang Huning. 1991. *Dangdai Zhongguo cunluo jiazu wen-hua: dui Zhongguo shehui xiandaihua de yixiang tansuo* [*The Culture of the Rural Family in Contemporary China: An Investigation of the Modernization of Chinese Society*]. Shanghai: Renmin chubanshe.

Wang Jingwei. 1905. "Minzudi guomin" [Citizens of a Nation]. In Zhang Nan, et al., eds., *Xinhai geming qianshinian jian shilun quanji* [*A Collection of Discussions of Issues in the Ten Years before the 1911 Revolution*], vol. 2, pp. 82–114. Hong Kong: Sanlian shudian (1962).

Wang K'e-wen. 1986–87. "The Left Guomindang in Opposition, 1927–1931." *Chinese Studies in History* 20, no. 2: 3–43.

Wang Tianjiang. 1963. "Shijiu shiji xiabanji Zhongguo de mimi huishe" [Secret Societies in the Latter Half of the 19th Century in China]. In *Lishi yanjiu*, vol. 2, pp. 83–100.

Warner, Michael. 1990. *The Letters of the Republic: Publications and the Public Sphere in Eighteenth Century America*. Cambridge, MA: Harvard University Press.

Washbrook, D. A. 1976. *The Emergence of Provincial Politics: The Madras Presidency, 1870–1920*. New York: Cambridge University Press.

Watson, James. 1985. "Standardizing the Gods: The Promotion of T'ien Hou ("Empress of Heaven") Along the South China Coast, 960–1960." In David

Johnson, et al., ed., *Popular Culture in Late Imperial China*, pp. 292–324. Berkeley: University of California Press.

Weber, Eugene. 1976. *Peasants into Frenchmen*. Stanford: Stanford University Press.

Weber, Max. 1958. *From Max Weber*, edited and translated by H. H. Gerth and C. W. Mills. New York: Oxford University Press.

———. 1969. *The Sociology of Religion*, translated by Ephraim Fischoff and with an introduction by Talcott Parsons. Boston: Beacon Press.

Weryho, Jan W. 1986. "The Persian Language and Shia as Nationalist Symbols: A Historical Survey." *Canadian Review of Studies in Nationalism* 13, no. 1: 49–55.

White, Hadyn. 1987. *The Content of Form: Narrative Discourse and Historical Representation*. Baltimore: The Johns Hopkins University Press.

Wo Fang. 1930. "Du 'Poqu mixin yu zongjiao cunfei wenti' yihou" [After Reading "To destroy Superstition and the Problem of Whether or Not to Preserve Religion"]. In *Fenggai*, pp. 113–15. Guangzhou: Guangzhou Tebie Shidangbu Xuanzhuanbu.

Wong, Young-tsu. 1989. *Search for Modern Nationalism: Zhang Binglin and Revolutionary China, 1869–1936*. Hong Kong: Oxford University Press.

Wright, Mary. 1968. "Introduction: The Rising Tide of Change." In Mary C. Wright, ed., *China in Revolution: The First Phase, 1900–1913*, pp 1–66. New Haven: Yale University Press.

Wu Weiruo. 1970. "Zhang Taiyan zhi minzuzhuyi shixue" [Zhang Taiyan's Historical Studies of Nationalism]. In Li Guoqi, ed., *Minzuzhuyi*, pp. 261–71. Taibei: Shibao Chuban Gongsi.

Wyman, Judy. 1993. "Social Change, Anti-Foreignism and Revolution in China: Chongqing Prefecture, 1870s to 1911." Ph. D. diss. submitted to the University of Michigan.

Yamada, Tatsuo. 1979. *Chūgoku Kokumintō Saha no Kenkyū [Researches on the Left Kuomintang of China]*. Tokyo: Keiyō Tsushin.

Yamamoto, Tatsuro, and Sumiko Yamamoto. 1953. "The Anti-Christian Movement in China, 1922–1927." *The Far Eastern Quarterly* 12, no. 2: 133–47.

Yamashita, Shigekazu. 1984. "Herbert Spencer and Meiji Japan." In Hilary Conroy, et al., eds., *Japan in Transition: Thought and Action in the Meiji Era, 1868–1912*, pp. 77–95. Rutherford: Fairleigh Dickinson University Press.

Yang, C. K. 1967. *Religion in Chinese Society*. Berkeley: University of California Press.

Yang Duanliu. 1922. "Zhongguo tongyizhi guoqu xianzai ji jianglai" [The Past, Present and Future of Chinese Unity]. *Taipingyang* 3, no. 7: 1–9.

Yang Shouren. 1904. "Xin Hunan" [New Hunan]. In Zhang Yufa, ed., *Wan Qing geming wenxue [Writings from the Late Qing Revolution]*, pp. 64–105. Taibei: Xinzhi zazhishe (1971).

Yokoyama, Hiroaki. 1986. "Chūgoku no kyōwa kakumei undō to himitsu kaisha" [China's Republican Revolutionary Movement and Secret Societies]. *Meiji Gakuin Daigaku Ronshū: Hōgaku Kenkyū* 396 (August): 125–89.

Young, Ernest. 1983. "Politics in the Aftermath of Revolution: The Era of Yuan Shih-k'ai." In John K. Fairbank and Dennis Twitchett, eds., *Cambridge History of China*, vol. 12, 209–59. Cambridge, UK: Cambridge University Press.

Young, Robert. 1990. *White Mythologies: Writing History and the West*. London: Routledge.

Yu, George T. 1962. *Party Politics in Republican China: The Kuomintang, 1912–1924*. Berkeley: University of California Press.

Yu Yingshi. 1987. *Zhongguo Sixiang Chuantongdi Xiandai Quanshi* [Contemporary Interpretations of the Chinese Intellectual Tradition]. Taipei: Lianjing.

Yuval-Davis, Nira, and Floya Anthias, eds., 1989. *Woman-Nation-State*. New York: St. Martin's Press.

ZMFH. Abbreviation for *Zhonghua Minguo Fagui Huibian* [*Collection of the Laws of the Chinese Republic*], 1933. Shanghai: Zhonghua Shuju.

Zeng Jue. 1930a. "Yin zi, si, guan, miaozhan hai yong baoliu ma?" [Do We Still Need to Preserve the Property of Immoral Shrines, Temples and Monasteries?] In *Fenggai*, pp. 116–19. Guangzhou: Guangzhou Tebie Shidangbu Xuanchuanbu.

———. 1930b. "Wo ye yitan 'sanminzhuyi yu zongjiao wenti'" [I too Wish To Say a Word about "The 3 People's Principles and the Problem of Religion"] In *Fenggai*, pp. 120–29. Guangzhou: Guangzhou Tebie Shidangbu Xuanchuanbu.

Zhaicheng cunzhi [*Gazetteer of Zhaicheng village, Ding county, Hebei*]. 1925.

Zhaicheng fukan [Appendix to Zhaicheng gazetteer]. 1925.

Zhang Li. 1980. "'Shunqing mieyang''mieqing jiaoyang' liangge kouhao zai Sichuande youlai jichi yinxiang" [The Causes and Influence of the Two Slogans, "Support the Qing and Exterminate the Foreigners" and "Exterminate the Qing and the Foreigners" in Sichuan]. *Shehui kexue yanjiu*, no. 6, pp. 20–28.

Zhang Pengyuan. 1981. "The Enactment and Enforcement of the Provincial Constitution in Hunan (1920–1925). In *Symposium on the History of the Republic of China*, vol. 2. Taipei: Institute of Modern History, Academica Sinica.

Zhang Qinshi. 1927. *Guonei jin shinianlai zhi zongjiao sichao* [*Trends in Religious Thought in China in the Last Ten Years*]. Beijing: Yanjing Huawen Xuexiao.

Zhang Shizhao (Qiutong). 1914. "Lianbang lun" [Discussing Federalism]. *Jiayin* 1, no. 1: 1–15.

———. 1915. "Lianbanglun da Fan jun Lishan" [Discussing Federalism. A Response to Mr. Fan Lishan]. *Jiayin* 1, no. 6: 1–7.

———. n.d. c. 1903. "Zhongguo gudai xianyi junquanzhi fa" [The Means of Restraining Imperial Power in Ancient China]. In *Guomin ribao huibian*, vol. 2, pp. 20–27.

Zhang Taiyan. 1899a. [1977 reprint.] "Fanzhen lun" [Discussion of the Feudatory System]. In Tang Zhijun, ed., *Zhang Taiyan Zhenglun Xuanji*, vol. 1, pp. 98–103. Beijing: Zhonghua shuju.

———. 1899b. [1977 reprint.] "Fenzhen" [Division into Military Jurisdictions]. In Tang Zhijun, ed., *Zhang Taiyan Zhenglun Xuanji*, vol. 1, pp. 104–8. Beijing: Zhonghua shuju.

Zhang Xin. 1991. "Elite Mobility, Local Control, and Social Transformation in Modern China: Henan, 1900–1937." Ph.D. diss. submitted to the University of Chicago.

Zhang Yufa, ed. 1971. *Wan Qing geming wenxue* [*Writings from the Late Qing Revolution*]. Taibei: Xinzhi zazhishe.

Zhuang Cheng. 1981. *Guofu geming yu hongmen huitang* [*Sun Yat-sen's Revolution and the Hongmen Society*]. Taibei: Zhengzhong Shuju.

INDEX

models of political community in, 56–61; Hong Kong, 203; Hui Muslims, 65, 144, 203; and imperialism, 23, 182, 202, 224; in Japanese colonial ideology, 224–25; Jin invasion, 57, 58, 67; *junxian* system, 153, 154; khanate of Kokand, 57–58; late imperial period, 25–26; localities, 177, 191; medieval period in, 35; modernity in, 226; modernization in, 206–7; modern period in, 35, 38; Mongol dynasty, 60, 116; Mongol invasion, 57; Mongols, 76, 105, 131; National Essence school, 132, 207, 208; the nation-state's future in, 232; New Armies, 134; north-south division of, 129–30; as only continuous historical nation, 41; Opium War, 206; overseas Chinese, 135–36, 232; periodization of Chinese history, 34, 35, 37–41; Ping-Liu-Li uprising, 134; popular novels, 150; printing press in, 150; Protect the Emperor Society, 74, 134, 135; public opinion, 157, 185; Qin, 38, 43; racial stereotyping of, 21; religion and politics in, 218, 220; remaking the people in, 32; representations of the nation in, 74–77; representation of women in, 11; resurgence of religion in post-Mao China, 112, 221; scientism in, 86, 93; self-strengthening movement, 206, 208; Seven Sages of the Bamboo Grove, 45; Song dynasty, 59, 131; southern narrative of, 203; state-building in, 159, 160; study societies, 154, 155, 157; Subei, 69; subethnic groups, 69; Sun Yat-sen on, 32–33; Suqian, 106; Taiping Rebellion, 68, 69, 116, 118, 179; Taiwan, 76, 203, 221; Tang dynasty, 187; Tanka boat people, 69; *tankuan* taxes, 166, 167; Ten Great Uprisings, 136; and theory of segmentary communities, 53; Tianjin, 165; Tibet, 76, 142; *ti-yong* thinking, 29, 206, 208; tribute trade system, 57–58; as true alternative to the West, 41; universal kingship in, 217, 222; warlords, 166, 173, 186, 187, 198, 202; Warring States period, 74, 187; as weak state with strong statist discourse, 170–74; Weber on, 24; Wei-Jin

period, 38, 44–45, 47; Western Jin, 38, 130; women as citizens of, 11–12; Wu, 74; Xinjiang, 76; Yellow Emperor, 75, 76, 132; Zhenjiang, 68; *zhongyuan*, 71. *See also* barbarians; Boxer Rebellion; Chinese Communist Party; Confucianism; federal self-government movement; *fengjian*; Han; Kuomintang; May 4th movement; Ming dynasty; provinces, the; Qing dynasty; race; religion; Republican period; Republican Revolution; rural China; secret societies; Sun Yat-sen
China-centered approach, 26
Chinese Communist Party (CCP): in anti-Christian movement, 103; Communists joining the Kuomintang, 202; criticism of federal self-government movement, 201, 229; Mao Zedong, 13, 189–91, 215; Northern Expedition, 203
Christianity: anti-Christian movement in China, 103–4; and imperialism, 104; Roman Catholic Church, 70, 122, 226; secret society attacks on, 121–23
Chu, 74
civil society: in China, 147, 148–52; defined, 148–49; and Enlightenment History, 152; *fengjian* narrative and, 152; hybrid narrative of, 152–60; in late Qing and Republican China, 149–52; and the public sphere, 148–49; and religion, 226; and the state, 147–75; and state-building, 160–70
class: as constitutive principle of citizenship in China, 80n.14; and the nation, 12–13
class nationalism, 12
clerisy, 52
coal miners, 122
Cohen, Paul, 26, 89
Cohn, Bernard, 22–23
colonialism, 23, 223–24, 227
Communist Party, Chinese. *See* Chinese Communist Party
communities: alternative conceptions of as threat to the nation-state, 230–31; believable self-image of the past in the present required for, 71; boundaries, 65–66; closure of, 65–69; culturalist view of, 76; culture as criterion of de-

history, 45, 47; objectivity, 48; periodization, 33, 34, 35, 37–41; as retrospective reconstruction serving present
needs, 51; Subaltern history, 6; and
translation, 73. *See also* bifurcation;
History, Enlightenment; past, the
History, Enlightenment (linear History):
the aporia of linear history and the
politics of nationalism, 27–33; bifurcating linear History in China and India,
51–82; birth of professional History,
21–22; Chinese adoption of, 25–27,
235; Chinese history as, 33–48; and
civil society, 152; and Confucianism,
90; critique of through culture, 207; critiques of, 233; evolutionism in, 20, 48;
failure to redress the aporia of time,
91; first history of China in the Enlightenment mode, 33, 173; Gandhi's
rejection of, 216, 227; Hegel on,
17–20, 86–87; Liang Qichao on nation-
state and, 34; as a mode of being, 17,
19–20, 27; the nation in, 4, 16; the nation as subject of, 27, 29; and the nation-state, 17–50, 229; possibility of
subject of, 55; progress, 33, 206, 210,
211; Ricoeur on, 101; schemas of, 34;
secular History of India, 77; self-
consciousness as telos of, 205
History of America (Bancroft), 30–31
Hobsbawm, Eric J., 21
Hobson, Marian, 72
hōken, 201
homeland, 71
Hong Bang (Red Gang), 117
Hong Kong, 203
Hongmen, 117, 129, 131, 133, 135, 136
Hongwu emperor, 131
Hsieh, Winston, 195, 197, 198
Huang, Martin, 44
Huang Shaodan, 100, 102, 103
Huang Zongxi, 59, 153, 154
Huang Zunxian, 154, 155, 171
Huaxia, 41, 43
Huaxinghui, 183
Hubei province, 188
Hu Hanmin, 141, 160
huiguan, 179, 183
Hui Muslims, 65, 144, 203
huitang. See secret societies

Hunan province, 155, 180, 182, 187,
188–93, 202
100 Days Reform, 154, 156, 207
Hu Shi, 47, 104, 132, 200, 201
Husserl, Edmund, 72–73

identity: defined, 7; Manchu identity,
67–69; political identities, 10, 15, 54.
See also national identity
imaginary communities, 54n
imperialism: anti-imperialism, 15, 111,
139, 143, 224; in China, 23, 182, 202,
224; and Christianity, 104; colonialism,
23, 223–24, 227; Liang Qichao on, 171;
national independence movements,
27; social Darwinist justification of,
22–23
India: Akbar, 77, 213; Aryavarta, 62, 63,
71, 78; Asoka, 77, 213; Ayodhya, 78;
Bengal Renaissance, 210; Bharatvarsha, 63; bifurcating linear History in,
51–82; British state-building in, 219–
20; Buddhism as cause of passivity in,
105; "colonializing of," 23; colonial
representations of, 223; dichotomy of
East and West in, 29–30, 78; Gandhi,
30n, 78, 206, 213–17, 222–27; Gujarat,
222; Guptas, 77, 213; Hegel on, 18–19,
61; historical models of political community in, 61–65; the house of Birla,
216; Indian National Congress, 77; in
Indo-European tradition, 41; Kang
Youwei on, 209; Liang Qichao on,
156; *Mahabharata*, 62; Maratha kingdom, 63–64; Marx on capitalism in,
23; modernity criticized in, 210–15;
Moghuls, 77, 213; Muslims in, 79,
80n.13; nation-state development in,
64n; Nehru, 77, 210, 212–13; new social movements, 217; notion of lack of
a state in, 61; pan-Hindu model of political community, 64; pilgrimage, 63;
Prithvi Raj II, 63; Punjab, 221; *Ramayana*, 62–63, 78, 80, 80n.13; religion
and politics in, 218; remaking the people in, 32; representations of the nation in, 77–80; secular History of, 77;
separatist movements in, 13; Sikh
kingdom, 63–64; Sikh religious revivalism, 221; Sri Partasarati Svami temple